young adult literature

young adult literature

from romance to realism

michael cart

AMERICAN LIBRARY ASSOCIATION
CHICAGO   2010

Michael Cart is a nationally known expert in young adult literature, which he taught at UCLA before his recent relocation to the Midwest. A columnist and reviewer for ALA's *Booklist* magazine, he is also the author or editor of twenty books and countless articles that have appeared in the *New York Times*, the *Los Angeles Times*, the *San Francisco Chronicle*, *Parents Magazine*, *American Libraries*, *School Library Journal*, and elsewhere. Cart served as president of both the Young Adult Library Services Association and the Assembly on Literature for Adolescents of the National Council of Teachers of English. He received the 2000 Grolier Award and was the first recipient (2008) of the YALSA/Greenwood Publishing Group Service to Young Adults Award. In addition, he appointed and chaired the task force that created the Michael L. Printz Award and subsequently chaired the 2006 Printz Committee.

ISBN: 978-0-8389-1045-0

Printed in the United States of America
15 14 13 12   5 4 3 2

While extensive effort has gone into ensuring the reliability of the information in this book, the publisher makes no warranty, express or implied, with respect to the material contained herein.

Library of Congress Cataloging-in-Publication Data
Cart, Michael.
  Young adult literature : from romance to realism / Michael Cart.
     p. cm.
  Includes bibliographical references and index.
  ISBN 978-0-8389-1045-0 (alk. paper)
  1. Young adult fiction, American--History and criticism. 2. Young adult literature--History and criticism. 3. Teenagers--Books and reading--United States. 4. Teenagers in literature. I. Title.
  PS374.Y57C37 2010
  813.009'92837--dc22

                                                                    2010013674

Book design in Liberation Serif and Museo Slab by Casey Bayer.

♾ This paper meets the requirements of ANSI/NISO Z39.48-1992 (Permanence of Paper).

ALA Editions also publishes its books in a variety of electronic formats.
For more information, visit the ALA Store at www.alastore.ala.org and select eEditions.

For Jack Ledwith
Still and always the best of friends

contents

Part One That Was Then

Part Two This Is Now

Part One
That Was Then

from sue barton to the sixties

What's in a Name? and Other Uncertainties

There is ready and well-nigh universal agreement among experts that something called young adult literature is—like the Broadway musical, jazz, and the foot-long hot dog—an American gift to the world. But the happy concurrence ends when you then ask those experts to explain precisely what this thing called young adult literature is, because doing so is about as easy as nailing Jell-O to a wall. Why? Because the term, like the gelatin, is inherently slippery and amorphous. Oh, the literature part is straightforward enough. Who can argue with the British literary critic John Rowe Townsend (1980, 26), who defines it as "all works of imagination which are transmitted primarily by means of the written word or spoken narrative—that is, in the main, novels, stories, and poetry" (to which, in due course, I will add narrative nonfiction). No, the amorphous part is the target audience for the literature: the young adults themselves. For it's anybody's guess who—or what—they are! Indeed, until World War II, the term *young adult*—like its apparent synonym *teenager*—was scarcely used at all. For while it was acknowledged that there were human beings who occupied an ill-defined developmental space some-where between childhood and adulthood, the idea that this space constituted a separate and distinct part of the evolution from childhood to adulthood was still foreign in a society accustomed to seeing children become adults virtually overnight as a result of their entering the full-time workforce, often as early as age ten. Who had the discursive leisure to grow up, to establish a culture of youth, to experience a *young* adulthood when there was so much adult work to be done? Indeed, as late as 1900, only 6.4 percent of American seventeen-year-olds postponed adult responsibilities long enough to earn high school diplomas (Kett 1977). No more than 11.4 percent of the entire fourteen- to seventeen-year-old population was even enrolled in school, and those who were received—on average—only five years of education (Mondale and Patton 2001). Simply put, until 1900 we were a society with only two categories of citizens: children and adults.

This situation was about to change, however—and in only four years, at that. The agent of impending change was G. Stanley Hall, the first American to hold a doctorate in psychology and the first president of the American Psychological Association. It was in 1904 that he "invented" a whole new category of human being with the publication of his seminal work *Adolescence: Its Psychology and Its Relations to Physiology, Anthropology, Sociology, Sex, Crime, Religion, and Education.* As the length of its title suggests, this was a massive, multidisciplinary, two-volume tome, which Joseph F. Kett (1977, 26) described as "a feverish, recondite, and at times incomprehensible book, the flawed achievement of eccentric genius."

It was flawed, because much of what Hall posited about this stage of life that he called adolescence has been discredited, especially his notion of recapitulation (i.e., child development mirrors that of the evolution of the human race). Nevertheless, his theories were enormously influential in their time, particularly among educators and a growing population of youth workers. The latter embraced Hall's view of adolescence as a time of storm and stress (a phrase that invoked the German Sturm und Drang school and visions of Goethe's sorrowful young Werther), along with inner turmoil, awkwardness, and vulnerability, all phenomena that invited, even required, adult intervention and supervision in such controlled environments as schools and a growing number of youth organizations like the Boy Scouts and the YMCA. Neither Hall nor his disciples used the term *young adult*, of course, but their definitions of adolescence generally embraced our modern sense of young adults as somewhere between twelve and nineteen years of age. Indeed, Hall was prepared to extend his definition's reach as far as the early twenties, but educators generally stopped at nineteen, and employers, at sixteen. In addition to these two groups, Hall inspired two other sets of influential devotees: members of the vocational guidance movement (Hall believed in teaching adolescents practical life and job skills) and the authors of "parents' manuals, which sought to guide the management of teenagers in middle-class and upper-middle-class homes" (Kett 1977, 221). Michael V. O'Shea, one of the most prolific writers of these manuals, was also among the first to capitalize on the potential economic importance of adolescents, so much so that Kett (1977, 224) dubbed him "the first entrepreneur of adolescence." As we will see, there have been many others.

As a result of this new focus on the perceived needs of adolescents, the percentage of young people in school gradually began to grow. By 1910, 15.4 percent of young people were enrolled (Rollin 1999), and the old model of the six-year high school was beginning to change, too, as, over the following decade, more and more junior high schools were created for students ages twelve to fourteen. "By 1920," Lucy Rollin (1999, 8) noted, "the pattern of the four-year high school was well established," and by 1930 almost half the adolescent population was enrolled. This was the good news for advocates of education, but the bad news was that slightly more than half of America's adolescents were still not in school but in the workforce, where they continued to be regarded as adults. But this, too, was about to change. Indeed, it had already begun to change as the workplace was employing increasingly sophisticated technology that required additional education, as—more forcefully—had a spate of compulsory education laws.

It took the economic devastation of the thirties, however, to effect truly seismic change. As Grace Palladino (1996, 5) has written, "The Great Depression finally pushed teenage youth out of the workplace and into the classroom." Lucy Rollin (1999, 85) concurred: "The Thirties were a fulcrum for this shift." The numbers, alone, are telling: by 1939, 75 percent of fourteen- to seventeen-year-olds were high school students, and by 1940 nearly 51 percent of seventeen-year-olds were earning diplomas (50.8 percent according to Kett [1977]).

The Emergence of Youth Culture

This influx of students into high school was an important step in advancing universal education, but what was even more important—in terms of the later emergence of young adult literature—is that putting young people into one another's company every day led to the emergence of a youth culture centered on high school social life, especially in the newly popular sororities and fraternities, which provided the context for a newish wrinkle in courtship rituals: dances and dating. Quick to recognize this was the already entrenched *Scholastic* magazine, which M. R. "Robbie" Robinson, another of the early entrepreneurs of adolescence, had founded in 1922. In 1936

Scholastic introduced a new column to its pages. Titled "Boy Dates Girl," the column was written by Gay Head (pseudonym for Margaret L. Hauser), whose columns would provide the fodder for a number of later books, including *First Love*; *Hi There, High School!* and *Etiquette for Young Moderns*. As the last title suggests, the column focused more on manners than on advice to the lovelorn. Among the topics Hauser addressed, according to Grace Palladino (1996), were how to make proper introductions, which fork to use at a dinner party, and whether to wait for a boy to open a car door. Although boys took pride of place in the column's title, its intended readers were clearly girls, who were admonished not to correct their dates, because boys did not appreciate "brainy" girls. In the early days of youth culture, it was obvious that the culture was already a male-centered one. This was a reflection of then prevailing cultural attitudes, of course, as was Hall's nearly single-minded focus on male adolescents in his own work. He had written so little about girls, in fact, that H. W. Gibson, an early disciple and social worker with the YMCA, dubbed adolescent psychology of the times "boyology" (Kett 1977, 224).

Although boys may have been the center of lavish attention, the stereotypical image of the male adolescent that emerged in popular culture was an unflattering one: the socially awkward, blushing, stammering, accident-prone figure of fun typified by William Sylvanus Thaxter, the protagonist of Booth Tarkington's best-selling 1916 novel *Seventeen* (Harper), the inspiration for Carl Ed's long-running comic strip *Harold Teen*, which first appeared in 1919. Twenty years later this image was still the rage, this time informing the spirit of radio's Henry Aldrich and the movies' Andy Hardy. (*The Aldrich Family* debuted on NBC in July 1939, and the first Andy Hardy movie, *A Family Affair*—starring Mickey Rooney—was released in 1937.) With the first appearance in 1941 of another soon-to-be youth icon, the comics' Archie Andrews (in *Pep Comics No. 22*, of December 22, 1941), it became clear that Hall's adolescent was fast morphing into a new kind of youth, the teenager. In fact, the first use in print of the term *teenager* occurred in the September 1941 issue of *Popular Science Monthly* (Hine 1999; see also Palladino 1996), and the term became commonplace in the decade that followed, though it wasn't until 1956 and Gale Storm's hit record *Teenage Prayer* that the term passed into currency in the world of popular music (the same year saw the debut of the singing group Frankie Lymon and the Teenagers).

The co-opting of the adolescent—now teenager—by popular culture did not mean that psychologists and other serious thinkers had abandoned the subject. Far from it. Two of the most significant works in the academic literature would appear less than a decade later: Robert James Havighurst's *Developmental Tasks and Education* and Erik Erikson's *Childhood and Soci-*

ety both appeared in 1950 and broke new ground in the field of psychology, especially with respect to stages of human development. Each writer defined specific stages of this development; Havighurst identified six and Erikson, eight. For both, two of the stages were "adolescence" and "young adulthood," which they identified as thirteen to eighteen and nineteen to thirty (Havighurst) and twelve to eighteen and nineteen to forty (Erikson). In short order, other significant work followed, most notably Jean Piaget's *The Growth of Logical Thinking from Childhood to Adolescence* (1958) on cognitive development and Lawrence Kohlberg's on moral development (intermittently throughout the 1970s).

All of this work—like that of Hall's—would have significant influence on therapists, youth workers, and especially educators, who found an equation between the tasks that Havighurst associated with each developmental stage and books for teens that dramatized the undertaking and accomplishing of those tasks. It's worth noting that the introduction of the term *young adulthood* into these various professional vocabularies may have been instrumental in the American Library Association's decision to form, in 1957, the Young Adult Services Division (YASD). This was a long-overdue professional acknowledgment not only of a now au courant term but also of the singular life needs of what we might as well now call young adults. Why *young adult* and not *adolescent*, though? Well, there is no definitive answer. However, the term *young adult* was not altogether foreign to the library world. The youth services librarian Margaret Scoggin had first used it in the professional literature as early as 1944 (Jenkins 1999), and Kenneth R. Shaffer, then director of the School of Library Science at Simmons College, recalled in 1963, "Our excitement of nearly a quarter of a century ago when we made the professional discovery of the adolescent—the 'young adult'—as a special kind of library client" (Shaffer 1963, 9). Also, one might presume that *adolescent* smacks a bit too much of the clinical, and some might even regard it as faintly patronizing, though *young adult* might not be much better. As we will see, such uncertainty as to precisely what to call youths has continued to invite much heated discussion and debate even to this date, though in 1991 YASD did finally decree, in concert with the National Center for Education Statistics, that young adults "are those individuals from twelve to eighteen years old" (Carter 1994).

A Literature for Young Adults

What impact did all of these developing attitudes and theories have on the writing and publishing of books targeted at such young people (however they might have been labeled and categorized at any given moment)? The short answer, one supposes, is "not much."

Because adolescents, teenagers, or young adults were—at least until the late 1930s—still widely regarded as children (even if the boys had mustaches and the girls, breasts!), there was no separate category of literature specifically targeted at them. However, as—over the course of the first four decades of the twentieth century (1900–1940)—opinions began coalescing around the viability of recognizing a new category of human being with its own distinct life needs, books aimed at these "new" humans began to emerge. This happened very gradually, though, and may have had its roots in the long-ago publishing world of the immediate post–Civil War years, when, as Nilsen and Donelson (2009, 42) have asserted, "Louisa May Alcott and Horatio Alger, Jr. were the first writers for young adults to gain national attention." The two authors' respective novels *Little Women* and *Ragged Dick* both appeared in 1868 and gave impetus to an era—already under way—of series fiction: dime adventure novels for boys and wholesome domestic stories like the Elsie Dinsmore books for girls. Then, as now, it was firmly believed there were girl books and boy books and never the twain would meet.[1] The always-opinionated G. Stanley Hall had much to say about this, too. In a 1908 *Library Journal* article, he allowed: "Boys loved adventure. Girls sentiment. Books dealing with domestic life and with young children in them, girls have almost entirely to themselves. Boys, on the other hand, excel in love of humor, rollicking fun, abandon, rough horse-play, and tales of wild escapade" (Nilsen and Donelson 2009, 52).

Series books for both sexes hit their stride with the formation of the Stratemeyer Syndicate in 1900. Edward Stratemeyer, who had worked as a ghostwriter for Alger, had the bright idea of hiring other ghosts to develop his own cascade of story ideas into novels. The result became what Carol Billman (1986) has called the Million Dollar Fiction Factory. Working pseudonymously, these otherwise-anonymous writers churned out hundreds of titles in endless series, most of them now forgotten, though a few—the Rover Boys, Tom Swift, the Bobbsey Twins, and Ruth Fielding—are still remembered with a twinge of pleasurable nostalgia.[2] Arguably the most successful of the Stratemeyer series and the ones that come closest to our modern conception of young adult fiction didn't appear until well after World War I. The Hardy Boys solved their first case (*The Tower Treasure*) in 1927, and Nancy Drew hers (*The Secret of the Old Clock*) in 1930.

Coincidentally, 1930 is the year the ALA formed its Young People's Reading Roundtable, whose annual list of best books for "young readers" (think "young adults" here) contained a mixture of children's and adult books. The first list, for example, ran the gamut from Will James's *Lone Cowboy* to Edna

Ferber's adult novel *Cimarron*. This situation obtained until 1948, when librarians—realizing the new but still amorphous group of older "younger readers" no longer had any interest in children's books—changed the name and content of their list to Adult Books for Young People (Cart 1996).

Meanwhile, prescient publishers, taking notice of the emerging youth culture of the 1930s, began cautiously publishing—or at least remarketing—what they regarded as a new type of book. One of the first of these was Rose Wilder Lane's *Let the Hurricane Roar*. Published in 1933, this story of two teenage pioneers by the daughter of the Little House books' author offered intrinsic appeal to contemporary teens. Recognizing this, its publisher, Longmans Green, quickly began promoting it as the first in its promised new series Junior Books, a frankly patronizing phrase that lingered in publishing like a bad odor in the refrigerator for nearly a decade. Nevertheless, it may have set the stage for another book that Little, Brown would publish in 1936.

This one caught the eye of the pioneering young adult librarian Margaret Alexander Edwards of the Enoch Pratt Free Library in Baltimore. Writing some years later in the *Saturday Review*, she reported Little, Brown's editorial bemusement when the publisher received a manuscript from the writer Helen Boylston. "While it was not a piece of literature, it was an entertaining story which did not fit into any category. It was too mature for children and too uncomplicated for adults. In the end Little, Brown took a chance and published the story under the title 'Sue Barton Student Nurse' *and the dawn of the modern teen-age story came up like thunder*" (Edwards 1954, 88, emphasis added).

The thunder was, presumably, the sound of fervent adolescent applause, as *Sue Barton* (for reasons that seem elusive to modern readers struggling through its turgid pages) quickly became one of the most popular books in the history of young adult literature. In 1947—eleven years after its publication—a survey of librarians in Illinois, Ohio, and New York chose the book as "the most consistently popular book" among teenage readers, and it remained in print for years thereafter along with its six sequels, which saw young Sue finish her training, serve in a variety of professional capacities (visiting nurse, superintendent of nurses, neighborhood nurse, staff nurse), and finally marry the young doctor she had met in book number one (Cart 1996, 41).

The popularity of the series may have derived in large part from its verisimilitude. Boylston was a professional nurse herself, and there's truth in the details of her settings, but there are also stereotypes in her characters and clichés in the dramatic situations in which they find themselves embroiled. Told in an omniscient third-person voice, the books betray their author's often too-smug, patronizing attitude toward her material and her characters—not only Sue but also, and especially, the "quaint" immigrants who are the chief patients at the big-city hospital where Sue receives her training.

Nevertheless, because of its careful accuracy regarding the quotidian details of the nurse's professional life, *Sue Barton* was the prototype of the career story, an enormously popular subgenre among the earliest young adult books.

Rivaling Sue for the affection of later nurse-story lovers was Helen Wells's own fledgling professional Cherry Ames, who debuted in 1943 (*Cherry Ames, Student Nurse*) and whose subsequent adventures filled twenty volumes. Wells also gave eager girl readers stories about the plucky flight attendant Vicki Barr. Still another writer who re-created occupational worlds that she was personally familiar with was the remarkable Helen Hull Jacobs, whose many books about the world of championship tennis and military intelligence reflected her own life as the number-one world tennis player and a commander in the Office of Naval Intelligence during World War II.

As for boys, they had been reading vocational stories since Horatio Alger offered his paeans to the rewards of hard work (and marrying the boss's daughter). More contemporary writers like Montgomery Atwater, Stephen W. Meader, and Henry Gregor Felsen offered fictions about such real-life jobs as avalanche patrolling, earthmoving, and automobile mechanics. In the years to come, other less talented writers would report on virtually every other conceivable career—in often drearily didactic detail.

A decade before Boylston's initial publication, another influential and wildly popular author for adolescents debuted: it was 1926 when Howard Pease published his first book, *The Tattooed Man* (Doubleday). A better writer than Boylston, Pease would soon rival her in popularity. In fact, a 1939 survey of 1,500 California students found that Pease—not Boylston—was their favorite author (Hutchinson 1973).

Like Boylston, Pease specialized in a literary subgenre: in his case, it was the boy's adventure story set—usually—at sea. And again, like Boylston, Pease knew his material from firsthand experience. For him, this was service in the U.S. Merchant Marine during World War I.

In 1938 still another important early writer, who also specialized in genre fiction based on personal experience, made his auspicious debut: John R. Tunis, the "inventor" of the modern sports story, published the first of his many novels, *The Iron Duke* (Harcourt). Tunis had played tennis and run track as a student at Harvard and, following service in World War I, had become a sportswriter for the *New York Post*. What set his work apart from that of earlier sportswriters was that he focused less on play-by-play accounts of the big game than on closely observed considerations of character, social issues, and challenges—not his characters' hand-eye coordination but, instead, their personal integrity and maturation.

The First Young Adult Novel?

In retrospect, any of these writers (though especially Pease, Boylston, and Tunis) could be reasonably identified as the first writer for young adults, but most observers (myself included) would opt to join the redoubtable Edwards (1954, 88) in declaring (on second thought in her case) that "it was in 1942 that the new field of writing for teen-agers became established."

The signal occasion was the publication of Maureen Daly's (1942) first—and for forty-four years her only—novel, *Seventeenth Summer* (Dodd, Mead). Amazingly, the author was only twenty-one when her history-making book appeared, though how old she was when she actually wrote the book is moot. Daly herself claimed she was a teenager, but the *New York Times* reported that only fifty pages of the book had been written before the author turned twenty (Van Gelder 1942). Daly was quick to point out, though, that her novel was not published as a young adult book. "I would like, at this late date," she wrote in 1994, "to explain that 'Seventeenth Summer,' in my intention and at the time of publication, was considered a full adult novel and published and reviewed as such" (Berger 1994, 216).

John R. Tunis was similarly—and unpleasantly—surprised to learn from his publisher Alfred Harcourt that *The Iron Duke* was a book for young readers. He was still fuming thirty years later when he wrote, "That odious term juvenile is the product of a merchandising age" (Tunis 1977, 25).

The merchandising of and to "the juvenile" had begun in the late 1930s, coincident with the emergence of the new youth culture. The movement picked up steam in the 1940s as marketers realized that these kids—whom they called, variously, teens, teensters, and finally (in 1941) teenagers—were "an attractive new market in the making" (Palladino 1996, 52). That market wouldn't fully ripen until post–World War II prosperity put money into the kids' own pockets, money that had previously gone to support the entire family. The wild success of *Seventeenth Summer* was, however, an early indicator to publishers of an emerging market for a literature that spoke with immediacy and relevance to teenagers. In the case of Daly's novel, these factors were due to not only her own youth and the autobiographical nature of her material ("What I've tried to do, you see," she told an interviewer, "is just write about the things that happened to me and that I knew about—that meant a lot to me" [Van Gelder 1942, 20]) but also the fact that she chose to tell her story of sweet summer love in the first-person voice of her protagonist, seventeen-year-old Angie Morrow.

For its time, the book was also fairly bold and, thus, further reader enticing in its inclusion of scenes showing teenagers unapologetically smoking and drinking. And yet to modern readers Angie seems hopelessly naive and much younger than her years. Her language now sounds quaintly old fashioned, and the pacing of her story is glacially slow, bogged down in far too many rhapsodic passages describing the fauna of Fond du Lac, Wisconsin (the book's setting). If Angie's diction is dated, so—more painfully—are her attitudes. Humiliated, for example, by the bad table manners of her new boyfriend, the otherwise-desirable (and always very clean) Jack Duluth, Angie frets, "His family probably didn't even own a butter knife! No girl has to stand for that!" (Daly 1942, 147) Clearly, Jack and his deprived family had never read Gay Head's column (or her books!).

Despite all this, *Seventeenth Summer* has remained tremendously popular; it's sold well more than a million and a half copies since its publication, and it's still in print in a smartly redesigned paperback edition.

Even more important than *Seventeenth Summer* to the cultivation of a readership for a newly relevant literature was the inaugural publication of the new girls' magazine *Seventeen* in September 1944. Teens were thrilled to be taken seriously at last. The first printing of four hundred thousand copies sold out in two days and the second—of five hundred thousand—in the same short time. One reader wrote the editors to thank them for "looking upon us teenagers as future women and Americans, instead of swooning, giggling bobbysoxers." Another chorused, "For years I have been yearning for a magazine entirely dedicated to me" (Palladino 1996, 91–92).

Here was a niche to be exploited, and the editors of *Seventeen* were quick to recognize it, making theirs one of the first magazines to actually survey its readers—not to determine their editorial interests but, instead, their taste and interests in consumables. Oddly, such research was "unheard of at the time in fashion magazines." But *Seventeen* quickly changed that by hiring the research company Benson & Benson to conduct the important market survey "Life with Teena" (the name of the hypothetical everygirl it conjured up to breathlessly report the survey's results). "Teena has money of her own to spend," the editors enthused, "and what her allowance and pin money earnings won't buy, her parents can be counted on to supply. For our girl Teena won't take 'no' for an answer when she sees what she wants in 'Seventeen.'" The not-so-subtle message to American business was "place your ads here." And the business wasn't confined to the manufacturers of sweater sets. "We're talking about eight million teenage girls who can afford to spend $170,000,000 a year on movies," the magazine trumpeted to motion picture producers (Palladino 1996, 103–6).

The year this happened was 1945. In Chicago, the nineteen-year-old shoe clerk Eugene Gilbert was wondering why so few teenagers were buying shoes in his store. His conclusion: "Stores and manufacturers were losing a lot of money because they were largely blind to my contemporaries' tastes and habits. I started then to become a market researcher in a virtually unexplored field." Four years later, as head of the Youth Marketing Company in New York, Gilbert was sagely observing, "Our salient discovery within the last decade was that teenagers have become a separate and distinct group in our society" (Palladino 1996, 109–10).

It was a revelation and a revolution, such a liberating experience for teens that the *New York Times* published the Teen-Age Bill of Rights (Rollin 1999, 107–8):

1. The right to let childhood be forgotten

2. The right to a "say" about his own life

3. The right to make mistakes, and find out about himself

4. The right to have rules explained, not imposed

5. The right to have fun and companions

6. The right to question ideas

7. The right to be at the Romantic Age

8. The right to a fair chance and opportunity

9. The right to struggle toward his own philosophy of life

10. The right to professional help whenever necessary

Oddly—if one is to judge by the gender of the pronoun employed throughout—these rights belonged exclusively to male teenagers! Odd, because—otherwise—the decade pretty much belonged to the girls, who certainly owned much of the media attention of the time. Not only did girls have *Seventeen*, but they could also read another popular magazine devoted to them. *Calling All Girls* actually antedated *Seventeen*; it launched in late 1941. Meanwhile, manufacturers and the motion picture industry kowtowed to girls, as did radio, which offered them such popular fare as *A Date with Judy, Meet Corliss Archer*, and *Your Hit Parade*, while newspaper comic strips served up daily doses of *Teena, Penny*, and *Bobby Sox*.

As for the fledgling young adult literature, imitation was definitely the sincerest form of flattery. For in the wake of *Seventeenth Summer*'s success, romance fiction quickly captured the hearts of American publishers. One of the earliest of the faux Angie Morrows that followed was sixteen-year-old Julie Ferguson, the heroine of Betty Cavanna's 1946 *Going on Sixteen* (Westminster). As its title suggests, the book is an almost homage to Daly. In fact, Cavanna's protagonist, Julie, actually mentions having "just last month read a newspaper account of a book written by a girl of seventeen" (Cavanna 1946, 89). This is offered in the context of Julie's longing for a career in publishing—not as an author but as an illustrator. In this regard, Cavanna borrows not only from Daly but also from career books like Boylston's. There are other similarities as well. Both books are about the interrelationship of dating and popularity; the book's dust jacket even claims that it offers "numerous useful tips on how to overcome shyness and how to become 'part of things.'"

Perhaps Cavanna's heroine read the book herself, because she finally does become part of things by finding true love (and dates) with her neighbor Dick Webster, who habitually calls her Peanut and Small Fry. One supposes these are intended as endearments, but they sound merely condescending. Consider the following: "'Hey!' Dick scolded, suddenly masculine. 'We've got to get going.' Dick looked at her Dad in a way that said 'Women!' and grabbed her hand authoritatively. 'Come on'" (Cavanna 1946, 220).

Girl readers were apparently quite ready to go along, too. Cavanna, ultimately the author of more than seventy books, became one of the most popular authors for adolescents of the forties and fifties. *Going on Sixteen* was the third most popular book in a 1959 survey of school and public libraries, close behind *Seventeenth Summer*.

Another romance author who rivaled Cavanna for popularity was Rosamund du Jardin (who was the only author to have two titles on that 1959 survey: *Double Date* and *Wait for Marcy*). Du Jardin's first book, *Practically Seventeen* (Lippincott) (do you detect a trend in these titles?) was published in 1949 and is yet another pale imitation of Daly.

Like *Seventeenth Summer*, for example, *Practically Seventeen* is told in the first person, in the dumbfoundingly arch voice of Du Jardin's protagonist Tobey Heydon (which sounds too much like *hoyden* to be a coincidence). Like Daly's Angie, Du Jardin's Tobey has three sisters—two older and one younger. Like Angie's father, Tobey's is a traveling salesman. He is fond of saying that, because he is "completely surrounded by females in his own home," he "would go crazy without a sense of humor and that he has had to develop his in self-defense." "But none of us mind," Tobey hastens to reassure the reader. "He is really sweet, as fathers go" (Du Jardin 1949, 4).

Like *Seventeenth Summer* (again), Du Jardin's book is a story of young love but much slighter in substance and much lighter in tone. Tobey's big dilemma—and the theme that unifies the book's highly episodic plot—is whether her relationship with her boyfriend Brose (short for Ambrose) will survive until he can lay hands on the class ring he has asked her to wear. Given the episodic structure of her first novel, it's no surprise to learn that Du Jardin had been a successful writer of magazine fiction, her short stories having appeared in such popular women's magazines as *Cosmopolitan, Redbook, Good Housekeeping,* and *McCall's*. Certainly, her work is slicker, more innocent, and funnier than Daly's. For at-risk teens of the current day, there is something pleasantly nostalgic and comforting in reading about peers (even long-ago ones) whose biggest problems are pesky younger sisters, who will take them to the big dance (the Heart Hop, in this case), and how to resolve a rivalry for a boy's affection with a visitor from the South named, appositely, Kentucky Jackson.

The book's dust-jacket blurb speaks, well, volumes not only about *Practically Seventeen* but also about the type of book that would prevail in publishing for young adults throughout the forties and fifties. Here's a sample paragraph: "In recent years, permanent recognition and popularity have been accorded the junior novel . . . the story that records truthfully the modern girl's dream of life and romance and her ways of adjusting to her school and family experiences. *Practically Seventeen* is such a book—as full of life as the junior prom," and about as relevant to today's readers as *Rebecca of Sunnybrook Farm*.

And yet were it and other such books relevant to and reflective of their contemporary readers' lives? Perhaps more than modern readers might realize. In 1951 J. B. Lippincott published the fascinating *Profile of Youth*. Edited by Maureen Daly (yes, *that* Maureen Daly), it collected profiles of twelve "representative" teenagers who had appeared in issues of *Ladies' Home Journal* throughout 1949 and 1950.

"We chose our young people from the North and South, the East and West," Daly (1951, 9) writes. "From the hangouts and the libraries; from the popular and the aloof; the leaders and the followers. Some are planning professional careers; others are preparing themselves for marriage. Some just want a job—any job. We asked them about their lives—and let them tell their own stories. We asked them about their problems—and joined with them on the solutions."

Although there are differences among the kids—especially in their circumstances (though none is homeless or impoverished)—the one thing they have overwhelmingly in common is, to twenty-first-century readers, an astonishing innocence. Almost none of them smokes or drinks; drugs are never mentioned; none of the students is gay or lesbian or a gang member. None is emotionally troubled or the victim of abuse. Instead, their biggest concern (the book calls it "A National Problem") is whether to go steady. They also "resent" parents who refuse to understand or recognize the importance of fads and customs in high school. (In her introduction, Daly [1951, 10] expresses hope that a parent reading this book "may listen with greater patience to a sixteen-year-old's plea for orange corduroy slacks or a red beanie when he realizes how vital 'fads' are to adolescent security."). Reading the profiles is eerily like reading the novels we have been discussing, especially when one comes to the editors' valedictory summing up of their findings ("American Youth—Full View"), where they affirm, "We have recorded, as told by youth itself, the things *they* find important—the good schools, the basketball rivalries, the college scholarships and Friday night dates" (Daly 1951, 256).

Perhaps life really was simpler back in the 1940s!

To the editors' credit, though, their book does differ from young adult literature of the 1940s by including one black teen (called Negro here), though one wonders how representative she may be. Her name is Myrdice Thornton, and she is the daughter of an affluent mother (her father, the first black member of the Chicago Park Police, was killed in the line of duty). Living in the North, she attends an integrated school in the Hyde Park neighborhood and seems to have experienced little racial prejudice or related problems, telling her profiler, "I never did feel different . . . I see no reason to act that way." Perhaps more indicative of reality was the reaction of the "Negro" boy who, when interviewed (though not profiled) expressed amazement that anyone would be interested in his opinion.

One other teen in the book, Hank Polsinelli, is also "different," the son of Italian immigrants. Alas, his parents are presented as the same kind of stereotyped and "quaint" eccentrics that Boylston featured in *Sue Barton*. Hank's mother, for example, is said to be "a real Italian mother; she believes it is her main business to cook, keep house and make a home for her husband and children and not ask too many questions." She does scold Hank when he misses Mass, "but Hank takes reprimands lightly and his mother understands men. 'He is a good boy at home,' she says, 'I don't know what he does outside'" (Daly 1951, 76).

That Hank and the several other working-class teens who are profiled seem much more mature than their privileged peers reminds us that adolescence, in its first several decades at least, was primarily an experience of middle- and upper-middle-class kids, who lived, for the most part, in all-white small towns. According to Kett (1977, 245), such "towns and small cities proved to be much more responsive to the institutions of adolescence than were rural and metropolitan areas, while a mixture of apathy and antipathy continued to mark the attitudes of lower class youth." Small wonder that urban settings and youths remained largely invisible in YA fiction until the social upheavals of the turbulent 1960s.

There are other disconnects between the idealized (fantasy?) world of early YA fiction and the real one. This is inadvertently reflected in the *Profile* book in a series of topical essays in which the editors and profilers step back from their individual subjects and do some actual research and investigative reporting, which leads to a somewhat less sunny picture of teenage life in the late forties. It's there we learn, for example, that "boys estimate that about half the eighteen and nineteen year old boys have had sex experience" (Daly 1951, 153), that "in almost all cases the boys feel it is up to the girls 'to keep things under control.' She should know how and when to say 'stop,' for after all it's just *natural* for a fellow" (152), and that "pregnancy itself is still considered a social disgrace and a personal disaster" (153). Also, "society as a group has little sympathy for the unwed mother" (154), especially if she is economically deprived. "These girls may be placed in a charitable institution, to be trained in sewing or a trade while waiting out the birth of a child" (154). Sex, of course, remained absent from YA fiction until the late 1960s, and it was equally absent from any serious discussion in the home. "Most teen-agers do *not* get sex information from their parents" (65). Nor did they get it from schools. "Oregon is the only one of the forty-eight states in which sex education is generally taught" (73). Nor, of course, did they get it from books—at least not the whole story. As one girl stated, "I read all about 'that' in a book when I was eleven. But nobody ever told me I was going to get so emotional about it" (155). Too bad, for that's what a good work of realistic fiction, a good work of fiction with fully realized characters whose lives invite empathy from the reader and with it emotional understanding can do—had there been any such books available. That there weren't may be evidence that adult authors (and publishers) did not yet trust YA readers with the truth of reality.

Another example of an invisible topic is the consideration—or lack thereof—of juvenile delinquency and the presence of gangs in teen life. Juvenile delinquency has been an issue in American life since the mid-nineteenth century; the 1930 White House Conference on Children and Youth formally defined it as "any such juvenile misconduct as might be dealt with under the law" (Kett 1977, 309). However, it wasn't until adolescents or teenagers had become a distinct—and distinctive—culture that popular attention turned, with a vengeance, toward the "problem." A significant catalyst was the universal hand wringing over the spate of unsupervised—and possibly out of control—youths during World War II, a situation that was the product of fathers at war and mothers at work. Thus, "during the first six months of 1943 alone, twelve hundred magazine articles appeared on this subject (juvenile delinquency)" (Palladino 1996, 81). One of these, "Are These Our Children?" which appeared in the September 21, 1943, issue of *Look* magazine, inspired RKO to produce a movie based on it. *Youth Runs Wild* was released in 1944, and ads promoting it featured such titillating headlines as "What Happens to These Unguarded Youngsters? The Truth about Modern Youth" (Barson and Heller 1998). The war ended in 1945 but not the fascination with "dangerous" kids. In 1947 Irving Shulman published his adult novel *The Amboy Dukes* about life in a Brooklyn gang. A host of original paperback novels, each more lurid than the last, followed in its wake. And then, suddenly, it was the 1950s and not only were delinquents and gang members big news (and bigger box office), so were teenage rebels. The movie *The Wild One*, starring a leather jacket–clad, motorcycle-riding Marlon Brando, was released in 1954 and contained an unforgettably culture-defining moment in a priceless exchange between a horrified adult and Brando. HA, "What are you rebelling against?" MB, mumbling, "What have you got?"

Adults were further outraged (and teens, enthralled) the following year when not one but two cinematic classics of youthful disaffection were released: *Rebel without a Cause*, starring the soon-to-be-iconic James Dean (who had died in an automobile crash only months before the movie was released), and *Blackboard Jungle*, a gritty film about an inner-city teacher's confrontation with his gang leader students. The most remembered aspect of the latter is the song that played over the movie's opening credits: it was, of course, Bill Haley and His Comets' "Rock around the Clock." Forgive a personal note here: I was thirteen when this movie was released and I'll never forget sitting in the balcony of the old Logan Theater in my hometown (Logansport, Indiana) and hearing this song, the likes of which I had never heard before and the likes of which I couldn't wait to hear again! It was a transfixing and transforming experience that captured the imaginations and sensibilities of every other teen in America, too, and, presto, rock and roll was born and nothing was ever the same again.

Except young adult literature of the fifties, that is! Well, that's not quite true. One aspect of the new, harder-edged reality of teen life did find a place in that fiction: the car gang, a franchise that Henry Gregor Felsen seemed to own; he capitalized on it in such novels as *Hot Rod* (1953), *Street Rod* (1953), *Crash Club* (1958), and others.

The wave of prosperity that accompanied the end of World War II had turned America into a nation of car-crazy kids. *Profile of Youth* devoted an entire chapter, "Teen-Age Drivers Talk Back," to the topic, in fact. It began, rather breathlessly, "Sixteen, when a driver's license can be taken out in most states, is a far more important milestone in the life of the typical American male than twenty-one, when he reaches his majority and can vote, because 'cars are more fun than anything else in the world'" (Daly 1951, 46). Inevitably, this phenomenon led to more adult hand-wringing ("I never close an eye any more until I know John or Mary is in at night!" [45]); a spate of popular songs about fatal car crashes involving teens; the magazine *Hot Rod*, which debuted in 1948; and a literary gold mine for Felsen.

The late forties and early fifties produced another wildly popular genre for boys. These books weren't about street rods but space rods! Science fiction found a welcoming home in young adult fiction with the publication of the already established adult author Robert A. Heinlein's first book for teens *Rocket Ship Galileo* (Scribner) in 1947. *Space Cadet* (Scribner, 1948) followed the next year and *Red Planet* (Scribner, 1949) the next. In short order, Heinlein was joined in the science fiction lists by Andre Norton (pseudonym of Mary Alice Norton), whose first YA novel, *Star Man's Son, 2250 A.D.* (Harcourt), appeared in 1953—many, many others followed.

As in the forties, the books of the fifties continued to focus on romance stories for girls and other genre fiction for boys, who—in addition to car books and science fiction—were reading novels of adventure, sports, and animals.

For both sexes, there was a soupçon of more serious literature that focused principally on historical fiction and what the educator G. Robert Carlsen called stories of foreign culture. The latter had been a mainstay of juvenile fiction since the turn of the twentieth century, though most of the titles, written by well-intentioned white Americans, were of the little-children-of-foreign-lands type (most seemed to be twins). But there were exceptions. Elizabeth Foreman Lewis had written knowledgeably and insightfully about the lives of young people in China, having lived and taught there herself. Similarly, Anne Nolan Clark wrote widely about Latin America. But the best work in the category came from abroad in the years immediately following World War II, "an era," according to the legendary editor and publisher Margaret McElderry (1994, 369), "in which American children's book editors actively sought out the best in writing and illustration from abroad." McElderry herself inaugurated this era when, in 1953, she published Margot Benary-Isbert's *The Ark*, the first German book to be published for American young readers following World War II. However, the strident imperative that books about other cultures could be written only by those from that culture did not appear until the 1980s and the advent of multiculturalism and political correctness.

For now, another advent—the arrival of a whole new decade and the dramatic changes it would visit on youth culture and the literature produced for it—is at hand. For a discussion of that, we begin a new chapter!

Notes

1. Speaking of *twain*, a singular work of fiction for boys—to match *Little Women* for girls—appeared in 1885: Mark Twain's *Huckleberry Finn.*

2. As Victor Appleton, Howard R. Garis wrote many of the Tom Swift books; under his own name, he created the more enduring literary character of Uncle Wiggily. Interestingly, his wife, Lillian, penned the Bobbsey Twins books under the pseudonym Laura Lee Hope. Their two children also wrote for Stratemeyer, thus turning the Garis household into a mini–fiction factory, though not, alas, a very happy one! See the ironically titled *House of Happy Endings* by Leslie Garis (Farrar, Straus & Giroux, 2007).

the sixties and the seventies

The Rise of Realism and the First Golden Age

Teenagers today want to read about teenagers today.

—S. E. Hinton, "Teen-Agers Are for Real," 1967

Hinton may have been writing in 1967, but she was echoing a concern that American educators had expressed for at least two decades. In 1946, for example, George W. Norvell wrote, "Our data shows clearly that much literary material being used in our schools is too subtle, too erudite." According to Nilsen and Donelson (2009, 59), Norvell went on to suggest that "teachers should give priority to the reading interests of young adults," concluding that "to increase reading skill, promote the reading habit, and produce a generation of book-lovers, there is no factor so powerful as interest."

Although I can't imagine any of them had read or even heard of Norvell, many teens of the early fifties featured in Maureen Daly's (1951) *Profile of Youth* echoed his views while acknowledging their personal dislike for reading. One senior boy, for example, reported switching to journalism from English literature because "they were giving us English writers of the seventeenth century and way back when" (41). A girl, it was reported, "doesn't like to read books and much prefers articles with many pictures" (62). It took another girl six weeks to get through the first hundred pages of *Pride and Prejudice*, and a horse-loving Wyoming boy asserted, "I read 'A Tale of Two Cities' last month for English class—didn't like it." "Another young cowboy," the profiler writes, "looked up. 'Last month,' he recalled morosely, 'last month we done 'Macbeth'" (215).

And so it goes. Would these teens have been more enthusiastic about reading if they had been permitted to self-select their books? Perhaps. The Dickens disliker did acknowledge reading about horses occasionally (though in farm and ranch magazines, not in books). And another boy demanded, "Why can't we read 'Cheaper by the Dozen' in class instead of some old has-been?" (96)

The problem, of course, was that even if teachers had been inclined to use young adult books in the classroom instead of books by old has-beens, it's obvious from our survey of the field that few works of young adult literature before 1960 would have qualified as literature. Indeed, many academics would have asserted that putting the words *young adult* and *literature* together was nothing but an oxymoron. And yet enough serious work was being done that the first tentative attempts at critical analysis had already begun to appear by the mid-1950s. Richard S. Alm (1955, 315), for example, noted in 1955 that "the last twenty years has seen the coming of age of the novel of the adolescent," perhaps, he ventured, because writers, "noting the heightened attention given to adolescents and their problems by psychologists, educators, and librarians, have turned to the personal concerns of the teen-ager."

Perhaps, but the writers of the novel for the adolescent whom Alm singled out for particular praise were all adult novelists like Maureen Daly, James Street, Dan Wickenden, William Maxwell, and Marjorie Kinnan Rawlings. This was consistent, though, with the approach Dwight L. Burton had taken in an earlier essay, "The Novel for the Adolescent," which is often cited as the first criticism of young adult literature. In it, Burton (1951, 362) devoted the lion's share of his attention to an analysis of work by four adult authors whose novels either showed "a keen perception of the adolescent experience" or "have a peculiar appeal to certain elements of the adolescent reading public." (For the record, the four authors were Dan Wickenden, Ruth Moore, C. S. Forester, and Thomas Wolfe.)

The point we infer from both of these early pieces of criticism is that, although there may—by the 1950s—have been a separate, identifiable body of books to be read by that separate, identifiable body of readers, young adults, too many of its constituent titles were what Alm (1955, 315) himself had glumly described as "slick, patterned, rather inconsequential stories written to capitalize on a rapidly expanding *market*" (emphasis added).

In 1956 a third early critic, Frank G. Jennings, was even blunter, grumbling, "The stuff of adolescent literature, for the most part, is mealy-mouthed, gutless, and pointless" (226). This may smack of overstatement for dramatic effect, but it is true, I think, that "much of the literature written for young adults from 1940 through 1966 goes largely and legitimately ignored today" (Nilsen and Donelson 1993, 574).

Books or Ladders?

Adolescence has always been viewed as a period of transition, of moving upward from one stage of development to another, and so it is not surprising that its literature, in the early years at least, should have been viewed as a ladder—or, more precisely, a rung on a ladder between children's and adult literature. This idea of reading ladders may have been the inspiration of Dora V. Smith, who, in the 1930s at the University of Minnesota, taught the first college-level course in adolescent literature. At least one of her most celebrated students, G. Robert Carlsen (1984, 29), thinks so, recalling that "in her classes we constructed ladders placing titles on the rungs according to our judgment of quality . . . through reading guidance a teacher was to move readers from one level to a higher one."[1]

Consistent with this concept is the corollary notion of stages of reading development (which echoes psychological stages of adolescent development!); that is, it is possible to identify certain specific types—or categories—of fiction that will appeal to young readers at certain specific ages or grade levels in school. In his influential 1967 work *Books and the Teen-age Reader* (Harper), Carlsen identified three such stages: (1) early adolescence, or ages eleven to fourteen, grades five to eight; (2) middle adolescence, or ages fifteen to sixteen, grades nine and ten; and (3) late adolescence, or ages seventeen to eighteen, grades eleven and twelve (Carlsen 1980). He then developed corollary categories of books that he believed offered unique appeal to students in each stage of development. For example, early adolescents would like animal, adventure, and mystery stories; middle adolescents would welcome war stories and historical novels; and late adolescents would dote on searches for personal values and books of social significance.

Carlsen linked these aspects of reading development to the University of Chicago psychologist Robert J. Havighurst's influential theory of developmental tasks, which seemed to suggest that if teenagers are to successfully climb the ladder of personal development from childhood to adulthood, they must successfully complete seven distinct life tasks: (1) achieve new and more mature relations with age mates of both sexes; (2) achieve masculine or feminine social roles; (3) accept their physiques and use their bodies effectively; (4) achieve emotional independence of parents and other adults; (5) prepare for marriage and family life; (6) prepare for economic careers; and (7) acquire a set of values and an ethical system as a guide to behavior (i.e., develop an ideology that leads to socially responsible behavior). "To accomplish [the tasks]," he claimed, "will lead to happiness and to success with later tasks, while failure leads to unhappiness in the individual, disapproval by society, and difficulty with later tasks" (Havighurst 1988, 61).

Havighurst's ideas influenced work other than Carlsen's. Evidence of this may be inferred from the Alm article. In it, the critic described what he perceived as the prevailing focus of young adult writers' attention: "In the main," he asserted, "these authors deal with an adolescent's relationships with others his own age, with his parents and other adults, and with such worries as deciding upon and preparing for a job, 'going steady,' marrying and facing the responsibilities of adulthood" (Alm 1955, 315). Though unacknowledged, this simply echoes Havighurst's list of development tasks.

Carlsen (1984, 29) was more candid, recalling of his own teaching methods: "I applied Robert Havighurst's concept of developmental tasks to adolescent books. It seemed to me that the most popular and successful titles, like Daly's 'Seventeenth Summer,' were books in which characters were dealing with one or more of the developmental tasks. So we looked not only at the story content, but also at the conflicts and turmoils besetting the characters."

Personally, I think the persistent attempt to transform literature into utilitarian ladders too often turned the early critics' attention from the work to the personal problems of the reader; that act, in turn, invited the transformation of a promising literature into the series of undemanding, formula-driven problem novels that would emerge in the sixties and seventies. I also think that frog-marching literature into ready-made category pens labeled for reading-age suitability homogenizes readers, smacks of the didactic and dogmatic, and threatens to turn literature from art to tool. Small wonder that young readers, beginning to feel manipulated, joined their voices in the chorus that greeted the looming new decade: "Never trust anybody over thirty."

The Times, They Were A'—Well, You Know . . .

This brings us to the 1960s, when the times and the literature would both be a-changin'! If one song—nasal balladeer Bob Dylan's 1964 release "The Times They Are a-Changin'"—epitomized the social mood of this turbulent decade, one novel did the same for the nascent genre soon to be called young adult literature. As had been the case in the 1940s with Maureen Daly and her *Seventeenth Summer*, the sea change would arrive with the appearance of a single young writer—again, a teenage girl—and the publication of her first novel. This time the book was *The Outsiders*, by S. E. Hinton of Tulsa, Oklahoma.

And so it is that we have two young women and two books, each with far-reaching influence on young adult literature and each with enormous popular attention because of the novelty of their authors themselves being teenagers. But there the similarities end and the differences begin. For starters, Hinton was writing about boys, not girls (one reason her publisher suggested she use her initials instead of her given name, Susan Elizabeth). And she wasn't writing about tree-shaded streets in small-town middle America. Instead, she was writing about mean urban streets where teenagers didn't have time to agonize over first love and dates for the prom; they were too busy agonizing over whether they would survive the next skirmish in their ongoing war with a rival gang.

For it was warfare that Hinton (1967a) was writing about—class warfare as symbolized by the two gangs that appear in *The Outsiders*: the Greasers and the Socs. *Soc* was short for "Socials, the jet set, the Westside rich kids" who "wreck houses and throw beer blasts for kicks" (10–11). (The Soc as a term and a social type had been around since the early fifties. One of the students in Daly's 1951 *Profile of Youth* is referred to as "a 'real sosh,' short for 'social.' That meant he was considered one of the right crowd, dated the right girls and went to the right dances" (109). As for the economically deprived Greasers, they are "almost like hoods" and are given to their own antisocial behavior—they "steal things and drive old souped-up cars and hold up gas stations" (11).

Significantly, Hinton's story is told in the first-person voice of one of the Greasers: fourteen-year-old Ponyboy Curtis, who lives with his older brothers Sodapop and Darry, the latter of whom acts in loco parentis, because the Curtis boys' real parents have been killed in a car wreck before the story begins. As Ponyboy reports, "The three of us get to stay together only as long as we behave" (11). They try to avoid the more lawbreaking Greaser activities, contenting themselves, instead, with wearing their "tuff" hair long, dressing in blue jeans and T-shirts, and lifting a fist in the inevitable rumble.

Hinton's was not the first novel to deal with gangs. Frank Bonham's story of Los Angeles, *Durango Street*, had been published in 1965, but there was something about *The Outsiders* that captured the imagination of its readers and spawned a new kind of literature, "books," as Richard Peck (1994, 154) has put it, "about young people parents thought their children didn't know." Hinton knew them, though; she went to school with them every day in Tulsa. She knew from personal observation what their lives were like, but as a reader, she didn't find that kind of first-person reality being depicted in the pages of young adult literature.

"The world is changing," she wrote in an impassioned *New York Times Book Review* article, "yet the authors of books for teen-agers are still 15 years behind the times. In the fiction they write, romance is still the most popular theme, with a horse-and-the-girl-who-loved-it coming in a close second" (Hinton 1967b, 26). Hinton continued, "Nowhere is the drive-in social jungle mentioned. . . . In short, where is the reality[?]" Hinton was not alone in wondering that.

In 1966 George Woods, then children's book editor of the *New York Times Book Review*, wrote, "One looks for modernity, boldness, for realism. The teen-age novel, especially, should grapple with the delights and the dilemmas of today's teen-agers. Delicacy and restraint are necessarily called for, yet all too often this difficult problem is resolved through avoidance. A critic in touch with the world and aware of the needs of the young expects to see more handling of neglected subjects: narcotics, addiction, illegitimacy, alcoholism, pregnancy, discrimination, retardation. There are few, if any, definitive works in these areas" (169).

Not quite four months before Hinton's piece appeared, Nat Hentoff delivered a similarly scathing indictment of young adult literature in the *Times*. Writing of his own first YA novel, he asserted, "'Jazz Country' failed, as have most books directed at teen-agers. . . . [M]y point is that the reality of being young—the tensions, the sensual yearnings and sometime satisfactions, the resentment against the educational lock step that makes children fit the schools, the confusing recognition of their parents' hypocrisies and failures—all this is absent from most books for young readers" (Hentoff 1967, 3).

A year later the Newbery Medal–winning author Maia Wojciechowska (1968, 13) joined the chorus, criticizing authors of books for the young who "keep going back to their own turn-of-the-century childhoods, or write tepid little stories of high school proms, broken and amended friendships, phony-sounding conflicts between parents and children, and boring accounts of what they consider 'problems.' The gulf between the real child of today and his fictional counterpart must be bridged."

Hinton's great success came in managing to bridge that gap and, by giving fictional counterparts to the real teenagers she knew, to introduce to young adult fiction new kinds of "real" characters—whether they were the alienated, socioeconomically disadvantaged Greasers or the equally alienated but socioeconomically advantaged Socs.

Her novel was innovative, too, in its introduction of thematic relevance. Hinton (1967b, 26) had been quite right when she pointed out, in her *New York Times* piece, that "violence, too, is part of teenagers' lives." Before her, though, authors had tended to ignore this basic reality of adolescent life. But Hinton used it as a tool to define the daily lives of her characters, both as individuals and as gang members, and this use was groundbreaking and consistent with the demands of the realistic novel.

As we have seen, Hinton rejected the literature that had been written for her generation, calling it "the inane junk lining the teen-age shelf of the library." And her rejection of the established literature for young adults is also consistent with the universal rejection of the status quo, which was such a hallmark of the iconoclastic sixties, a decade that belonged to the young.

Because of her own youth, Hinton came to symbolize that rejection as well as its replacement by a new kind of literature. Richard Peck (1993, 19), writing of the authors, including himself, whose work would follow hers, has said she "may be the mother of us all." The Young Adult Library Services Association confirmed that assessment in 1988 with the presentation, to Hinton, of the first Margaret A. Edwards Award, which recognizes lifetime achievement in writing young adult books.

So Hinton's significant place in the evolution of young adult literature is secure, yet reading her first novel today, one is struck by what an odd hybrid it is: part realistic fiction and part romantic fantasy that, at its self-indulgent worst, exemplifies what the critic Terrence Rafferty (1994, 93) has called "morbid adolescent romanticism." Her Greasers are such romantically idealized figures, in fact, that it is small wonder that Ponyboy is, himself, enchanted by other romantic figures, the Southern cavaliers of Margaret Mitchell's *Gone with the Wind*. There is some verisimilitude in this, however. The sociologist Frederick Thrasher had earlier, in his 1929 study of 1,313 Chicago gangs, pointed out that gang members placed a high value on physical prowess, peer loyalty, and even chivalry (Kett 1977).

Another element of romanticism is Hinton's sometimes-sentimental treatment of her theme of lost innocence, which may, in turn, invite some revisionist comparisons with J. M. Barrie's *Peter Pan* and his band of Lost Boys.

This loss of innocence was also the theme of J. D. Salinger's *The Catcher in the Rye* (Little, Brown, 1951), a more distinguished work of fiction that, though published for adults, is also a more viable model for the modern young adult novel than is Hinton's. *Catcher*'s most powerful contribution is the idiosyncratic, first-person voice of its narrator, Holden Caulfield. But the book is also quintessentially adolescent in its tone, attitudes, and choice of narrative incidents, many of which are rite of passage, including the obligatory (and obligatorily embarrassing) encounter with a prostitute. The latter introduction of sexuality may explain why none of the early critics of YA books—Alm, Burton, Jennings, Carlsen—included *Catcher* in their analyses (*Catcher* did make it into Carlsen's 1971 revision).

Wry, cynical, funny, and intensely self-conscious, Holden's voice is one of the more original in American fiction, and the story he tells is a marvel of sustained style and tone. Even more than *Seventeenth Summer, Catcher* helped establish a tradition of first-person narrative voice for young adult fiction.

Holden's tone and manner are clearly echoed in the work of Paul Zindel, whose own first novel *The Pigman* was published in 1968, a scant year after Hinton's. Zindel's debt to Salinger is the more obvious, as his characters, like Salinger's, hail from the urban East—New York City, to be precise. Another YA pioneer, John Donovan, whose first novel *I'll Get There, It Better Be Worth the Trip* was published in 1969, also employed the New York setting and, like Zindel, echoed Holden's unmistakable voice and attitude.

Because Zindel was an accomplished playwright and a demonstrated master of dialogue (he won the Pulitzer Prize for Drama in 1971), it's not surprising that he chose to tell his story in not one but two first-person voices: those of teenage friends John and Lorraine, whose brash, colloquial tone invites further comparison with Holden's. There are other similarities: John, like Holden, is both "extremely handsome" and a prodigiously gifted liar. He hates school, too, and has a horror of being a "phony in the crowd" (Zindel 1968, 71).

Further, Holden's favorite word is *madman,* and after having some kind of indeterminate breakdown, he tells his story "about this madman stuff" from a sanitarium where he has been sent "to take it easy" (Salinger 1951, 1). There are numerous references to mental illness in *The Pigman,* too. Lorraine tells readers "how really disturbed" two of her classmates are and believes herself to be paranoid. For his part, John announces he is a lunatic. Neither of the two is really insane, of course, only terminally smart-alecky.

Zindel's biographer, Jack Forman (1994, 933), summarized critical opinion: "'The Pigman' was a groundbreaking event because—along with S. E. Hinton's 'The Outsiders'—it transformed what had been called the teen 'junior novel' from a predictable, stereotyped story about high school sports and dances to one about complex teenage protagonists dealing with real concerns."

Complex? Real? Perhaps—but John and Lorraine seem more types of disaffected modern youths than real characters (and, frankly, their narrative voices are so similar as to be sometimes indistinguishable). Compared with their parents, however, they are positively Chekhovian in their complexities. Zindel seems to have taken George Woods's thoughts about adult hypocrisy to heart, for John's and Lorraine's parents are one-dimensional cartoon versions of prevailing adult stereotypes. John thinks, "I would rather be dead than to turn into the kind of grown-up people I knew" (Zindel 1968, 178).

Given their respective romanticism and dramatic hyperbole, it's a bit surprising that Hinton and Zindel have traditionally been accorded the lion's share of the credit for ushering in a new age of modern, realistic young adult fiction. Especially when a third writer, whose first young adult novel was also published in 1967, served up an authentically realistic work of fiction in terms of theme, character, setting, style, and resolution. I refer to Robert Lipsyte, whose gritty, often hard-edged novel *The Contender* (1967) offers a richly realized theme—becoming an individual and transforming the self—that speaks to the quintessential adolescent experience. His protagonist, Alfred Brooks, is a black teenager living with his aunt in a tiny Harlem apartment. For Alfred, the future offers nothing but dead ends—until he discovers Donatelli's Gym and learns that, though he may not have the killer instinct necessary to become a successful boxer, he does have the necessary strength of character to become a contender in the larger arena of life.

Lipsyte, like Zindel, was already an established writer before turning to young adult fiction. At the age of twenty-seven, he was one of two internationally syndicated sports columnists for the *New York Times.* His experience as a journalist, trained to search for the telling detail and for reporting the unflinching, though often unpleasant, truth guaranteed a book that is a marvel of verisimilitude in the details of its setting: the boxing world and its gritty, New York streets backdrop. The characters, even the minor ones, are real people, not conventional types. They have believable motivations and authentic reactions to one another and to the situations in which they find themselves. With four decades of hindsight, it now seems that it is *The Contender* and not *The Outsiders* or *The Pigman* that is a model for the kind of novel that Woods, Hentoff, and Hinton herself had called for in the articles cited earlier in this chapter. This revisionist critical opinion was reflected in the long-overdue awarding of the Margaret A. Edwards Award to Lipsyte in 2001.

Regardless of who was first responsible, it is inarguable that, in the late sixties, YA literature was in a hectic period of transition from a literature that had traditionally offered a head-in-the-sand approach to one that offered a more clear-eyed and unflinching look at the often unpleasant realities of American adolescent life.

It would be an uphill battle, though, for not only are young adults inherently romantic; they are also inherently reality denying. Richard Peck (1994, 159), as usual, put it well: "In depicting reality our books are often on a collision course with our readers' most deeply felt beliefs: that they cannot die or be infected with sexually transmitted diseases, or get pregnant unless they want to, or become addicted to anything. Our books regularly challenge their conviction that the rules don't apply to them. There are limits to the amount of reality the novel form can encompass. Young adults test the boundaries."

Lipsyte—and Hinton and Zindel and Donovan, and even Bonham and Hentoff—were among the first to test these boundaries and, in the process, to set aside certain shibboleths that had contributed to the rosy unreality of previous YA novels. The taboos that had hobbled the literature in terms of subject and style had flourished in the complicity of silence that authors had maintained in the forties and fifties. But in the late sixties and early seventies, a new and bolder generation of authors began to break the silence with the power and candor of their voices. "Authors [now] wrote the way people really talked—often ungrammatically, sometimes profanely" (Nilsen and Donelson 1988, 275).

Zindel had written the way two people really talked; in 1973 Alice Childress would go him ten better and write in twelve different voices while also addressing the hard-edged issue of heroin abuse in her novel *A Hero Ain't Nothin' but a Sandwich* (Coward, McCann). Hinton would also write about drug abuse (*That Was Then, This Is Now*, Viking, 1971). As for other taboo topics, Zindel would write about abortion (*My Darling, My Hamburger*, Harper, 1969); Norma Klein would write about a happily unwed mother (*Mom, the Wolfman, and Me*, Pantheon, 1972); John Donovan would break one of the strictest taboos of all when he introduced the subject of homosexuality (*I'll Get There, It Better Be Worth the Trip*, Harper, 1969); and, in the era of the Vietnam War, Nat Hentoff explored the ethics of the military draft and the hot issue of avoiding it (*I'm Really Dragged but Nothing Gets Me Down*, Simon & Schuster, 1968).

Robert Cormier and the Seventies

In retrospect, the period from 1967 to 1975 is remarkable for the boldness with which writers began to break new ground, in terms of both subject and style. The single most important innovation of the seventies, however, came at the very end of this period, with the 1974 publication of Robert Cormier's first young adult novel, *The Chocolate War*. In it, this working journalist and already established author of adult fiction single-handedly turned the genre in a dramatic new direction by having the courage to write a novel of unprecedented thematic weight and substance for young adults, one that dared to disturb the comfortable universe of both adolescents and the adults who continued to protect their tender sensibilities. It did this by boldly acknowledging that not all endings of novels and real lives are happy ones. In this story of Jerry Renault, a teenage boy who resolutely refuses to sell chocolates in his school's annual fund-raiser and thereby challenges the accepted order of things with dire consequences, Cormier took his young adult readers into the very heart of darkness for the first time, turned the lights on, and showed them what the landscape there looked like. Alas, it looked alarmingly like the real one we all inhabit and read about in our morning papers and see depicted daily on the evening news. In that novel, and in the fourteen that would follow before Cormier's death in 2000, he continued to disturb the too-comfortable universe by challenging complacency, by reminding us that, as he himself later said, "adolescence is such a lacerating time that most of us carry the baggage of our adolescence with us all our lives" (Sutton 1982, 33).

Dark forces are at work in the world Cormier limned not only in *The Chocolate War* but also in such other indispensable novels as *I Am the Cheese, After the First Death, Fade, The Bumblebee Flies Anyway, We All Fall Down,* and so many more. Cormier's is a deterministic view that sees evil—sometimes institutionalized—in a world where conventional morality may not prevail and where there are powerful, faceless forces that will destroy us if we disturb them. Such a revolutionary view opened enormous areas of thematic possibility for writers who would come after him. In turn, this amazing author was always quick to acknowledge his own debt to a writer who came before him: Grahame Greene, whom he called "the writer-mentor of my mature years" (Cart 2000) and whom he was fond of quoting: "The creative writer perceives his world once and for all time in childhood and adolescence and his whole career is an effort to illustrate his private world in terms of the public world we all share" (Cormier 1998, 22). Students of young adult literature will know how brilliantly he succeeded.

Had the seventies produced no other writer than Robert Cormier, they would be remembered as the first golden age of young adult literature. Wonderfully, however, the decade also saw the first work of at least half a dozen others who would become grand masters of the field upon receiving the Margaret A. Edwards Award (Cormier himself received the honor in 1991). These others include Judy Blume, whose first novel *Are You There God? It's Me Margaret* appeared in 1970; M. E. Kerr, whose first YA novel *Dinky Hocker Shoots Smack* was published in 1972; Richard Peck, who debuted the same year with *Don't Look and It Won't Hurt*; Lois Duncan, whose *I Know What You Did Last Summer* came along in 1973;[2] Walter Dean Myers, with *Fast Sam, Cool Clyde, and Stuff* in 1975; and Lois Lowry, with *A Summer to Die* in 1977. What an extraordinary roster—what an extraordinary decade!

The emergence of a serious body of literature expressly written and published for young adults was also acknowledged—however belatedly—when the Young Adult Library Services Association (YALSA), in 1973, finally began considering YA titles for inclusion on its annual Best Books for Young Adults list (the list had been called by that name since 1966 but had included only adult titles). Three young adult novels were selected for the historic 1973 list, which also contained thirty-one adult titles: Alice Childress's *A Hero Ain't Nothin' but a Sandwich*, Rosa Guy's *The Friends*, and Robert Newton Peck's *A Day No Pigs Would Die*.

The Problem with the Problem Novel

Unfortunately, success and innovation often breed not only more success and innovation but also pale imitation, as new techniques are turned into recycled formula, making subject (think "problem") and theme the tail that wags the dog of the novel. Such was the case in the later seventies with the appearance and swift ascendancy of what has come to be called the problem novel.

The Canadian critic Sheila Egoff (1980, 196) has described the characteristic deficiencies of the problem novel as well as any other observer: "It was very strongly subject-oriented with the interest primarily residing in the topic rather than the telling. The topics—all adult oriented—sound like chapter titles from a textbook on social pathology: divorce, drugs, disappearing parents, desertion and death." Or think of it this way, and you'll understand the problem with the problem novel: it is to young adult literature what soap opera is to legitimate drama.

Just why the new novel of realism so often degenerated into the single-issue problem novel may be an unanswerable question. But it surely has something to do with the rapid pace of change overtaking the lives of young people in the late sixties and early seventies and the perhaps belated recognition by writers and publishers that the novel, if it is to have any hope of offering relevance and revelation to its readers, must keep pace with the ever-changing and ever-more-sophisticated ingredients of their daily, real-world lives.

Looking back at the seventies, Egoff (1980, 194) pointed out that "adolescents had been steadily assuming more and more of the attributes, perquisites, and problems of their elders. Like adults, teenagers now had money, cars, jobs, and also drugs, liquor, sex, and the assorted difficulties arising therefrom." The powerful newness of those difficulties and the intoxicatingly sudden freedom to write about them caused some writers to forget the totality of the realistic novel's mission: it must portray not only real-life circumstances—problems, if you must—but also the real people living in real settings. Hence, this thought from critic—and later *Horn Book* editor—Roger Sutton (1982, 33): "Instead of a character being the focus of the novel, a condition (or social concern) became the subject of examination." Or, as Sheila Egoff (1980, 67) argued,

"The realistic novel grows out of the personal vision of the writer," while the problem novel "stems from the writer's social conscience."

The writer who, by this measure, apparently boasted the most highly developed social conscience of the sixties and seventies was Jeanette Eyerly, who might be called the queen of the problem novel. One remembers her many, many books not by the richness of their settings or the complexities of the characters but, instead, by the problems her interchangeable kids were forced to deal with. Thus, *Drop-Out* (1963) is not about people but about the perils and consequences of dropping out of school; *A Girl Like Me* (1966) is about the wages of teenage pregnancy; abortion is all we remember of *Bonnie Jo, Go Home* (1972); similarly, the only memorable aspect of *The World of Ellen March* (1964) is the divorce of the title character's parents; and, in this ongoing inventory of woe, there appear suicide (*The Girl Inside*, 1968), drugs (*Escape from Nowhere*, 1969), runaways (*See Dave Run*, 1978), and—well, you get the idea.

It's ironic, however, that while such books were receiving scorn and disapproval from adult reviewers, they were enjoying enormous success with young adult readers. "Teens," Sutton (1982, 33) wryly observed, "don't even read these books so much as they gobble them like peanuts, picking them up by the handful, one right after the other." Deny though they might the relevance of the problems to their own lives (pace Richard Peck), teens seemed to dote on reading about how they plagued other people's lives. In retrospect, it seems that the problem novel offered readers the same sort of appeal that horror fiction would a decade later: the frisson of reading about darkness from the comfort of a clean, well-lit room.

If the problem novel received an often well-deserved drubbing from reviewers, the early novels of realism did not escape unscathed, either. As early as November 1969, Diane Gersoni Stavn (1969, 139) noted that "an unusual number of juvenile novels aimed at an audience of young teens and attempting realism" had been published in 1968 and 1969, but "these stories [were] often written according to the language, structure, and content specifications of children's books."

The next broadside came in 1976, with Jane Abramson's "Still Playing It Safe: Restricted Realism in Teen Novels," in which the author argued that "the restrictions on teen fiction result in books that succeed only in mirroring a slick surface realism that too often acts as a cover up. . . . Books that set out to tackle painful subjects turn into weak testimonies to life's essential goodness" (38). There is nothing wrong with testimonies, of course, unless they compromise aesthetic inevitability by forcing an unrealistically happy ending on an otherwise realistically downbeat story: suppose, for example, it turns out that the woman Oedipus slept with wasn't his mother after all and, at story's end, a gifted eye surgeon is found whose uncanny abilities enable him to restore the self-blinded king's eyesight. *Rex redux!*

This kind of manipulation transforms realism into romance and demonstrates the kind of "cockeyed optimism" and "false notes of uplift" that Abramson objected to in teen novels (38). I think she was quite correct in this aspect of her criticism. However, it should be remembered that the kind of realistic novel that was being written in the late sixties and early seventies was still firmly rooted in the traditions of nineteenth-century American realism and its essentially optimistic view that goodness would prevail and that man had the power of free will to make it so. It was not until Cormier's *Chocolate War* arrived in 1974 that there was the first hint of determinism and the notion that evil might conceivably carry the day. But it could also be argued that Cormier was operating not in the tradition of realism at all but in that of naturalism, which views human beings as hapless victims of social and natural forces.

Be that as it may, I suspect most readers will be happy simply to acknowledge that whatever these novels were, they were at least different from those of the forties and fifties, and the best of them were good enough for some to call the seventies a golden age of young adult literature.

Others, those who use the phrase "problem novel" as a pejorative, will be less sanguine. Though technically the problem novel and the realistic novel are synonymous ("What's a novel without a problem?" Marilyn Kriney, the former publisher of HarperCollins Children's Books, asked cogently), there are, practically speaking, differences that we have already discussed (Cart 1996, 71). As the seventies drew to a close, those differences loomed large, indeed. For if—despite its occasional lapses—the novel of realism was gradually evolving into something richer and more rewarding, the problem novel was evolving into something, well, ridiculous. As competition for readers' attention became ever brisker, the problems being addressed had to become ever more sensational until the problem novel reached an arguable nadir in two books whose publication bracketed the decade. The first was *Go Ask Alice* by Anonymous (Prentice-Hall, 1971) and the second was Scott Bunn's *Just Hold On* (Delacorte, 1982).

Though presented as the "authentic" diary of a "real" fifteen-year-old girl who ultimately dies of a drug overdose, *Go Ask Alice* was actually a work of fiction coauthored by two adults: Beatrice Sparks and Linda Glovach. Nevertheless, as late as the 1998 Aladdin paperback edition, it was still being touted as "the harrowing true story of a teenager's descent into the seductive world of drugs." Over the years, the question of the book's authenticity has become something of a cause célèbre and the issue is even discussed at the urban legends website Snopes.com.

Perhaps because its treatment of the dangers of drug use is so sensational, lurid, and over the top, *Go Ask Alice* has been hugely successful, never going out of print and selling millions of copies to credulous teenagers. Most modern readers find it unintentionally hilarious in its melodramatic overstatements and, though originally aimed at high school–age students, principally middle school students now read *Alice*.

Scott Bunn's *Just Hold On*, a more serious effort at the tragic consequences of being a teen, proved less enduringly successful, though not for lack of its own sensational content. *Time* magazine helpfully summarized its plot: "Heroine Charlotte Maag, 16, is raped by her father, an Albany pediatrician. She befriends fellow loner Stephen Hendron, who is hiding the shame and rejection of his own physician-father's alcoholism. By mid-story Charlotte is on the sauce, Stephen is involved in a homosexual affair with a football star named Rolf, and both tumble into bed with another couple after a bourbon and pot party. At novel's end Stephen is near catatonia and Charlotte is institutionalized" (Reed 1982, 66).[3]

This kind of wretched excess suggested that the genre was not only over-ripe but also overdue for satire. The irrepressible Daniel M. Pinkwater took the cue and responded with his own *Young Adult Novel* (Crowell, 1982), a hilarious take off on the problem novel. A nice coincidence is that Pinkwater's novel was published the same year as Bunn's book, sounding the death knell for the subgenre it represented. Unfortunately, by this time, the shrill sensationalism of the subgenre had exhausted readers, and accordingly, they rejected not only the problem novel but also the novel of realism and maybe even reality itself. And small wonder, for while it may be true that, in popular culture, "The Seventies are often considered a joke decade, defined by shag carpet, pet rocks, streaking, polyester leisure suits, and the thump-thump of Beethoven to a disco beat" (Rollin 1999, 241), it is also true that it was the decade of the Kent State shootings, the forced resignation of Vice President Spiro Agnew, Watergate, the resignation of President Richard Nixon, the ignominious end of the Vietnam War, the economic hard times of the Carter administration, the Iran hostage crisis, anxiety over the environment (the first Earth Day was held in 1970), the kidnapping of Patty Hearst, and the violent deaths of her captors. Times were hard; the daily business of life was unsettling, and young readers began turning for relief to a resurgence of the sweetly unrealistic romance novel. Welcome, reader, to the 1980s.

Notes

1. Much of the analysis of early YA literature came from professors of education, that is, teachers who were teaching prospective teachers. Critical writing from teachers of

library science came later, as—still later—did work from university English and comparative literature departments.

2. Duncan had actually begun publishing in the 1960s, but her early work was, for the most part, forgettable formula romance.

3. It's worth noting that the mass media only takes note of YA literature when it's at its most outrageous.

the eighties—
something old,
something new

The Rise of the Paperback Series, Multicultural Literature, and Political Correctness

If the laws of physics applied to young adult literature, for every action (read "innovation"), there would be an equal and opposite reaction. One doubts that it was physics—more probably a combination of publishing economics and weariness with hard-edged realism—but it is a fact that just such a reaction followed the decadelong emergence of such realism, with its relatively unsparing and unrelenting focus on life's darker aspects. That this should have manifested itself as an early eighties renaissance of forties- and fifties-style romance fiction may, at first, seem surprising until one remembers the conservatively nostalgic climate of a country that had also swept a forties movie star and former host of the fifties television series *Death Valley Days* into the White House.

The critic Margo Jefferson finds effect in this cause. Writing in 1982, when the romance revival was still in its early innings, she concluded that the emotionally recidivist titles were "grown-up nostalgia repackaged for the young, very like those remakes of 1950s and 1960s songs by people in their 30s and 40s pretending to be ten or twenty years younger" (Jefferson 1982, 613).

As early as 1974, the journalist Edwin Miller was warning readers of *Seventeen* magazine about just such a grown-up nostalgia that seemed to be skewing Hollywood's portrayal of teens in the seventies. "Young people have become more troublesome in recent years," he wrote. "Even nice kids. If [however] you have a teen-ager pinned down in the past like a butterfly under glass, you've got the upper hand" (Rollin 1999, 262). This sounds a bit paranoid, but it's true that Hollywood was busily harvesting the past for display both on America's large and small screens. *American Graffiti*, George Lucas's sentimental salute to the early sixties, was a box-office sensation in 1973, and *Happy Days*, a nostalgic nod to the simpler—and arguably happier—times of the 1950s, was the number-one-rated television show of the 1976–1977 season.

When it was their turn, publishers cranked the clock back even farther, to the 1940s, with their fictional treatment of the innocent romantic lives of young people who Barson and Heller (1998), in their amusing book *Teenage Confidential,* call "Kleen Teens."

If the adolescent lives portrayed in the eighties' romances were an eerie replication of those already unreal lives found in the pages of the forties and fifties versions, their packaging at least was different this time around. Although there had been a certain sameness to the content of the earlier titles, they were, at least, published as individual hardcovers by writers whose names—Janet Lambert, Betty Cavanna, Anne Emery—quickly became household words. The new romances, however, had little individual identity; they were slick, mass-market paperback series appearing at the rate of one new title per month under such saccharine rubrics as Wildfire, Caprice, Sweet Dreams, First Love, Wishing Star, and so on and on. If they were branded, it was with the name of their series, not that of their authors.

The decision to revive romance was not made in a vacuum, however; marketing decisions seldom are. The editor Pamela Pollack (1981, 25) explained, "Mass market paperback publishers gave teens what they 'want' as determined by market research, rather than what they 'need' based on their problems as reflected by social statistics."

In fact, what they wanted in the eighties was what their parents had already been demanding—and getting—for a decade or more: genre romances and formulaic bodice-ripper-of-the-month gothic paperbacks. The latter—the adult gothics—had hit the paperback racks at least two decades earlier, led by the 1960 publication of Victoria Holt's *Mistress of Mellyn* (Doubleday).

However, it was not until the seventies, according to Kristin Ramsdell, that the (adult) romance boom really began. Although historical romances were especially popular at first, "light, innocent, Category (usually contemporary) Romances were popular, as well" (Ramsdell 1987, 8). It was this latter type that began trickling down into YA publishing at about the time that President Reagan's trickle-down theories of economics hit the marketplace.

Both offered what many readers have always, not unreasonably, wanted: escape from life's cares and woes. The author Jane Yolen told *Seventeen* magazine that "the trend is a teenager's way of saying 'enough.' Teenagers have seen their adolescence taken away by graphic television shows and movies and books. The return to romance is a way to return to the mystery and beauty of love, even if only on a superficial level" (Kellogg 1983, 158).

Well, maybe. But it's worth noting that Yolen is, most famously, an author of fantasy, and the lives portrayed in romances had more of the never-never to them than reality. Here's how Pollack (1981, 28) described them: "The heroines—shy, inexperienced, small-town girls—live in happy homes and tend to have names that end in 'ie.' Their primary interest in life is boys; having a steady ensures a place in the high school hierarchy. They are not interested in college or career and are not involved in the women's movement. Their mothers are their role models. Their fathers are shadowy but benign bread-winners. There are no grandparents—in fact, there are few elderly, black, or handicapped people to be found."

The predictably hand-wringing adult reaction to this was not long in coming. As early as 1981, when the romance boom was only two years old, a coalition of organizations led by the Council on Interracial Books for Children issued a report charging, among other things, that these books "teach girls that their primary value is their attractiveness to boys; devalue relationships and encourage competition between girls; discount the possibility of nonromantic friendships between boys and girls; depict middle-class, white, small-town families as the norm; and portray adults in stereotypical sex roles" (Ramsdell 1983, 177).

Apparently, however, stereotypes sell, for the new romance series were wildly successful from their very inception. Scholastic's Wildfire, which debuted in 1979, sold 1.8 million copies of sixteen titles in one year. Dell's Young Love followed in February 1981; Bantam's Sweet Dreams, in September 1981; Simon & Schuster's First Love, in February 1982; and in 1985 the first YA novel ever to reach the *New York Times* paperback best-seller list, the Sweet Valley High super edition *Perfect Summer*. Created by Francine Pascal, the Sweet Valley empire soon spawned countless spin-offs; by the end of the eighties, there were 34 million Sweet Valley High books in print (Huntwork 1990).

Speaking, still, of sales, another significant difference between the new romance and that of the forties was that, for the first time, teens themselves were the targeted consumers. Affluent though the eighties may have been in consumer terms, they were a period of economic hardship for schools and libraries. With this traditional market for YA literature in eclipse, publishers began looking for a new one. As Ramsdell (1987, 19) points out, Scholastic's launch of its Wildfire series "changed the way materials were marketed to young adults. . . . Previously publishers had concentrated on reaching young adults indirectly through the schools and libraries; now they tried selling to them directly with spectacular results."

By the early 1980s American teens were spending a staggering $45 billion per year on nonessential consumables, and new marketing companies like Teen Research Unlimited, of Northbrook, Illinois, had been founded to poll them and otherwise study their tastes and habits. It was another example of history's repeating itself. It was in the 1940s, remember, that teens were first identified as potential consumers and, to study them, the pioneer marketing maven Eugene Gilbert founded his Youth Marketing Company.

By 1986, 93 percent of high school students in one national survey had worked for pay. "You want to talk revolution?" *Forbes* magazine cynically asked. "Not to this generation of adolescents. They have seen the future—and they want to buy it, not change it" (Rollin 1999, 282).

And where were they buying it? In the new American consumer paradise, the shopping mall. The first enclosed shopping mall in America had opened in 1957 in Edina, Minnesota, and in the succeeding two decades the mall had become such a fixture of American life and home away from home for America's teenagers that Richard Peck had become its unofficial laureate with his 1979 novel *Secrets of the Shopping Mall* (Delacorte).

The omnipresence of the malls quickly led to the evolution of the chain bookstore. Announcing Pacer Books, a new line of YA paperbacks from Putnam, then editor in chief Beverly Horowitz explained that Pacer titles would be found in display racks in these new fixtures of the omnipresent malls, "hangout places where kids go on a boring Saturday. You will find Pacer positioned right between the fast-food haven and the record store. There is a teen-aged consumer force out there, and the only way to reach them is to go where *their* action is" (Baldwin 1984, 15).

George Nicholson, then editor in chief of Dell/Delacorte Books and a pioneer in paperback publishing for young readers with Dell's Yearling Books, agreed, explaining that chain bookstores in malls "demystified the traditional bookstore concept for kids. Now they can buy anything they want. They have the power to come in, pay their money, and out they go, without being harassed. No one questions them" (Baldwin 1984, 18).

The stupendous success of paperback romance series soon inspired other genre incursions into the marketplace, most notably horror. Christopher Pike is generally credited with creating the bloodcurdling stampede with the 1985 publication of his novel *Slumber Party*. However, R. L. Stine quickly followed with his first foray into horror (writing as Jovial Bob Stine, he had previously been known as an author of joke books); his *Blind Date* was published in 1987. Both authors became phenomenally popular, though Stine took the lead with the 1990 introduction of his Fear Street series and the 1992 debut of the Goosebumps books. By 1994 there were twenty-one Goosebumps titles, and each had sold in excess of 1 million copies in paperback (Cart 1996).

As were the romance series, horror fiction was formula driven, produced according to multipage specification sheets that virtually guaranteed predictable plots and cardboard characters. Settings were as blandly white, middle class, and suburban as those of romance novels and equally devoid of sex (though gouts of blood were always welcome).

New Voices and Multicultural Stirrings

Despite the glut of paperback series, the eighties also saw the debut of a number of literarily and culturally important new voices, including the likes of Francesca Lia Block, Bruce Brooks, Brock Cole, Chris Crutcher, Ron Koertge, Gary Paulsen, Cynthia Voigt, and Virginia Euwer Wolff (Block, Crutcher, Paulsen, and Voigt would go on to receive the Margaret A. Edwards Award for their contributions to the field).

Meanwhile, already established voices continued to be heard; such stalwarts as Sue Ellen Bridgers (*Permanent Connections*, 1987); S. E. Hinton (*Tex*, 1980, and *Taming the Star Runner*, 1988); Robert Cormier (*The Bumblebee Flies Anyway*, 1983; *Beyond the Chocolate War*, 1985; and *Fade*, 1988); M. E. Kerr (*Little Little*, 1981; *Me, Me, Me, Me, Me: Not a Novel*, 1983; and *Night Kites*, 1986); Robert Lipsyte (*Summer Rules*, 1981, and *The Summer Boy*, 1982); and Richard Peck (*Remembering the Good Times*, 1985, and *Princess Ashley*, 1987) published major work.

As the legendary editor Charlotte Zolotow—who worked with Block, Kerr, Lipsyte, Zindel, and others—noted, "The more original you are in publishing, the harder it is to be commercially successful but good writing survives trends," adding that young adult novels in the eighties were "becoming more honest and realistic, authors writing out of heart, feeling, and genuine motivation" (Baldwin 1984, 17).

Another legendary editor, Jean Karl, who had founded the children's book department at Atheneum, agreed: "Young adults are moving into new areas of their lives," she said, "where they need to find books which will provide them with *literary* experiences that will broaden their view of the world" (Baldwin 1984, 20, emphasis added).

Clearly, this view needed broadening, because the world of the 1980s that young (and old) adults inhabited was changing dramatically. One of the most significant changes had begun quietly enough back in 1965, when the U.S.

Congress passed certain amendments to the Immigration and Nationality Act that not only placed a ceiling on immigration from European countries for the first time but also set it lower than the newly established limits for those from other parts of the world. The result was a major change in patterns of immigration. The numbers of immigrants from Europe began dropping precipitously, while those from Asia and the West Indies increased dramatically. In 1940, 70 percent of immigrants had still come from Europe. By 1992 only 15 percent came from there, whereas 37 percent were coming from Asia and 44 percent from Latin America and the Caribbean ("Numbers Game" 1993). Moreover, not only did the pattern change, so did the scope. The 1980s began seeing the greatest wave of immigration to the United States since the nineteenth century (8.9 million people entered the United States legally between 1980 and 1990 and roughly 3 million more illegally) (Mydans 1993). Significantly, most of the new immigrants hailed from such countries as Mexico, the Philippines, Haiti, South Korea, China, the Dominican Republic, India, Vietnam, and Jamaica—all of which had previously been represented only modestly.

Just as it had taken a decade for adult romances to trickle down into the YA field, so it would take nearly a decade and a half—from 1965 to 1980—for publishers to begin to take cognizance of these new facts of demographic life and to start offering a new body of literature, called multicultural, that would give faces to these new Americans.

And not a moment too soon.

According to "Kids Need Libraries" (Mathews et al. 1990, 202), a position paper promulgated by the youth-serving divisions of the American Library Association and adopted by the Second White House Conference on Libraries and Information, "Kids need preparation to live in a multicultural world and to respect the rights and dignity of all people."

A search for those rights had brought yet another huge immigrant swell to U.S. shores: political refugees who came to America from countries like Iran, El Salvador, and Cuba seeking not only economic opportunity but also sanctuary.

The arrival of both groups of new peoples created enormous problems of acculturation not only for them but also for established residents, as each category tried to cope with innumerable daily crossings of the borders of strange languages and baffling customs and mores. In this potentially explosive, newly multicultural environment, books had never been more important, for—as Hazel Rochman (1993, 9) wisely put it—"The best books break down borders."

The editor and publisher Margaret K. McElderry (1994, 379)—who had been the first to publish a children's book from Germany following World War

II—had this to say: "What is of immense importance now, as I see it, is to find writers among the new wave of immigrants, authors who can portray creatively what it is like to adjust to life in the U.S., what their own experiences have been, written in either fictionalized form or as expository nonfiction."

Such writers had already appeared in the world of adult publishing: authors like Gish Jen, Bharati Mukherjee, Gus Lee, Maxine Hong Kingston, Amy Tan, Sandra Cisneros, Nicholasa Mohr, Gary Soto, David Wong Louie, Bette Bao Lord, Gita Mehta, Frank Chin, and still others. Who would match their eloquence in the world of young adult literature?

Before we can answer that question, we need to pause for a belated word or two of definition. *Multiculturalism* is an expansive word, containing in its definition and in its resonant connotations as many concepts—and sometimes hotly expressed opinions—as a suitcase full of unmatched socks.

I have been using the word *multiculturalism* to refer simply to aspects of the cultural and social lives and experiences of the newly immigrant populations who began arriving here in the seventies and the eighties. For others, however, the issues surrounding the word were more complex—and controversial.

Sarah Bullard explained: "Educators disagree, first, over which groups should be included in multicultural plans—racial and ethnic groups, certainly, but what about regional, social class, gender, disability, religious, language and sexual orientation groupings?" (Smith 1993, 341).

Similarly, Masha Kabakow Rudman (2006, 111) has written, "Multiculturalism can be defined simply as the inclusion of, appreciation of, and respect for all cultures; but a more complex formulation includes a challenge to the power structure that subordinates people on the basis of race, ethnicity, class, gender, sexual orientation, ability, age, and religion." This more expansive definition conjures up the image of a very—almost unmanageably—large tent, and so, when addressing this issue in the context of the decade of the eighties, I agree with Karen Patricia Smith, who argued—in a 1993 article about the concept of multiculturalism and literature—that "it is . . . necessary, for the sake of coherence, to narrow the scope of one's discussion." For her purposes—and for mine, at least in this chapter—"the term will be used to refer to people of color; that is, individuals who identify with African-American, Hispanic, American Indian, Eskimo or Aleut, and Asian or Pacific Islander heritage" (Smith 1993, 341–42).

Color is an important consideration, because—until the end of the sixties—it was nearly absent from the world of books for young readers. It was in 1965 that the educator-writer Nancy Larrick published a hugely influential—and, again, controversial—article in the *Saturday Review*. Titled "The

All-White World of Children's Books," the article excoriated American publishers for failing to give faces to the growing populations of children of color. Surveying the 5,206 books for young readers published between 1962 and 1964, she found that only 6.7 percent contained any reference in text or illustration to blacks. And 60 percent of that 6.7 percent were set either outside the United States or in the period before World War II. And even when blacks did appear, they were too often presented as caricatures and stereotypes in books that, as Henrietta Smith (1995, 5) has observed, "were replete with the exaggerated use of dialect and illustrations that showed the Negro child with heavy lips, bulging eyes, night-black skin and wooly hair."

But it was still the sixties, and the times were actually a-changin'. In the wake of Larrick's seminal article, of the burgeoning civil rights movement, and of such long-overdue legislation as the Voting Rights Act of 1965, the world of American blacks as depicted in literature began changing dramatically. Within five years, a black literary renaissance was under way, marked by the emergence of such celebrated illustrators as Jerry Pinkney, Ashley Bryan, John Steptoe, and Tom Feelings, and such distinguished writers as Rosa Guy, Alice Childress, Walter Dean Myers, Julius Lester, Mildred Taylor, and Virginia Hamilton, who—in 1975—became the first black writer to win the prestigious Newbery Medal for *M. C. Higgins the Great*. Two years later, Taylor became the second for *Roll of Thunder, Hear My Cry*. To further encourage this creative flowering, the American Library Association, working through its Social Responsibilities Roundtable, established the annual Coretta Scott King Awards in 1969 to recognize outstanding works written and illustrated by black authors and artists.

It was in the mid-seventies that Chinese Americans also found an early literary representative of their own in Laurence Yep, who began writing about their cultural experience in his second book, *Dragonwings* (Harper, 1975). Yep's own experience of growing up as an outsider between cultures had actually found expression—though metaphorically—in his first book, a fantasy titled *Sweetwater* (Harper, 1973). Yep continued to write powerfully about his experience throughout the seventies and eighties in such other novels as *Child of the Owl* (1977), *Sea Glass* (1979), *The Serpent's Children* (1984), and *Mountain Light* (1985).

Although Japanese Americans also found their faces and stories represented in the early work of Jeanne Wakatsuki Houston, Lensey Namioka, and Yoshiko Uchida, it would not be until the nineties that the true diversity of other Asian peoples found expression in young adult literature. In the preface to his important anthology *American Dragons* (Harper, 1993), a collection of creative short work by twenty-five contemporary Asian American writers,

Yep stressed the diversity of Asian cultures in America. "Asian Americans," he noted, "come not only from China and Japan but from the many countries around the Pacific rim, including the Philippines, Korea, India, and even Tibet. Recently there have been new waves of immigrants, especially from Southeast Asia, countries such as Vietnam, Thailand, Cambodia, and Laos" (Yep 1993, xi–xii).

This is an important point, because the umbrella term *Asian American* tends to treat individuals from dramatically different countries and cultures as a single, homogeneous whole, and, obviously, nothing could be further from the truth. The same problem has plagued literature about Native Americans and, especially, about Latinos and Latinas, who come from a world so diverse (twenty-one different nations comprise Latin America alone) that no one can even agree on a uniform term to embrace it. Although I will typically use *Latino* or *Latina*, others prefer *Hispanic* as a broader term that emphasizes the common denominator of the Spanish language, even though there is no one universal form of the language in this hemisphere, and the more politically conscious regard *Hispanic* as too Eurocentric (and too often a language of oppression, to boot).

These disagreements aside, there is universal agreement that no viable body of literature for and about Latinos existed until the 1970s and 1980s, and even then, the growing size of the populations that remained, in large part, invisible far outpaced the amount of work available. There were a number of interrelated reasons for this, beginning with the very language of Latino literature. "Most of what we write," Roberto Rodriguez and Patrisia Gonzales (1994, B7) declared, "is considered noise, foreign chatter at best. We are often unable to find a medium for our rich and textured prose—the amalgam of Spanish, English, Indian and *calo* (street talk). Many publishers not only find our writing unacceptable; they can't read it."

Why they can't read it brings us to a second reason: there were—and, perhaps, still are—too few Latinos working in children's book publishing, which has resulted in a lack of knowledge of how to acquire, evaluate, and publish for this market. And a reason for that is there was no significant tradition of creating an indigenous literature for young readers in most Latin American countries, as the few available books there were imported from Spain. And much of that was drearily didactic and moralistic. As a result, most of the Latino and Latina writers for young people who began appearing in the seventies and eighties were already established authors for adults; writers like Rudolfo Anaya, Gary Soto, Nicholasa Mohr, Sandra Cisneros, and others. It was not until the nineties and the creation of literary prizes like the Pura Belpré and Americas awards for excellence in Latino literature that a new generation of writers began focusing exclusively on writing for young readers. Further encouragement came from mainstream publishers' creation of Spanish-language imprints (e.g., Rayo from HarperCollins, Mirasol from Farrar, Straus & Giroux, and Libros Viajeros from Harcourt) and from the emergence of small independent publishers like Arte Público, Lee and Low, and Children's Book Press.

Even then, books for and about young people from other cultures remained a hard sell. Donald Barr (1986, 50), writing in the *New York Times Book Review*, noted, "American adolescents, for the most part, have little interest in their own traditions and almost none in anyone else's." Six years later, Margaret McElderry (1994, 379) agreed, noting in her 1994 May Hill Arbuthnot lecture, "The number of such books has drastically diminished in the last fifteen or twenty years. In part this has happened," she continued, "because our young readers some while ago seemed to lose interest in other countries, other peoples, other ways, tending instead to concentrate on themselves and their peers and their life-styles."

Political Correctness

Nevertheless, this began gradually to change in the later eighties as the sheer numbers of foreign born demanded that attention be paid. But that raised the vexing question "By whom?" If the question were applied to the creators of multicultural literature, an increasing number of critics were questioning the authenticity of literature being created by those writing from outside a cultural experience. Writing in *Library Trends*, Karen Patricia Smith (1993, 345) noted, "For years, minority populaces have been written about and 'described' by essentially white authors who are outside the cultures about whom they are writing or illustrating . . . the question posed and often debated is whether or not material written by so-called 'outsiders' is actually valid material."

As I pointed out in chapter 1, this issue was being debated as early as the 1950s and may be one that can never be satisfactorily resolved, for at its core, it asks an unanswerable question: can a writer's imagination be powerful enough to create a viable work of fiction about a culture he or she has observed only from the outside?

Richard Peck (1993, 21–22), for one, believes it can: "Now in the nineties," he asserted, "we're being told to march to the beat of multiculturalism. This baffles novelists who thought we'd been celebrating the cultural mix of this country well before the textbooks touched on it. . . . Unless a book is to be judged by the race or ethnicity of its author. In which case we are standing at the edge of an abyss. Fortunately a novel need not brand the race of its characters as a film must. A novel can begin at the next epidermal level down, to explore what we all have in common."

Jane Yolen (1994, 705) added a similarly cautionary thought: "What we are seeing now in children's books is an increasing push toward what I can only call the 'Balkanization' of literature. We are drawing rigid borders across the world of story, demanding that people tell only their own stories. Not only does this deny the ability of gifted storytellers to re-invigorate the literature with cross-cultural fertilization, but it would mean that no stories at all could be told about some peoples or cultures until such time as a powerful voice from within that culture emerges."

Both Peck's and Yolen's observations bring us to the brink of another abyss: that aspect of multiculturalism that, in the later 1980s, came to be called political correctness, or what I have dubbed "multiculturalism without a sense of humor." It is related to a certain stridency that accompanied efforts to maintain the cultural identity and separate integrity of the newly immigrant populations. The traditional image of America as a melting pot seemed to be in the process of being replaced by a new metaphor, America as stir-fry, the ingredients of which, of course, remain distinct.

Hazel Rochman (1993, 17), who came to the United States from South Africa, was fearless in her indictment of this movement: "*Multiculturalism* is a trendy word, trumpeted by the politically correct with a stridency that has provoked a sneering backlash. There are P.C. watchdogs eager to strip from the library shelves anything that presents a group as less than perfect. The ethnic 'character' must always be strong, dignified, courageous, loving, sensitive, wise. Then there are those who watch for authenticity: how dare a white write about blacks? What's a gentile doing writing about a Jewish old lady and her African-American neighbors? The chilling effect of this is a kind of censorship and a reinforcement of apartheid."

Of course, this works both ways. One of the Latino books that Anglo censors most often challenge is Rudolfo Anaya's *Bless Me, Ultima*, which—according to the watchdogs—celebrates witchcraft in its story of a New Mexican boy's magical encounter with a *curandera*, a healer, and her owl spirit. Rodriguez and Gonzales (1994, B7) explain: "The objections to Anaya's book indicate that those who would ban it do not understand Latino culture or its indigenous roots: the practice of healing is part of our indigenous memory."

Native American culture has been particularly subject to misrepresentation and, accordingly, has engendered some of the hottest debates, including challenges to the authenticity of the treatment of Native Americans in Laura Ingalls Wilder's Little House books, in the work of Jamake Highwater (three of whose novels were selected as ALA Best Books for Young Adults), and in individual titles by Lynn Reid Banks, Ann Rinaldi, Gerald McDermott, and others.

In 1970 the futurist Alvin Toffler (1970, 4) coined the now-familiar phrase "future shock," which he defined as "the shattering stress and disorientation that we induce in individuals by subjecting them to too much change in too short a time." Future shock had certainly played a part in the first great wave of immigration that occurred in the late nineteenth century but to a lesser degree, certainly, than in the one that followed in the 1980s, principally because the former was more gradual, spread out over some four decades (roughly from 1880 to 1920). The second great wave about which I've been writing in this chapter came crashing on our shores in the space of only a single decade, however, bringing with it future shock in spades! Too few people deal well with such rapid change; it induces in them not only disorientation but also fear—principally fear of the unknown, which is why good, information-providing books about the culture and the individual human conditions of new immigrant lives are so important.

Even by the dawn of the new decade of the nineties, the issues continued to be so complex and so various as to baffle minds and perplex hearts. But I believe, as I wrote in the first edition of this book, that it remains literature, whether imported from other lands in other languages, imported in translation, written in English in this country by immigrants who describe the invention of new selves here or recall the realities of former lives in the lands of their national origins—it is literature that will prove the place of illumination, the neutral center where all of us can go to find out about one another and, come to think of it, ourselves. "We" need to read books about "them," and "they" need to read about "us," and in the process, perhaps we will find that we are all simply "we."

the early nineties

A Near-Death Experience

As the new decade of the nineties dawned, Connie C. Epstein, former editor in chief of Morrow Junior Books, reflected on the condition of young adult publishing. Noting "weakening sales for what had come to be called 'problem stories,'" she reported that "some editors, marketing directors, and subsidiary rights directors, discouraged by this downturn, have been wondering whether the young adult novel was ready for burial, and certainly most would agree that the genre is in turmoil" (Epstein 1990, 237).

Four years later, in 1994, the critic Alleen Pace Nilsen (1994, 30) agreed that assessing "the health of the genre" had become tantamount to "gathering at the bedside of an ailing loved one," though she qualified her diagnosis by explaining she was referring specifically to "the realistic problem novel" rather than "the entire body of modern young adult literature."

But what else, one is tempted to ask, was there? Well, there was horror, of course, the market for which continued to thrive in the early nineties. "Adolescents now constitute a booming niche market for the peddling of published gore and violence," Paul Gray (1993, 54) explained in *Time* magazine, noting that Christopher Pike had 8 million copies of his books in print in 1993 and that R. L. Stine boasted 7.6 million copies of his books. Shortly thereafter, the entertainment journalist Ken Tucker, in a reference too good not to mention, dubbed Pike and Stine the "Beavis and Butthead of horror." "It's easy to understand why young adult horror is so popular," he continued. "It's a combination of youth's eternal desire to shock its elders and a budding interest in all things odd and uncomfortable" (Tucker 1993, 27).

That interest was reflected not only in books but also in the spate of increasingly violent slasher movies that had been dominating the box office since the eighties, starting with Sean Cunningham's *Friday the Thirteenth* and Wes Craven's *Nightmare on Elm Street*. The interest in the "odd and uncomfortable" was also finding expression in the popularity of the daytime confessional reality shows that had started with Phil Donahue in 1972; had come of age with Oprah Winfrey, whose show debuted in 1986; and had then taken a swan dive into the sensational in the early nineties, with increasingly over-the-top programs hosted by the likes of Jerry Springer, Sally Jesse Raphael, Geraldo Rivera, Ricki Lake, Maury Povich, and others. As a result, the Penn State sociologist Vicki Apt said, "Television emphasizes the deviant; if you really are normal, no one cares" (Roan 1994, E1).

Nilsen felt that this was another reason for the decline in realistic YA fiction. "The daily media glut of stories about the personal foibles and tragedies in which young people get involved . . . leaves little unexplored territory for authors to mine," she said (Nilsen 1994, 32).

Although it was small comfort, this decline was not confined to literature for young adults. Adam Hochschild (1994, 11), founder of *Mother Jones* magazine, offered a similar observation about adult fiction in the 1990s: "One reason people write fewer traditional realist novels these days is that modern readers are jaded. Film, radio, first-person journalism, prying biographers and, above all, TV have saturated us with reality."

Small wonder, then, that readers continued to search for escape in the borderline fantasy pages of series romance, which, accordingly, continued to sell every bit as briskly as horror, with Sweet Valley setting a particularly blistering pace. According to the series' publisher, Bantam Doubleday Dell, there were more than 81 million copies of Sweet Valley titles in print in 1994, with more to come, for, as the publisher trumpeted, "Sweet Valley continues to offer teens all the racy romance, drama, and adventures they're looking for in a series" (Bantam Doubleday Dell 1994, 90).

In the meantime, African American teens were being represented in a romance series of their own. According to Bantam Doubleday Dell, Walter Dean Myers had "created" the series 18 Pine Street.

Historical romances were flourishing, too. Titles in the Pleasant Company's American Girl series for preteens routinely enjoyed six-figure sales. For older teens, Jennifer Armstrong's Wild Rose Inn books had been added to Bantam's long-standing Starfire imprint.

The popularity of such genre series is perhaps the most durable phenomenon in the ongoing history of publishing for young readers. Such series were, as we have seen, staples of the twenties and thirties, thanks in large part to the Stratemeyer Syndicate. Today's writing factories, which are still turning out similar titles on the creative assembly line as fast as kids can read them, are no longer called syndicates, however, but packagers. Their typical function is to develop an idea for a series, sell it to a mainstream publisher, and then assemble the talent—including author, editor, and illustrator—necessary to produce a finished product for delivery to (and manufacture and distribution by) the publisher. One of the leading packagers of the eighties was Daniel Weiss Associates, which produced ten series a month in "a market-driven style and standard," according to Elise Howard, who was then the company's vice president (Cart 1996, 148). Packagers would become even more important and influential, as we will see, in the late nineties and early aughts with the explosion of what came to be called chick lit.

For the moment, it bears repeating here that teens themselves were purchasing these original paperback genre series—unlike hardcover novels of realism, which adult librarians and teachers usually bought—and usually at a mall-based chain bookstore. And fewer and fewer hardcovers were being published and purchased. Thanks to a combination of taxpayer revolts (spearheaded by California's notorious Proposition 13), diminishing federal funding, and the American economy's recessionary malaise, the institutional market continued its precipitous decline throughout the eighties and into the early nineties. If anything, the school library market was even punier than that of the public library, as educators were increasingly spending their dwindling resources on new technology instead of books. By 1993 the industry magazine *Publishers Weekly* noted that the market had dropped from 80–90 percent institutional to only 50–60 percent (Dunleavy 1993). As a result, Nilsen observed, major publishing houses "moved from the past practice of bringing out about 80% fiction and 20% nonfiction to doing 80% nonfiction and 20% fiction"—the point being that, while cash-strapped institutions were avoiding "nonessential" fiction, they continued to buy nonfiction to support curricular needs. The publisher Beverly Horowitz confirmed this, citing growing pressure to increase profit margins by eliminating whatever books or kinds of books that didn't turn a profit, "both quick and high" (Eaglen 1990, 54).

Middle School Literature

Something else equally significant was happening to young adult books: the typical age of their protagonists was decreasing from sixteen or seventeen to as young as twelve or fourteen. This radical change was due to several interrelated factors. First was the rise of the middle school movement. From 1966 to 1981, the number of these new schools—which typically served grades 6–8—increased from 499 to 6,003. Unlike the old junior highs, which might have been described as high schools with training wheels, these new schools were specifically designed to meet the unique developmental needs of eleven- to fourteen-year-olds, young people who were no longer children but not quite young adults, either. As Lucy Rollin (1999, 252) notes, "The term 'middle school' emphasized a separate identity, a school and a group of students who were not 'junior' to anything but in transition." As had happened in the thirties with the emergence of the first generation of teenagers, this new group offered a de facto challenge to publishers to create a new kind of literature expressly for them, one that publishers continued to call young adult but that targeted this new, younger age range. Simultaneously, the amount of traditional YA literature continued to dwindle, as fewer and fewer books appeared for high school–aged readers. As a result, though it might have appeared to the casual observer that the age of YA protagonists was simply decreasing, what was actually happening was that a new kind of literature—middle school literature—was being born (and the traditional form was, well, dying). This shift dovetailed nicely with the sales strategies of the chain bookstores, many of which were morphing into superbookstores. The Barnes & Noble chain led this evolution, opening 105 superstores between 1989 and 1992. Though much larger than the earlier chain stores, none of the new behemoths contained separate young adult sections; instead, everything labeled "YA" was simply—and summarily—shoved into the children's department. This practice further encouraged the "youthening" of protagonists, because at the same time, the stores avoided stocking any titles containing controversial subjects or themes. As George Nicholson noted in 1990, the chains would not buy a novel "with anything difficult in it" (Cart 1996, 150). No wonder that another legendary editor, Richard Jackson, flatly declared in 1994, "Young adult [now] stops at fourteen" (Cart 1996, 150).

Unfortunately, the new middle school YA literature did have at least one thing in common with the traditional form: it didn't sell well in hardcover. In fact, in 1993 hardcover sales to both the institutional and the retail markets were down for the first time, though paperback sales continued to soar. As a result, publishers—though they still produced small hardcover editions of a thousand copies or less for the institutional market (Eaglen 1990)—were typically acquiring for hardcover release only titles that promised steep sales when they would be published a year later in their paperback editions, editions that were sold directly to teens through the chain bookstores.

Recognizing the dwindling market for hardcovers, why didn't publishers begin issuing quality fiction in original trade paperback formats for those largely ignored older teens? After all, adult publishers were finding success with this more cost-effective strategy. One reason was that the children's book review media tended not to cover paperbacks (hence the continued small-run hardcover releases), and many libraries remained reluctant to stock such an ephemeral format. Another reason was the claim that chains would not stock such paperbacks; and still another was authors' alleged preference for the implicit cachet of hardback publication, along with the more practical reason that publishers paid larger advances for hardcovers than for paperbacks. To its credit, the publisher Harcourt, Brace did experiment with issuing selected titles in simultaneous hard and soft editions in a uniform trim size but, unfortunately, had little or no success.

Ave, YA?

Thanks to all these many factors, the number of YA titles continued to decline, though it is difficult to ascertain by how much with any degree of precision. Publishers and the reference media have historically (and a bit unceremoniously) lumped statistics for children's and YA books together into one generic children's books category. Nevertheless, Audrey Eaglen (1990, 54) in her *School Library Journal* column noted that "even the biggest publishers seldom do more than a dozen or so YAs a year."

What did editors have to say about this? A panel of five leaders in the field shared their views with participants in a 1994 YALSA conference preceding the annual American Library Association Conference and Exhibition, held that year in Miami Beach. The five were Marc Aronson, of Henry Holt; David Gale, of Simon & Schuster; Richard Jackson, of Orchard Books; Robert Warren, of HarperCollins; and Linda Zuckerman, of Harcourt, Brace. Two of them—Jackson and Zuckerman—had their own imprints (Richard Jackson Books and Browndeer Press, respectively). With five strong-minded, independent individuals on the platform, consensus on some issues was predictably elusive; however, there did seem to be agreement that young adult publishing—though still alive—was ailing. Aronson delicately called it "a time of transition." Zuckerman was probably the least sanguine of the five, saying frankly, "I think young adult literature is dying." She explained that there was only a limited amount of time and risk that publishers were willing to take with developing new authors. As a result, she predicted, the YA field would continue to diminish, becoming increasingly focused on series and on the work of a handful of established name authors.

There was consensus that publishers were, indeed, increasingly target-ing the twelve- to fourteen-year-old reader. In fact, of the five, Gale was the only one who was still actively searching for books for older readers, though he acknowledged that he had to exercise caution in accepting manuscripts with too much sex or violence, as an increasingly conservative school library market might reject them. He also agreed that books for older readers were "nonexistent" in bookstores, echoing Nilsen's earlier comment that fiction didn't sell particularly well in the prevailing market and that fewer novels were being published.

Several of the editors also acknowledged that a major factor in their decision to publish a book in hardcover was its demonstrated potential for paperback reprint sales. "Do paperback sales drive the market?" Warren asked rhetorically and answered categorically: "Yes." Warren then turned the discus-sion from a focus on the field of YA to the individual writer, and he reminded the audience, "We're not publishing a genre; we're publishing an author. And a good book will always, always be published" (Cart 1996, 163).

This salutary affirmation aside, an overall air of the valedictory pervaded a conference that found little to celebrate in the present but much to laud in the past. Indeed, the principal business of the conference attendees was the selection of the one hundred best YA books published between 1967 and 1992.

This 1994 list—the Top One Hundred Countdown—included a number of titles that, in terms of their topical and thematic content, were historically important. *Go Ask Alice* and *A Hero Ain't Nothin' but a Sandwich* were, for example, classic treatments of drug abuse, whereas Richard Peck's *Are You in the House Alone?* was the first YA novel to deal with rape. As did Paul Zindel's earlier *The Pigman*, Lois Duncan's *Killing Mr. Griffin* continued to explore the important issue of adolescent acceptance of responsibility, also a theme of her earlier classic *I Know What You Did Last Summer* (Little, Brown, 1973). Felice Holman, in her *Slake's Limbo* (1974), introduced an element of allegory into the prevailing mode of YA realism; her story of young Artemis Slake's 121-day odyssey in New York's subways also gave readers a classic story of survival. Last, Barbara Wersba's *Run Softly, Go Fast* (1970) explored another timeless theme: the uneasy relationship of fathers and sons, a topic that also informed such other novels of the seventies as Robert Newton Peck's *A Day No Pigs Would Die* (Knopf, 1973) and Richard Peck's *Father Figure* (Viking, 1978).

Despite its golden past, young adult literature was, by 1994, clearly at risk of extinction. Ironically, so were young adults themselves, whose lives were becoming increasingly endangered by societal and personal problems that ranged from poverty to homelessness, from fractured families to violence (in 1991 one fifteen- to nineteen-year-old was murdered every three and a half hours!), from increased drug use to sexual harassment, rape, and—perhaps as a result of all this—an exponential increase (200 percent in the preceding four decades) in teenage suicide (Waters 1994, 49).

Sadly, these issues coincided with a continuing decline in the purchasing power of school and public libraries and a critical shortage of trained young adult librarians who might have helped endangered young adults weather their stormy lives. According to a 1988 survey conducted by the National Center for Education Statistics, only 11 percent of America's libraries had young adult specialists on staff. A later survey, conducted in 1992 by the Young Adult Library Services Association, confirmed this, reporting a continued "dearth of qualified staff" and the prevailing feeling, among librarians, that YA funding was the first area to be cut at times of fiscal crisis and that "the loss of library funding" had become "a national epidemic" (Latrobe 1994, 238).

How, I asked in the first edition of this book (which I wrote in the immediate wake of the 1994 Miami Beach conference), can we solve problems of such magnitude? How can we even comprehend them? Well, if knowledge is power, there was no shortage of powerful nonfiction being published to describe the shape and scope of the problems. More important, a trend in early nineties nonfiction was the inclusion, through interviews, of the authentic voices of the young people themselves, especially those whose lives were at risk or who lived at the narrower margins of society. Such books included Susan Kuklin's *Speaking Out: Teenagers Take on Race, Sex and Identity* (Putnam, 1993), Judith Berck's *No Place to Be: Voices of Homeless Children* (Houghton Mifflin, 1992), and Susan Goodwillie's *Voices from the Future: Our Children Tell Us about Violence in America* (Crown, 1993). Such books gave not only voices but also faces to those too-often-invisible young people. But, good as those books were, we needed more.

"We need more than information," I argued in "Of Risk and Revelation," my keynote speech at the 1994 conference. "We need *wisdom*. And for that we must turn to fiction—to young adult fiction, which is written for and about YAs and the unique problems that plague and perplex them. Why fiction? Because of its unique capacity to educate not only the mind but the heart and spirit as well. The late Italo Calvino put it this way in his *Six Memos for the Next Millennium*: "My confidence in the future of literature consists in the knowledge that there are things only literature can give us by means specific to it" (Calvino 1988, 1).

"Really good fiction," the novelist and critic John Gardner once wrote, "has a staying power that comes from its ability to jar, to turn on, to move the whole intellectual and emotional history of the reader" (Yardley 1994, 3). If young adult literature is to have a future, it must be more than formula-driven fiction that begins and ends with a problem. It must be as real as headlines but more than the simple retailing of fact. It must also be enriched by the best means literature can offer: an expansive, fully realized setting; a memorably artful narrative voice; complex and fully realized characters; and unsparing honesty and candor in use of language and treatment of material. Young adult literature, in short, must take creative (and marketing) risks to present hard-edged issues of relevance so that it may offer its readers not only reality but also revelation and, ultimately, that desired wisdom.

This is the spirit in which I wrote the first edition of this book, and it remains one of the guiding principles by which I evaluate the success or failure of the literature that followed in the second half of the 1990s. For more about that, we turn to the next chapter and a consideration of the balance of that formative decade.

the rest of the nineties

Revival and Renaissance

In retrospect, the 1994 Miami Beach conference turned out to be a dramatic turning point for young adult literature, marking not the death of the genre as had been predicted but, instead, its rebirth and the beginning of a remarkable period of renaissance that has continued to the present day (2010).

The first stirrings of this revival had actually taken place in U.S. schools in the late eighties and early nineties in the form of the nascent whole-language movement, a method of teaching reading that employed trade books instead of classic basal readers (Dick and Jane, anyone?). Although at first the movement primarily affected the children's book market, it would have a longer-range and salutary impact on young adult literature by bringing contemporary books into the classroom. As Lori Benton, then with the Book Shop in Boise, Idaho, told *Publishers Weekly,* there's "a huge demand for us to give in-service workshops. Teachers want help finding what literature is available and appropriate" (Ohanian 1991, 127).

Another phenomenon of equal if not greater importance arrived in 1992 when, following a fifteen-year period of decline, America's teen (twelve to nineteen) population spiked significantly, growing 16.6 percent from 1990 to 2000, when it totaled 32 million. That rate of increase was widely expected to outstrip that of the general population before peaking in 2010.

In the meantime, January 1994 saw the publication in *School Library Journal* of Chris Lynch's important article "Today's YA Writers: Pulling No Punches." Himself an emerging writer of hard-hitting literary fiction for young adults, Lynch underscored the importance to the field of allowing authors the luxury of "taking the gloves off" when writing for young adults. "My plea is authenticity," he wrote, adding "the teen experience is unlike any other and it deserves its own literature" (Lynch 1994, 37–38).

An early intimation that this process was already under way was a new column on young adult literature that had debuted in the venerable *Horn Book* magazine in its September–October 1993 issue: "The Sand in the Oyster," by the writer, critic, and editor Patty Campbell. In her first column, Campbell (1993, 568) promised "to do some heavy breathing, since [the] subject will be controversial books and issues in young-adult literature, focusing not only on sex and censorship but also on debatable matters of literary style and other social and intellectual concerns." Lynch's article and Campbell's column would be the first of a series of similar writings to help spur the revival of young adult literature. In June 1994, for example, I began my own monthly column, "Carte Blanche," in *Booklist* magazine. And 1995 saw both Marc Aronson's memorably titled "The YA Novel Is Dead, and Other Fairly Stupid Tales," in *School Library Journal*, and my own "Of Risk and Revelation: The Current State of Young Adult Literature," in *Journal of Youth Services in Libraries*.

In retrospect, it's clear that 1996 marked another significant turning point in young adult literature's coming of age as literature. In a radical departure from its previous focus on scholarship and research in children's literature, the Children's Literature Association devoted the entire contents of the spring issue of its quarterly journal to "Critical Theory and Young Adult Literature." That fall the theme of the annual workshop of the National Council of Teachers of English's Assembly on Literature for Adolescents (ALAN) was "Exploding the Canon," which offered true believers another opportunity to trumpet the news that young adult literature was now *literature* that deserved a long-overdue place in a literary canon. Surely, conferees argued, YA books deserved a place in America's classrooms, where they could be taught and appreciated in the company of long-established—but increasingly dusty—classics.

This argument found more discursive expression that same year in two book-length publications: Sarah H. Hertz and Don Gallo's *From Hinton to Hamlet: Building Bridges between Young Adult Literature and the Classics* (1996) and the first edition of this book (HarperCollins, 1996). Scarcely a year later, another important book appeared, John Noell Moore's *Interpret-*

ing Young Adult Literature: Literary Theory in the Secondary Classroom (Boynton/Cook, 1997).

How Adult Is Young Adult?

In summer 1996 YALSA presented still another significant program, "How Adult Is Young Adult?" Held at the American Library Association's Annual Conference and Exhibition, in New York, the program attracted a standing-room-only audience and excited considerable discussion and debate. Campbell (1997, 366), in fact, devoted one of her "Oyster" columns to its content, noting, "We have lost the upper half of YA—those fourteen- to nineteen-year-olds who were the original readership for the genre."

How to recover and even expand that audience was, in fact, the central purpose of the program's co-conveners (the literary agent George Nicholson and myself). To that end, a number of influential speakers addressed the importance of redefining and expanding the audience for young adult literature. As moderator, my role was to provide context, and accordingly, I noted, "The borders of the land of young adult have always been ill-defined and subject to negotiation and many titles that have found their way onto YALSA's annual Best Books for Young Adults list have slipped across from the land of children's literature as well as from the world of books published for adults."[1]

The editor Marc Aronson picked up on this theme in noting that the most successful titles in his own EDGE imprint at Henry Holt were those that crossed markets. "They reach YA and Asian American adult [readers]; YA and Latino adult, YA and Jewish adult, YA and African American adult." In fact, he suggested, "We have frozen our terms around a late sixties reality that no longer exists and we may be doing ourselves harm by calling books that deal with older teenage life or deal with coming of age in a sophisticated way, 'YA.'" His point, of course, was that *YA* had become synonymous with *middle school literature*, and therefore the term was an implicit turnoff for older readers, as was Barnes & Noble's policy of shelving YA titles in its children's departments. In that respect, there was good news from another of the speakers, Carla Parker, senior buyer for the Barnes & Noble chain, who reported—to loud applause—that Barnes & Noble would reconfigure old stores and create separate, stand-alone YA areas in all of its new stores, so that by 1997 all of the YA sections would be "outside of, not in, their children's departments."

What to call these new departments—and the more sophisticated literature they might stock—excited considerable discussion. For example, another speaker, the writer Francesca Lia Block, suggested the term *X-Over* to describe the department's multigenerational, crossover appeal, the same appeal that her category-denying Weetzie Bat novels had excited among both teens and readers in their twenties.

Whatever it might be called, as Anna Lawrence-Pietroni (1996, 34) had written in that landmark issue of the *Children's Literature Association Quarterly*, "Young adult fiction defies easy categorization, and by its nature proposes a more liberating view of genre as process rather than as circumspection and definition." Block seemed to echo this view at the YALSA program: "Society is beginning to understand that childhood and adulthood are not really as separate as people think they are. . . . Childhood is filled with darkness, the need for love, the search for acceptance. Why can't we create a category which all the barriers will cross? This is the intention in bookstores and libraries: books that appeal to young and old, gay and straight, open-minded and representative of different racial backgrounds. Maybe we can begin here to use literature as a way to connect rather than to divide."

The issue, however, was not so much what such a new, free-ranging category of literature might be called or could offer in the way of connections but how it might be created, published, marketed, and sold. In 1992, the editor and publisher Stephen Roxburgh, then still at Farrar, Straus & Giroux, had written, "Publishing, in order to work, has to fit into boxes. One has to be clear on whether the publishing strategy for a title is adult or YA. A book's primary support, in terms of advertising and the review media must be defined" (Lodge 1992, 38).

Because of the undefined composition of her multigenerational readership, Block acknowledged that most readers found her books by word of mouth. Speaking to the same issue in her address, Parker suggested, "We need to see more book reviewing and advertising done on MTV and in the magazines that teens actually look at: *Seventeen*, *Savvy*, and *Spin*. I don't think YA is dead. I think it's changed and we must change with it."

Some strategies for change that were suggested during the program included the cross-promotion of titles by listing them in both children's and adult catalogs, as Houghton Mifflin had done with David Macaulay's *The Way Things Work*. The literary agent George Nicholson, another speaker, offered the model of Robert Cormier's novel *Fade*, with which he had been involved when he was publisher of books for young readers at Dell/Delacorte. This most ambitious of Cormier's books was published, he explained, in both adult and young adult editions and was listed in both catalogs. Another possibility broached was the publication of adult paperback editions of more sophisticated

YA titles, as had been done with *Fade*, Walter Dean Myers's *Fallen Angels*, and A. M. Homes's *Jack*.

By program's end, the panel had carved out an ambitious agenda that publisher Andre Schiffrin seemed to be describing in another context (the venturesome creation of his nonprofit company the New Press): "We would need," he wrote in *American Bookseller*, "to show that audiences deemed unreachable [think sixteen- to twenty-five-year-olds here] by many publishers will respond to materials and formats designed to reach them. The search for new audiences is, of course, as essential to the future of the bookstore as it is to that of publishers. We hope to be increasingly successful at finding new ways to reach those readers with meaningful, affordable books" (Schiffrin 1995, 17).

Hope keeps dreams alive, of course, but much of what the panelists were calling for seemed, at the time, to be just such a dream—and an impossible one at that, given the rapidly changing world of publishing. The traditional model of the private, often family-owned, small company had morphed, through relentless mergers and acquisitions, into a new model: the multinational, publicly held, infotainment conglomerate. According to a 1997 special issue of the *Nation*, one of eight such behemoths (Hearst, News Corporation, Pearson, Viacom, Advance Publications, Bertelsmann, Time Warner, and Holtzbrinck) owned virtually every publisher in America. Many of these were headed by a new kind of executive "brought in, often from finance or banking, with a commitment to their new owners (international media conglomerates) to increase profits, which now are gauged against those of other conglomerate holdings" (which were often television and motion picture companies) (Schiffrin 1995, 17).

This constant pressure to perform resulted in the increased commodification of books, publishers' focus on the next hot new property to be exploited. Morgan Entrekin, of Grove/Atlantic, one of the few surviving independents, said, "Nowadays, there is a burning impatience to find the next big hit, to pigeonhole authors and books in easy categories. The large corporations that control American publishing care more about product than prose" (Getlin 1997, E5).

The massive size of publishing operations further encouraged the status quo rather than the sort of experimentations that the YALSA panel had called for. Imagine asking a giant ocean liner to turn on a dime, and you have a good idea of the condition of American publishing in the late nineties. And as publishing grew, so did the noninstitutional market. By 1997 Barnes & Noble operated more than a thousand stores (454 superstores and 559 smaller mall outlets), and retail outlets controlled 85 percent of the market (Campbell 1997).

And yet progress did continue to be made. For example, another important advance took place in 1995, when the National Book Foundation reestablished a long-moribund category for its prestigious National Book Award: a prize for the most distinguished book of the year for young readers. The first award, presented in 1996, went to the young adult novel *Parrot in the Oven*, by the California writer Victor Martinez. In the succeeding six years, the award would go four times to a young adult book (the remaining two were awarded to children's titles). Two years later, recognizing the increasing artistic sophistication of young adult literature, the *Los Angeles Times* added the category "Young Adult Novel" to its roster of annual book awards. The founding judges—Patty Campbell, Selma Lanes, and myself—selected Joan Bauer's wonderfully funny and heartfelt *Rules of the Road* as the first recipient of the major new award.

Inarguably, however, the most important of the new YA literary prizes would be YALSA's Michael L. Printz Award, which was created in 1999 and presented for the first time in 2000. I have more to say about the creation of this new award for a new millennium and its far-reaching significance later in this chapter.

A Renaissance of Youth Culture

It was clear by the mid-1990s that there was "a renaissance of youth culture in this country" (Bernstein 1996, 25). This was, once again, a largely market-driven phenomenon, rooted in the extraordinary growth of this segment of the population, which would grow by 4.5 million between 1990 and 2000 (a 17 percent increase). Record numbers of students were enrolled in U.S. schools in 1996 and 1997, with "the bulk of the increase at the high school level," according to the U.S. Department of Education. "From the fall of 1997 through 2007, the nation's schools can expect a thirteen percent increase in grades nine through twelve" (American Library Association Washington Office Newsline 1977, 73).

That this record number of young people commanded record amounts of disposable income was catnip to the American marketplace. According to the *New York Times*, "In 1995 people between 13 and 19 spent $68.8 billion on personal items, up from $49.8 billion in 1985. 'The teen market has got tremendous buying power and is growing by leaps and bounds,' said Page Thompson, the head of United States Media at the ad agency DDB Needham. 'If you take a look down the line, four or five years from now, it's going to be huge. Long term, it's a bonanza'" (Pogrebin 1996, C8).

Seldom in our history had so much attention been lavished on teens, who now seemed omnipresent, not only in America's malls and galleries but also in every medium of popular culture: magazines, movies, television, and more.

Among magazines, *Teen People* debuted to much fanfare in 1998 and quickly became second only to the venerable *Seventeen* magazine in its popularity (*Teen* and *YM* rounded out the big-four magazines for this demographic). *CosmoGirl* followed in 1999 and *Elle Girl* and *Teen Vogue* in 2001 and 2003, respectively. Oddly there have been no general interest magazines for boys with the possible exception of *MH-18*, which debuted in 2000 but folded in less than a year. There have, however, been a number of special interest magazines for boys including *Thrasher*, *Transworld Skateboarding*, and *Game Pro*.

If no single director dominated teen-oriented motion pictures in the nineties as John Hughes had in the eighties, movies continued to capture the teen zeitgeist, none more cleverly than two 1995 releases: Amy Heckerling's *Clueless* and Kevin Smith's *Mallrats*. The former, according to *Time* magazine, "is about conspicuous consumption: wanting, having and wearing in style," whereas the latter telegraphs its message when a character walks into the mall that is the film's setting and exclaims, "I love the smell of commerce in the morning" (Corliss 1995b, 77–78).

Television began its increasingly single-minded focus on teens in 1989 with the series *Saved by the Bell* (followed in 1993 by *Saved by the Bell: The New Class*). The trash classic *Beverly Hills 90210* followed in 1990. In 1992 MTV launched its hugely popular and influential series *The Real World* (which still airs today and has become the network's longest-running series). *My So-Called Life* and *Party of Five* debuted in 1994, and *Sabrina the Teenage Witch* and *Clueless* followed in 1996. Meanwhile, in 1995, the teen-oriented WB television network launched and, within five years, had become home to such blockbuster teen-centric series as *Buffy the Vampire Slayer, Dawson's Creek, Felicity, Charmed, Roswell, Popular*, and *Angel*. "In network TV, WB defines hot because (1) its audience is young, (2) it's the only network to make solid ratings gains this past season, and (3) its audience is young," the television critic Rick Kushman (1999, G1) noted sardonically. The most critically acclaimed of all the youth-oriented series, *Freaks and Geeks*, came along at the very end of the decade, in 1999, a year when eighteen of the thirty-six new shows starred people in their teens or early twenties (Kushman 1999).

According to *Time*, "The economics alone don't explain the high school vogue, nor why the shows include a couple of the fall's better premieres. 'Adolescence is a great period of time to write about,' says Jason Katims, creator of the acclaimed "Relativity." 'It's where so much of you is formed and the themes that will follow you your whole adult life are born' " (Poniewozik 1999, 77–78).

Publishers already knew this, of course, and were publishing not only books for adolescents but also a new genre of books—for adult readers—about adolescents. One of the first of these was Grace Palladino's lively and informative *Teenagers: An American History* (1996). Another important title—and one that would be widely imitated—was journalist Patricia Hersch's moving and unsparing *A Tribe Apart: A Journey into the Heart of American Adolescence* (Fawcett Columbine, 1998); Hersch, the mother of four adolescent boys, spent three years in the company of eight other teenagers in Reston, Virginia.[2] William Finnegan's *Cold New World* was a sobering look at adolescent alienation and impoverishment (Random House, 1998), and Peter Zollo's *Wise Up to Teens: Insights into Marketing and Advertising to Teenagers* (New Strategist, 1999) examined the lives and consuming interests of more privileged teens, as did Don Tapscott's *Growing Up Digital* (McGraw-Hill, 1998), which profiled the emergence of the "net" generation.

No longer limited to the traditional twelve- to eighteen-year-old demographic, this new culture embraced young adults as old as thirty, giving shape and form to the previously amorphous Weetzie Bat readership and acknowledging the growing commercial and cultural influence of the MTV demographic. Booksellers were starting to call this group the alternative audience, and a number of venturesome small presses—Last Gasp, Serpent's Tail, City Lights, Manic D—were starting to publish quirky, offbeat titles for them. Significantly, the phenomenon was not limited to major urban centers. "In the suburbs kids are absolutely starving for, and fanatical about, anything that is weird, funky, extreme," publisher Katherine Gates told *Publishers Weekly*. "Also don't forget that books are the current required accessories of hipdom, the way CDs used to be" (Bernstein 1996, 26). As a result, such "hip" outlets as Tower Records and Virgin Atlantic began to carry books for these wired and with-it young readers right alongside their staple music products.

The Advent of the Edgy

All of the elements I've been discussing breathed new life into the nearly moribund YA genre, sparking a rapid and energetic recovery from its near-death experience. With a newly expanded reader demographic and a new retail marketplace in which to reach them, publishers began issuing a newly hard-edged and gritty fiction of realism that targeted a crossover readership.

Quickly dubbed "bleak books," the new subgenre excited considerable discussion and even more controversy.

The movies had anticipated this turn to darkness in 1995 and 1996 with such landmark noir films as Larry Clark's horrifying *Kids* (with a screenplay by teenager Harmony Korine) and—from Britain—Danny Boyle's *Trainspotting* (based on the sensationally popular novel of the same title by Irvine Welsh).

As the *New York Times* critic Jon Pareles (1995, sec. 2, 1) correctly noted, "'Kids' is, for now, the most extreme of a long line of films in which teens are amoral, irrational, hormone-crazed and oblivious to consequences."

Bellwether book titles in this new genre began appearing in 1997, including Brock Cole's *The Facts Speak for Themselves* (Front Street), Norma Fox Mazer's *When She Was Good* (Levine/Scholastic), Robert Cormier's *Tenderness* (Delacorte), Han Nolan's *Dancing on the Edge* (Harcourt, Brace), and Adam Rapp's *The Buffalo Tree* (Front Street). Not only was the content of these books newly sophisticated (subjects ranged from pedophilia to insanity, murder, rape, juvenile incarceration, and serial slaying); so, also, was the physical design of the books. *Publishers Weekly* took notice of this in the article "Hipper, Brighter, and Bolder" (Stevenson 1997), which acknowledged the importance of the new retail market (which also included the online retailers Amazon.com and BarnesandNoble.com, both of which would create new, separate teen sections at their websites in 1998—and the competition there for the attention of YA consumers). In the same spirit, the editor and publisher Arthur Levine told me in an interview, "It's first of all important to pay careful attention to the dust jacket art in order to excite all of your potential audiences" (Cart 1997, 553).

While all this dynamic activity was happening, libraries remained a staple—though slightly diminished—market for these books, and the institutional world was actually the first to acknowledge the changes sweeping the YA world—for good or for ill. In fact, one of the very first strands of spirited discussion on the newly created electronic book discussion forum YALSA-BK was "Bleak Books." Soon thereafter, *Booklist* magazine's children's books editor, Ilene Cooper, wrote a thoughtful article, "Facts of Life," about Cole's *The Facts Speak for Themselves* and followed this with "Publishing on the Edge," coauthored with the YA books editor Stephanie Zvirin. At the 1998 ALA conference, *Booklist* sponsored the important panel discussion "On the Edge: Personal Perspectives on Writing for Today's Young Adults." The speakers included the authors Brock Cole, Annette Curtis Klause, Norma Fox Mazer, and Han Nolan, and the editor Richard Jackson, the publisher of the controversial bleak book by Virginia Walter, *Making Up Megaboy,* the story of a suburban white California teen who inexplicably murders a Korean shopkeeper.

The eloquent Jackson (1998, 1985) put the entire controversy in perspective: "When reviewers today worry about bleak stories, they are worrying, on behalf of the audience, about the readiness of young readers to face life's darkest corners. But in America there are kids *living* in those dark corners, and they need our attention as much as the feisty, pert, athletic, and popular youth so reassuring to adults. Even children in the sun will enter the darkness. They *all* need our tenderness. And we need our tenderness as art inspires us to feel it."

This should have been the last word on this controversy, but there would be many more to come as the mainstream media belatedly discovered the debate, and a yearlong spate of increasingly sensational stories about this "new" trend in publishing began appearing. The media hubbub seems to have started with an article that appeared in the *New York Times Sunday Magazine* on August 2, 1998. Written by Sara Mosle and titled "The Outlook's Bleak," the article was a hand-wringing account of the eruption of edgy young adult novels that were offering unsparingly dark looks at the lives of contemporary teens. By reading bleak books, Mosle argued, teens were growing old before their time, "shouldering burdens far beyond their years."

And so they were—but not because they were reading young adult books. Rather, it was because they themselves were a generation at risk. The first edition of this book was chockablock with statistics demonstrating that reality. This time around it is sufficient to quote Thomas A. Jacobs (1997, 39), who—in his book *What Are My Rights? 95 Questions and Answers about Teens and the Law*—wrote, "In the Forties the top discipline problems in school were talking, chewing gum, making noise, running in the halls, getting out of turn in line, and not putting trash in the wastebaskets. In the Nineties, the top problem [was] alcohol and drug abuse, followed by pregnancy, suicide, rape, assault, arson, murder, vandalism, and gang fights."

Nevertheless, the *Times* piece proved only the tip of the iceberg, as a titanic number of similar articles began appearing in such outlets as *Time, U.S. News and World Report, Wall Street Journal*, and *Brill's Content*, all of them tut-tutting the spurt in bleak books. The titles of the articles betray the sensational slant of their content: "Reads Like Teen Spirit," "Frank Tales Tempt Teens," "Luring Today's Teen Back to Books," and "Sex, Serial Killers, and Suicide." Use of words like *tempt* and *luring* suggested, to overcredulous adults, that publishing had become a dirty old man approaching a group of innocent teens and wheezing, "Hey, kids, wanna see some—heh, heh, heh—*books*?"

Such oversimplification did both publishers and the new young adult literature a disservice. In retrospect, it seems more than likely that the mainstream media were not responding to any perceived changes in or problems with young adult literature but, instead, simply riding the crest of the wave of interest in young adults themselves and in some of the darker aspects of their real lives, including an inarguable increase in teenage drug use (Bass 1997; Wren 1997) and a wave of gun-related school violence that crested (but did not end) with the Columbine shootings in 1999.

The result, unsurprisingly, was a rise in the adult demonization of youth. "According to a new poll," the late columnist Molly Ivins (1997, A19) wrote in 1997, "we don't like our own children. A public policy research group called Public Agenda found that only 37 percent of adults polled believe that today's youngsters will eventually make this country a better place. It seems we consider our teenagers, whom we have long disliked, to be 'rude,' 'wild,' and 'irresponsible.'"

The reporter Lynn Smith (1997, E3), writing in the *Los Angeles Times*, made a cogent point in this connection: "Some youth advocates said such perceptions may be misinformed, largely because many adults shape their opinions from sensational news coverage and studies that focus on problems, rather than actual contact with young people."

As for those young people themselves, a New York teen named Julia Rosen (1998, 347) may have spoken for her entire generation when she wrote, in *VOYA* magazine, "Reading 'bleak books' helps us to realize what kinds of problems actual teens have. They broaden our outlook and help us become less apathetic about the world's problems. Until we live in a world where no problems exist, where adults always behave responsibly, and where there are always happy endings, adults must learn to accept that some of the books we read will describe the harsh realities of life."

The journalist David Spitz (1999, 49) noted what else such reading could do. "Teen books," he wrote in *Time*, "may not be able to compete with the visuals of 'The Matrix' but they do provide for a few hours what teens may need most: time to think. And there's nothing bleak about that."

A Profusion of Prizes

Even though the cutting edge of the new YA literature was inarguably sharper than before, its art was even more acute. *The Facts Speak for Themselves* was a finalist for the National Book Award, after all, and *Dancing on the Edge* was the winner of the award that same year. Also, *Tenderness* and *When She Was Good* were both selected as ALA Best Books for Young Adults, as were *Blood and Chocolate* and *Making Up Megaboy*.

The editorial latitude being given authors for new candor, vigorous truth telling, ambiguity in their fiction, and sharing the sad truth that not all endings are happy ones may have resulted in occasional eruptions of bleakness, but it was also clearly elevating young adult literature to new heights of artistry.

Hence, as noted earlier, a profusion of new awards began appearing to acknowledge this salutary aesthetic reality. Surely, true believers in the viability of young adult literature felt, the time was right for the creation of another award, one that would serve the same purpose for young adult literature that the Newbery Medal did for children's literature: to recognize the most distinguished contribution to American literature during the preceding year for its intended readership. A noble purpose but one not easily realized. The creation of awards can be a fraught process, I discovered when I became president of the Young Adult Library Services Association in 1997 and found myself taxed with effecting a decision that an earlier YALSA board had made in 1995: to accept, in concept, the proposal of author Amelia Elizabeth Walden to fund the creation of an annual book award for young adults. Walden, the author of some forty-three YA novels published between 1946 and 1977, had, in 1971, established a testamentary trust in the amount of $25,000 for that purpose. And in 1991 the trust had been increased to $50,000.

Such munificence seemed the answer to a YA believer's prayer, until its specific petitions were examined to reveal that, in her offer, Walden had stipulated that the award committee be required to choose a book relevant to teens, preferably fiction; give equal consideration to literary merit and popularity; and choose a book that reflects a positive approach to life. Alas, the latter two criteria were inherently contentious. As long as there has been a young adult literature, there has been a raging debate over the relative importance, in evaluating it, of merit and popularity. Worse, at a time when YA was finally able to eschew forced happy endings and acknowledge, with candor, the often *bleak* realities of contemporary teen life, the requirement that the winning book "reflects a positive approach to life" seemed, at best, limiting and, at worst, self-defeating.

Dirk P. Mattson (1997) reported the ensuing brouhaha, at painful length, in his article "Should We Beware of Donors Bearing Book Prizes? Questioning the Walden Award," and I needn't elaborate further on it here, except to say that, in retrospect, the incident brought new urgency to the discussion of what might constitute a meaningful award. Ultimately, after much debate, the

YALSA board chose not to take action on the offer, tacitly consigning it to the department of benign neglect. A decade or so later, the Assembly on Literature for Adolescents (ALAN) of the National Council of Teachers of English revived it and in 2008 announced its creation of the Amelia Elizabeth Walden Award. To be presented annually to the author of a young adult book selected by an ALAN committee, the $5,000 prize would recognize a book "demonstrating a positive approach to life, widespread teen appeal, and literary merit."[3]

Plus c'est change . . .[4]

The Printz of Prizes

Many of us were still determined to seize the day, however. With the enthusiastic support of YALSA's deputy executive director, Linda Waddle, and the YALSA Executive Committee (consisting of Pam Spencer Holley, Deborah D. Taylor, and Joel Shoemaker), I appointed—in the spring of 1998—a nine-member task force (with myself as chair) to investigate "the feasibility of an annual award for the best young adult book based solely on literary merit, to establish criteria for selection with necessary policies and procedures, and to explore the mechanisms for effectuating the award."[5]

I felt it was imperative that the other eight members reflect the diversity of audience and opinion that is the world of young adult literature and YALSA. To that end, I appointed two young adult book editors—Marc Aronson (Henry Holt) and David Gale (Simon & Schuster); a professional reviewer and critic, Hazel Rochman, of *Booklist* magazine; the reading specialist Dr. Gwendolyn Davis; two public librarians, Kirsten Edwards and Ed Sullivan; and two school librarians, Frances Bradburn and Mary Purucker. Geographically, the task force represented the West (California and Washington), the Midwest (Illinois), the South (North Carolina), and the East (New York).

Although the task force members came from different segments of the young adult world, the members quickly arrived at a happy commonality of opinion on many major issues that might have been contentious. For example, they found themselves in unanimous agreement that an award for best young adult book was not only feasible but also long overdue. They also agreed that *Booklist* should sponsor it, and they concurred on a number of necessary definitions: *best* meant books of exemplary literary merit but not of immense popularity; *young adult* meant persons ages twelve through eighteen; and *young adult book* meant a book published expressly for that readership. Thus, books published for adults—even though they might find a young adult audience—would not be eligible. The reasoning? This was to be an award for the best young adult book, not the best book for young adults. This distinction set the proposed award apart from YALSA's Best Books for Young Adults list, which does include titles published for adults and includes popularity as a factor to be considered in selecting books for the list.

The second part of the mission—"to establish criteria with necessary policies and procedures"—was a bit more problematic, though again many points were quickly and unanimously agreed on. Here are the most important: The winning book must have been published in the United States during the year preceding its selection; however, it may have been published in another country first. Eligibility is not confined to novels; anthologies are eligible, as are poetry and other works of nonfiction. Works of joint authorship are eligible, too. In addition to a winning title, as many as four honor books can be named. And if no title is deemed sufficiently worthy in a given year, no award will be given.

Following six months of intensive work, the task force presented its recommendations to the YALSA board at the 1999 Midwinter Conference. They were unanimously adopted and—just like that—the Michael L. Printz Award became a reality.[6]

From the beginning, the task force members believed that an award recognizing literary merit was essential not only as acknowledgment that some of the most risk-taking, artful, and creatively stimulating work in publishing was happening in the field of young adult literature but also as evidence that teenagers need books that are created for them, books that are relevant to their interests and to their life needs. It was, finally, our belief that the Michael L. Printz Award would stimulate the further publication of such books, books that have the enduring power to change the lives of their readers—and perhaps the world they inhabit—for the better. This, as we will see in the next chapter, proved to be the case, guaranteeing that the Michael L. Printz Award would be one not only for a new millennium but also for all times and for all seasons.

Notes

1. Direct quotations in the following section come from an unpublished manuscript of transcripts of the participants' speeches.
2. Hersch was one of the more memorable keynote speakers at the YALSA President's Program at the 1998 ALA Conference in Washington, D.C.
3. ALAN Online, "Amelia Elizabeth Walden Award," http://www.alan-ya.org/amelia -elizabeth-walden-award/.
4. The first Walden Award was presented at the 2009 ALAN conference to Steve Kluger for his antic novel *My Most Excellent Year: A Novel of Love, Mary Poppins, and Fenway Park* (Dial, 2008).
5. Quoted from the official charge of the 1999 Printz Task Force (internal memo).

6. Of course, it wasn't that simple. Those who are interested in a more detailed account of the award's creation are referred to "Creating the Michael L. Printz Award," *Journal of Youth Services in Libraries* 12 (Summer 1999): 30–33.

Part Two
This Is Now

a new literature for a new millennium?

The Renaissance Continues

History was made on January 17, 2000, when—at the ALA Midwinter Meeting in San Antonio, Texas—the first-ever winner of the Michael L. Printz Award was announced, along with three honor titles. Together the four books exemplified the newly literary, inventive, and diverse nature of young adult literature, which the award had been created to recognize.

Ever since 1989, when Francesca Lia Block, in her first novel *Weetzie Bat,* introduced magical realism and the verbal strategies of imagist poetry to YA literature, the field had become increasingly open to experiments in style, structure, and narrative form. Walter Dean Myers's *Monster*—the winner of the first Printz—is an excellent example. Originally conceived by the author as a screenplay, the resulting novel about Steve Harmon, an African American teenager on trial for his life, is told in two different but interrelated dramatic forms: the first is a screenplay, written by the boy himself, who observes of his surreal experience, "I feel like I have walked into the middle of a movie"; the second is his journal (printed on gray paper and set in a handwriting-style font) in which he is able to record the more visceral reality of his interior life and emotional responses (of the prison he writes, "The best time to cry is at night when the lights are out and someone is being beaten up and screaming for help").

Reflecting the increasingly visual context of contemporary teens' Internet-ridden lives, the book also includes a number of black-and-white, often digitally manipulated photographs—the work of Myers's gifted artist son, Christopher—that further ratchet up the reader's interest and engagement.

Though notable for its innovations, *Monster* is also very much of its time, rooted—as it is—in adult America's abiding fear and distrust of teenagers, especially those of color. The title of the book, in fact, is a reference to the prosecuting attorney's reference to Steve as being a monster.

Two of the three Printz honor books—Ellen Wittlinger's *Hard Love* and Laurie Halse Anderson's *Speak*—are also notable for their innovative formats and structures. The former, an ill-starred love story, includes pages from teen zines (self-designed, self-written, self-published magazines that captivated teen energies and imaginations in the late nineties), along with such other anomalies as handwritten letters, poems, and pages from journals.

The latter is also notable for its nontraditional structure. Eschewing chapters, Anderson divides her debut novel into four sections that reflect a school year's traditional grading periods. The story is then presented in a series of short scenes told in the first-person voice of the protagonist (and outcast) Melinda, who brings a sense of imperative action to her almost-cinematic accounts by using the present tense and introducing scenes with headings ("Hard Labor," "Death by Algebra," "Lunch Doom") that recall title cards from silent films.

Though more traditional in its structure, David Almond's *Skellig*, the third honor title, is a departure in two other senses. First published in England, it evidences that young adult literature—born though it might have been in the United States—has become a global phenomenon. Second, the novel is a metaphysical exercise in ambiguity, raising—but never resolving—the central question of the identity of the eponymous Skellig while tacitly acknowledging the aesthetic and intellectual influence on its author of the British mystic William Blake. A staple of literary fiction, ambiguity had been largely absent from young adult literature, but it is an essential constituent of both *Skellig* and *Monster* (the question of Steve's guilt is essentially left to the reader to adjudicate), and its use is another herald of the coming of age of young adult literature. In this context, it should be added that *Hard Love* also represents the maturation of fiction addressing gay and lesbian issues and experiences. Its protagonist, John, falls in love with an out lesbian named Marisol, but the bittersweet reality is that—though the two appealing teens are kindred spirits—Marisol is not emotionally equipped to reciprocate John's tender feelings and, at the book's end, the two part.

The decade that has passed since the publication of these four landmark titles has, in retrospect, only reinforced the validity of what I wrote about them in my "Carte Blanche" column of March 15, 2000: "Clearly, each of these books is extraordinary in its own individual way, but each has in common with the others innovation, creative courage, unimpeachable style, and, in sum, literary excellence" (Cart 2000a, 1370).

Those words also serve to describe the Printz winners and honor titles in the years that have followed. Many of them also exemplify innovations and new trends that have characterized the literature's continued aesthetic evolution and, all in all, confirm one of the most exciting trends of the new decade: the emergence of the literary novel for young adults.

Defining Literary Merit

For the reviewer, critic, and serious reader, one of the most interesting opportunities for discussion of this new literature is that matter of exactly what constitutes literary excellence or merit or quality. The Printz Award Task Force acknowledged that challenge when it wrote the policies and procedures to guide the selection process. Accordingly, it's worth quoting the "Criteria" section here in full:

> What is quality? We know what it is not. While we hope the award will have a wide *audience* among readers 12 to 18, *popularity* is not the criterion for this award. Nor is *message*. In accordance with the Library Bill of Rights, *controversy* is not something to avoid. In fact, we want a book that readers will talk about. . . .
>
> Having established what the award is not, it is far harder to formulate what it is. As every reader knows, a great book can redefine what we mean by quality. Criteria change with time. Therefore, flexibility and an avoidance of the too-rigid are essential components of these criteria. . . . [Thus] the following criteria are only suggested guidelines and should in no way be considered as absolutes. They will always be open to change and adaptation. Depending on the book, one or more of these criteria will apply: Story, Setting, Theme, Voice, Accuracy [remember that nonfiction is eligible], Illustration [as are graphic works], Style, Characters, Design (including format, organization, etc.).
>
> For each book the questions and answers will be different, the weight of the various criteria will be different.[1]

Given this latitude for uncertainty and interpretation, the Printz committees that have served in the years since 2000 have done a heroic job of finding and honoring titles that will stand yet another taxing test of excellence: time. Having myself chaired the 2006 Printz committee, I can testify that the process of selecting the single best YA book of the year is no easy task. It is a process, for many, many worthy books are nominated both from within the committee and from the field. Discussion and sometimes heated debate follow (book lovers are passionate people!), and it is unlikely that the first choice of every single member of every single committee will be the title to receive the top award (or even to be named an honor title). Nor has every choice been a universally popular one with the reading public. And yet, as the following list of winners evidences, these books are not only timely in speaking with relevance to the lives of their contemporary adolescent readers but also timeless in the universality of their art and in their ability to expand the meaning of the word *excellence* as applied to young adult literature. Consider the Printz winners:

2000—*Monster* by Walter Dean Myers

2001—*Kit's Wilderness* by David Almond

2002—*A Step from Heaven* by An Na

2003—*Postcards from No Man's Land* by Aidan Chambers

2004—*The First Part Last* by Angela Johnson

2005—*How I Live Now* by Meg Rosoff

2006—*Looking for Alaska* by John Green

2007—*American Born Chinese* by Gene Luen Yang

2008—*The White Darkness* by Geraldine McCaughrean

2009—*Jellicoe Road* by Melina Marchetta

2010—*Going Bovine* by Libba Bray

No matter how diverse and disparate they are, what all the winning titles have in common is richness of character, an attribute that, more than any other, separates literary from popular fiction, in which character often takes a backseat to plot. This is not to say that the Printz Award books are thinly or awkwardly plotted or do not have compelling, reader-involving stories to tell. They do—all of them. But story in these books is always in service to character. And although the actions of the characters may often contain an element of ambiguity, they are never arbitrary or dictated by the needs of a formula or a plot device. It is because they feature such fully formed, beautifully realized, multidimensional characters that these books will endure, just as the human spirit.

In addition to this stirring and life-affirming commonality, their diversity also distinguishes the books, which is emblematic of the wonderful welter of innovations redefining the meaning of *young adult literature*. For example, five of the eleven winners to date were first published in a country other than the United States (*Kit's Wilderness, Postcards from No Man's Land, How I Live Now*, and *The White Darkness* were first published in England, and *Jellicoe Road* in Australia). *American Born Chinese* is the first graphic novel to win the Printz and augurs well for the continued aesthetic growth of a form that was once dismissed, sniffily, as just comics. That two winners—*Looking for Alaska* and *A Step from Heaven* are both first novels also evidences the field's attraction of powerful new voices (as does the recent establishment of YALSA's William C. Morris First Book Award).

In the case of several of the books, the task force proved almost prescient: "Controversy is not something to avoid. In fact, we want a book that readers will talk about." Three of the Printz winners were particularly notable for exciting controversy and discussion: *Postcards from No Man's Land, How I Live Now*, and *Looking for Alaska* all invited visceral reactions from some readers (and reviewers) for their inclusion of sexual content. In the case of *Postcards*, it was the homosexuality of several characters and the ambiguous sexuality of the protagonist; with *How I Live Now*, it was the inclusion of a sexual relationship between two young cousins, which many regarded as incestuous; and with *Alaska*, the grumbles revolved around a scene involving oral sex (and others involving teenage drinking and smoking—lots of smoking!).

Equally, if not more, controversial has been the regular appearance, in discussion, of another *C* word that was invoked—and invited—by the task force: *complexity*. Many observers have charged that the complexity of plots and characterizations in such winning titles as *Jellicoe Road, The White Darkness, Postcards from No Man's Land*, and *Kit's Wilderness* made them uninviting or inaccessible to teen readers. "In particular," Sarah Cornish and Patrick Jones (2002, 353) wrote, "the buzz about several 2001 winners was that while they might be great literature, they would be a hard sell to many young adults."

The title that has most often excited this objection is not a Printz winner, however, but a Printz honor title: M. T. Anderson's epic novel *Octavian Nothing: Traitor to the Nation*. Published in two volumes (each of which received an honor), this ambitious historical novel of the American Revolution as seen through the eyes of a sixteen-year-old slave has been much criticized (another

C word) not only for the complexity of its plot, structure, and theme but also for the elaborate eighteenth-century voice Anderson has created for his first-person protagonist. Some (myself included) find such criticism particularly egregious in its wholesale discounting of the abilities of its intended audience of readers. Anderson himself has addressed this issue: "I think people don't always give teens credit for how well they read," he told an interviewer in 2008. "I think kids are excited by language, and they've not always been given credit for that" (Sellers 2008).

In addition to the two volumes of *Octavian Nothing*, the Printz committees have named an additional thirty-five honor titles, many of which are notably sophisticated in their use of language, their structure, and their thematic content. Among them are Margo Lanagan's *Tender Morsels* (2009), Sonya Hartnett's *Surrender* and Markus Zusak's *The Book Thief* (both 2007), Jennifer Donnelley's *A Northern Light* (2004), and Chris Lynch's *Freewill* (2002). Still other honor titles evidence emerging trends that we will discuss later, including the emergence of literary nonfiction (e.g., Jack Gantos's compelling memoir *Hole in My Life* and Elizabeth Partridge's ambitious biography of John Lennon, *All I Want Is Truth*). Also in evidence is the renaissance of the short story (*Black Juice* by Margo Lanagan, 2006) and poetry for young adults (*Your Own Sylvia* by Stephanie Hemphill [2008]; *A Wreath for Emmett Till* by Marilyn Nelson [2006]; *Keesha's House* by Helen Frost [2004]; *Heart to Heart*, a poetry anthology edited by Jan Greenberg [2002]; and *True Believer* by Virginia Euwer Wolff [2002]).[2]

But Will They Read It?

Despite the Printz Award's success in recognizing and encouraging literary excellence while serving as a bellwether for exciting new trends in YA literature, the prize—as noted earlier—has not been without its critics. It was dealt something of an implicit rebuff at the 2005 YALSA Best of the Best preconference. The 127 conferees were charged with selecting the best-of-the-best YA books published in the decade between 1994 and 2003. Not only were three of the five Printz winners from that period excluded (*Kit's Wilderness*, *Postcards from No Man's Land*, and *A Step from Heaven*), so were ten of the eighteen honor titles.[3]

Printz winners have fared little better in another de facto best-of-the-best ranking: YALSA's annual Best Books for Young Adults (BBYA) top ten list. Long part of the process of selecting the BBYA list, the BBYA committee also chooses the top ten. Once the master list has been selected, each member then votes for his or her personal top ten books from it. The ballots are tabulated, and the books receiving the most votes constitute the top ten for that year. Through 2009, only four of the ten Printz winners and twelve of the thirty-seven honor titles had made the list. Though it (and its parent BBYA list) is supposed to represent a balance of literary quality and reader popularity, it would seem that the scales have definitely been tilted in the direction of popularity—or participating librarians' notion of what will be popular with teens (though, to be fair, teen input is solicited throughout the BBYA selection process). The long-standing dialectic between popularity and literary merit will probably never be resolved, and such debate can be a healthy and intellectually stimulating process. Nevertheless, when one is talking about selecting best books, popularity alone is no measure of merit. If it were, the Printz would automatically be awarded to Stephenie Meyer (Twilight series) each year, and there would be no need for discussion. Nor is it enough simply to toss an aesthetically noteworthy title into a new book bin and expect it to sell itself. After all, one reason adult gatekeepers—librarians and teachers—are involved with young adult literature is to bring their maturity of judgment and their greater experience of reading to the process of putting teens and excellent books together. Sometimes this means fast talking and strenuous selling, but surely a successful sale is worth the labor, no matter how herculean.

If literary fiction is often regarded as more popular with adults than with teens, the same is routinely said of two of its constituent forms, the short story and poetry, which have also experienced a period of rapid revival and growth in the wake of the overall YA renaissance. Again, this lack of popularity seems counterintuitive. After all, the defining aspect of the short story—its shortness—would seem to be an irresistible lure for attention-span-challenged teens. Poetry, too, is often an exercise in brevity, and teens seem to love the emotionally cathartic experience of writing it. But the received wisdom is that teens resist every effort to persuade them to read either short stories or poetry. Is the received wisdom wrong? Let's examine each form in turn and try to find out.

The Short Story Revival

The short story as an American literary form dates back to the early 1800s and the work of Washington Irving, Nathaniel Hawthorne, and Edgar Allan Poe. Later in the same century, it flourished in the hands of Stephen Crane, Jack London, Frank R. Stockton, Bret Harte, O. Henry, and—in the early twentieth century—Sherwood Anderson. The form hit its stride in the 1930s and 1940s in the work of F. Scott Fitzgerald and Ernest Hemingway and, in the 1950s, of J. D. Salinger, John O'Hara, John Cheever, and the whole coterie of *New Yorker* magazine writers who redefined the form. But then in the sixties and seventies, the market for the short story began to decline as the general interest magazine, which had always been its home, went into eclipse. But the story is a durable form, and it rebounded in the eighties in the minimalist work of Raymond Carver, Richard Ford, Tobias Wolff, and others. This was also the decade in which MFA programs in creative writing began appearing in U.S. universities and fastened on the short story as "the instructional medium of choice." "The majority of people who enroll in these programs want to be novelists," Charles McGrath (2004b, B1) wryly wrote in the *New York Times*, "but novels don't lend themselves very readily to the workshop format, and so would-be novelists these days spend at least part of their apprenticeship working on stories."

This equation of the form with the academic suggests a major reason short stories have been such a hard sell to teens. They have traditionally been used for instructional purposes in America's high school classrooms. Worse, like most other required reading, they have too often been dusty works from the adult literary canon that offer little of relevance to the lives or interests of contemporary teens. This situation began to change in the eighties when—encouraged by the renaissance of the form in adult publishing—pioneering young adult anthologists like Donald Gallo and Hazel Rochman began assembling thematically related collections of short stories, many of them written specifically for the collection by established young adult authors.

Gallo, who must be regarded as the godfather of the contemporary YA short story collection, published his first, *Sixteen*, in 1985. This was followed by *Visions* in 1988 and *Connections* in 1990. Rochman's first, *Somehow Tenderness Survives*, a collection of stories about South Africa, appeared in 1988 and was followed in 1993 by *Who Do You Think You Are? Stories of Friends and Enemies* (coedited with Darlene Z. McCampbell).

Rochman has written about the necessary characteristics of such anthologies. "It's helpful," she noted in a 1998 "YA Talk" piece for *Booklist*, "for teen readers, especially reluctant ones, to have a theme that grabs them, a cover that looks like them, and some connection to lead them from one story to the next" (Rochman 1998, 1234).

This new kind of anthology—the theme-driven collection of original work commissioned expressly for the book—quickly became enormously popular. In 1997 a half dozen were included on YALSA's Best Books and Quick Picks lists. In the meantime, well-known YA novelists had begun assembling anthologies, too, among them Harry Mazer, Anne Mazer, Lois Duncan, Marilyn Singer, Judy Blume, James Howe, and others. Such name authors certainly excited new interest among young adult readers already familiar with and well disposed to their work.

Of perhaps greater interest in literary terms, however, was the quick emergence of single-author collections. Among the first of these were Gary Soto's *Baseball in April* (1990) and Chris Crutcher's *Athletic Shorts* (1991). Others have followed by a veritable who's who of writers, including David Almond, Francesca Lia Block, Bruce Coville, Diana Wynne Jones, Kelly Link, Chris Lynch, Beverly Naidoo, Graham Salisbury, Tim Wynne-Jones, and many others. In terms of sheer literary excellence, such collections hit a new peak with the publication of Australian author Margo Lanagan's *Black Juice*, a brilliantly imaginative collection of speculative stories selected as a 2006 Printz honor title. (Though a single-author collection, it is also an example of another newish kind of anthology in which genre, not theme, provides the basis for commonality: for example, Kelly Link's *Pretty Monster* and Deborah Noyes's *Gothic!*)

The popularity of the short story (and the decreasing attention span of teens) is also responsible for a new literary form that began to emerge in the 1990s: the novel as collection of linked stories. Among the first of these were three heart-stoppingly good books: Bruce Brooks's *What Hearts*, Chris Lynch's *Whitechurch*, and E. R. Franks's *Life Is Funny*. Other notable works in this form that have followed include Kathi Appelt's *Kissing Tennessee*, Walter Dean Myers's *145th Street*, Richard Peck's *A Long Way from Chicago* and *A Year Down Yonder*, Ellen Wittlinger's *What's in a Name?* and—most recently—Margo Rabb's critically acclaimed *Cures for Heartbreak*. The constituent parts of such books usually have stand-alone coherence and, thus, appeal to those time- and attention-span-challenged teens, but the stories cannot be read at random like those in a collection. They must be read in the order of their presentation, as one would read a novel. This experience of reading is, I think, wonderfully like that of living. After all, human lives themselves are series of sometimes-significant moments that seem individual and isolated until enough time has passed to offer opportunity for reflection and the attendant emergence of context. The same is true of these books. Each story is individual, yet at the end, the reader can see how the apparently discontinuous is, in fact, part of a larger continuity and that the isolated is, in fact, linked, connected to other events that, together, offer coherent sense (and, in the case of books, sensibility). We will examine what part another exercise in isolation and linkage, the Internet, may play in the evolution of fiction in a later chapter. But for the moment, suffice it to say that the short story, presented in imaginative forms and formats, seems to have overcome original reader reluctance to become an exceedingly durable form. But what about poetry?

A Poetry Renaissance

As the evergreen appeal of Mother Goose evidences, small children love cadence and rhyme. However, their taste for poetry seems to decrease as an inverse function of their age. By the time they have finished elementary school, most kids are no longer engaged by verse (nor are critics: I confess I gave no attention to this form in the first edition of this book, while Nilsen and Donelson [2009] devote only 10 pages to it in the 491-page eighth edition of their textbook). Once again, this diminishing interest is pretty clearly a function of adolescents' association of poetry with the classroom and the dreaded phrase "required reading." Holly Koelling (2007) discusses this lack of popularity (and audience!) in her analysis of the Best Books for Young Adults lists from 2000 to 2006. There she notes that only three works of poetry (0.5 percent of the total) appear on the seven annual lists. This is hardly an anomaly. In looking at the six Best of the Best Books lists that YALSA has assembled periodically since 1974, one finds only six works of poetry represented out of 530 titles (0.01 percent)! Four of the titles are anthologies— Stephen Dunning's *Reflections on a Gift of Watermelon Pickle*, R. R. Knudson and May Swenson's *American Sports Poems*, Paul B. Janeczko's *The Place My Words Are Looking For: What Poets Say about and through Their Poems*, and Lori Carlson's *Cool Salsa: Bilingual Poems on Growing up Latino in the United States*—and two, Mel Glenn's *Class Dismissed: High School Poems* and Cynthia Rylant's *Something Permanent*, are single-author works.

As is the case with short story anthologies, theme is of overarching importance. The poet and anthologist Janeczko says, "If poetry is to do more than furnish answers on a multiple-choice test, we must relate poetry to the real world, finding poems that are connected with something that happened at school, in the community, or in the world" (Cart 2001, 1390).

Another successful anthologist, Ruth Gordon, agrees that "a theme that will appeal" makes a successful collection but notes that a fundamental cause of poetry's lack of popularity is that "so many people are afraid of it because of the form and its perceived formality; they have been taught to read incorrectly and they are not taught how to read poetry for themselves" (Cart 1997, 1570).

Something of a sea change began visiting poetry in the mid-nineties, when American culture began taking new cognizance of the form. In 1996 the Academy of American Poets, with the support of a number of other organizations, including the American Library Association, succeeded in having April designated as National Poetry Month. A decade earlier, in 1986, the librarian of Congress had appointed Robert Penn Warren as America's first official poet laureate, raising the public profile of the literary form. Public television and the Internet also made poetry vastly more accessible, as did the surge in popularity of coffeehouses, which—shades of the beat poetry movement of the 1950s—began sponsoring open-mic poetry nights and poetry slams, events that young adult librarians discovered and that became, almost overnight, staple fixtures of their programming for teens.

Ironically, the same teens who have traditionally been reluctant readers of poetry have, nevertheless, always loved writing it. "Poetry is a perfect medium for adolescence: it lends itself to the fierce dramas and false clarities of these years," the author and teacher Katie Roiphe (2009, 14) writes in the *New York Times Book Review*.

The Internet has begun providing teens exciting new opportunities for writing and hearing poetry. A number of sites like the former poet laureate Robert Pinsky's own (www.favoritepoem.org) and the *Atlantic Monthly*'s Unbound Poetry Pages (www.theatlantic.com/unbound/poetry/) present opportunities for hearing both poets and ordinary Americans reading work. Such sites as www.teenpaper.org, "Scriveners," and "Writes of Passage" were only three of many that offered teens abundant opportunities for publishing their work online. Book publishers, too, began issuing collections of teen-written work. Betsy Franco's *You Hear Me? Poems and Writing by Teenage Boys* was selected as a 2001 Best Book for Young Adults. Other collections include Lee Francis's *When the Rain Sings: Poems by Young Native Americans* and Lydia Omolola Okutoro's *Quiet Storm: Voices of Young Black Poets*.

Franco (the mother of the celebrated young actor James Franco) is one of a new generation of anthologists—others are Naomi Shihab Nye, Liz Rosenberg, and Lori Carlsen—who have brought enhanced popularity to poetry for teen readers. Nye and Carlsen have also enriched multicultural literature by editing anthologies of poetry from the Middle East (Nye) and from Latin America (Carlsen). Jan Greenberg, known for her many books about art and artists, received a Printz honor for her innovative anthology *Heart to Heart: New Poems Inspired by Twentieth Century Art*.

Another measure of the new popularity of poetry may be found in the annual Top Ten Best Books for Young Adults. Since this list was established in 1997, a total of eight works of poetry—of 130 total titles—have been included (a fairly robust 6 percent of the total).

Arguably, the most visible manifestation of poetry's new popularity, however, is the profusion of novels in verse (book-length works of narrative poetry). Hardly a new form (Homer, anyone?), the modern verse novel began to excite interest about the same time as poetry did. One of the early examples from adult literature is Vikram Seth's *The Golden Gate*, which was published in 1986 and became a surprise best seller. In the young adult world, two of the first were Mel Glenn's *My Friend's Got This Problem, Mr. Candler* (1991) and Virginia Euwer Wolff's *Make Lemonade* (1994). Interestingly, Wolff does not herself consider *Make Lemonade* or its two sequels (*True Believer* and *This Full House*) to be novels in verse. "Reviewers have called my books 'novels in verse,'" she told *Publishers Weekly*, but "I consider them as written in prose but I do use stanzas. Stanza means 'room' in Latin, and I wanted there to be 'room'—breathing opportunities to receive thoughts and have time to come out of them before starting again at the left margin. I thought of young mothers reading my books, and I wanted to give them lots of white space, so they could read entire chapters at a time and feel a sense of accomplishment" (Comerford 2009).

The accessibility of verse novels—pages set with short lines surrounded by white space—has made them popular for use with reluctant readers as well as those who speak English as a second language. The narrative nature of their content is also an inducement to teen readers, and because almost all of them are written in free verse, no one need fear the rigors of form or any perceived formality.

Though free verse sometimes invites self-indulgent writing that has more to it of prose than poetry, it can—when properly executed—prove not only reader friendly but also exceedingly artful. Karen Hesse's *Out of the Dust*, published in 1997, is an example of the latter. Set in Oklahoma during the Dust Bowl, this elegantly composed story of family loss and hardship is a demonstration of the stark capacity of verse to capture and stir the deepest human emotions. Another example is the California poet Sonya Sones's first book, *Stop Pretending: What Happened When My Big Sister Went Crazy* (Simon & Schuster, 1999). Telling the story of the emotional breakdown and subsequent institutionalization of the narrator's older sister, the first-person poems from the point of view of a thirteen-year-old girl have a cumulative emotional power that is quietly devastating—which makes the first evidence of the older girl's recovery dizzyingly cathartic: "I blink / and there you suddenly are / inhabiting your eyes again . . . and I'm feeling all lit up / like a jar filled / with a thousand fireflies."

Sones's subsequent works—*One of Those Hideous Books Where the Mother Dies, What My Mother Doesn't Know*, and *What My Girlfriend Doesn't Know*—similarly demonstrate the capacity of poetry to record the personal and, through the use of figurative language, rhythm, verbal economy, emotional insight, and honesty, to translate it into the universal. Small wonder that Sones has become one of the most popular (with both readers and reviewers) practitioners of the verse novel form.

Another notable practitioner is the versatile Ron Koertge. The author of such celebrated prose novels as *The Arizona Kid, Stoner and Spaz*, and

Margaux with an X, Koertge is also an award-winning adult poet who demonstrated his skills in his YA novels in verse, *Shakespeare Bats Cleanup* and *The Brimstone Journals*, an ALA Best Book for Young Adults. The latter, told in the different voices of fifteen members of the graduating class of Branston High School, fluidly demonstrates poetry's wonderful capacity for presenting multiple points of view; other notable titles that do this are Nikki Grimes's *Bronx Masquerade* and David Levithan's *The Realm of Possibilities*.

A few writers—Helen Frost and Marilyn Nelson among them—have written verse novels employing either traditional or newly created poetic forms. Nelson, for example, wrote her Printz Honor Award–winning *A Wreath for Emmett Till* in the exquisitely difficult form of a heroic crown of sonnets. Frost, another Printz honor winner for *Keesha's House*, which is written in the form of sonnets and sestinas, also specializes in creating forms that match the thematic or narrative material of her novels in verse. In *The Braid*, for example, she has, as she notes in an afterword, "invented a formal structure for this book, derived in part from my admiration for Celtic knots" (Frost 2006, 91).

All in all, the book-length work of verse has proved marvelously versatile, lending itself to a variety of forms and genres, including biography and memoir (Stephanie Hemphill's *Your Own Sylvia: A Verse Portrait of Sylvia Plath* received a Printz Honor Award), mystery (especially in the work of Mel Glenn), fantasy (Lisa Ann Sandell's novel of the Lady of Shalott, *Song of the Sparrow*), historical fiction (Jen Bryant's two novels about the Scopes trial, *Trial* and *Ringside, 1925*), and even problem novels (see, for example, Ellen Hopkins's *Crank, Glass, Burned, Identical*).

Trends are transient, and doubtless the novel in verse will pass in and out of favor with writers and readers for years to come. But one thing seems certain: poetry itself will remain one of literature's most durable—and versatile—forms.

Notes

1. American Library Association, "The Michael L. Printz Award Policies and Procedures," www.ala.org/ala/mgrps/divs/yalsa/booklistsawards/printzaward/aboutprintz/michaell printz.cfm.
2. A complete list of Printz winners and honor titles is available online at www.ala.org/ yalsa/.
3. Those interested in reading more about this preconference might look at my "Carte Blanche" column in the September 15, 2005, issue of *Booklist*.

romancing the retail

Of Series, Superstores, Harry Potter, and Such

Not every twenty-first-century trend in young adult literature has evidenced the field's artistic evolution. Some have demonstrated its ever-expanding commercial possibilities, instead. Principal among these is the inexorable (and apparently never-ending) rise of what has come to be called chick lit: those often (though not always) humorous novels aimed at female readers in pursuit of romance and/or designer labels. Arguably the first of these epidemic novels was Helen Fielding's adult title *The Diary of Bridget Jones*, published in England in 1996. Wildly popular, the book quickly inspired a host of similar titles, and thus a major trend—"perhaps the only new one of the past 25 years," according to Laura Miller (2004, 27)—was born. The phenomenon arrived in the United States with the 2000 publication here of the British comedian Louise Rennison's *Angus, Thongs, and Full-Frontal Snogging*. To the surprise of many, this became a 2001 Printz honor title, turning the usual controversy on its head as—for once—a book was criticized as being too popular to receive Printz recognition! Be that as it may, *Angus* was so successful that at last count, eight more addled adventures of its protagonist Georgia Nicholson have followed, clearly demonstrating that the operative word in any discussion of chick lit is *popular*, followed closely by *commercial*.

For many readers, the first indication that a new genre was in the offing was the unheralded appearance of book display tables at their neighborhood Barnes & Noble bookstores bearing signs that read, simply, "Chick Lit." This suggested several things: the principal market for this new kind of genre fiction was retail, not the traditional institutional market, and the major chain bookstores (principally Barnes & Noble) were playing an increasingly active role in the process of publishing books for young readers and were able to create and develop trends. One of the earlier indicators of this had been an article that appeared in the August 12, 1997, *New York Times.* In it, the reporter Doreen Carvajal noted, "Publishing executives in search of oracles have begun turning to the dominant chains like Barnes & Noble and Borders for guidance about a broad range of issues—from dust jacket colors and punchy titles to authors' precise sales histories and forecasts of customer demand—that could determine a manuscript's destiny." To affirm this, Carvajal (1997, C5) quoted Ira Silverberg, then Grove Press's editor in chief: "Barnes & Noble and Borders have an increasing presence, so we really must spend more time with them to get our books across to a wider audience."

Silverberg, of course, was an adult publisher, but a similar influence was being felt on the juvenile side of publishing houses. The children's book reviewer Barbara Elleman (1998, 44) noted in a 1998 *School Library Journal* article, "Juvenile trade marketing staffs have begun close contact with bookstore chains, as their adult counterparts have done for some time. Barnes & Noble has 35 central buyers who make the [purchasing] decisions for all the stores across the country. In the children's field, there are only one or two buyers. Their selections are usually based on an author's reputation, the number of awards he or she has won, the 'spin' the sales and marketing people have put on the book, and how much money the publishers are willing to put into marketing it in the bookstore."

Whether these buyers have ever actually exercised veto power over the publication of any particular book is moot, but I know from personal experience that their opinions are taken very seriously, indeed. When, in the late nineties, I served as a consultant to Houghton Mifflin on the development of their prospective new YA series the Best American Nonrequired Reading (the term *young adult literature* was considered too noncommercial!), I was flown to New York for a meeting with Joe Monti, then children's book buyer for Barnes & Noble, to solicit his views on the viability of the series and whether it should be published as a YA or an adult title. Later, when I was developing *Rush Hour*, my own short-lived YA literary journal, its publisher Delacorte also sought advice and feedback from Barnes & Noble regarding marketing, jacket art, and price points.

The growing influence of the chains affirmed another equally significant trend: the growing purchasing power of the young adults themselves. "Attracting teens' business has become a Holy Grail for marketers," the reporter Dave Carpenter (2000, D1) wrote in a November 2000 article, adding that American teens were projected to spend "a staggering" $155 billion that year.

Two years later, the *Washington Post* reported: "Teenagers are the demographic that almost everyone in the book industry—librarians, publishers, booksellers—wants. As the number of teenagers in the population has risen [the 2000 census had shown 5.5 million more ten- to nineteen-year-olds than in 1990], so has teen buying power for all kinds of items, including books" (Bacon 2002, B1).

The *Los Angeles Times* defined precisely how much buying power when it reported in a 2001 article that literature for young adults (which it defined— à la YALSA—as twelve- to eighteen-year-olds) had become a $1.5 billion industry (DiMassa 2001). That same year *USA Today* reported that teens ages fourteen to seventeen had bought 35.6 million books in 2001, an increase of about 6 million over the previous year.

One noteworthy aspect of teens' new spending patterns was an equally new penchant for hardcover books in a field where paperbacks had reigned supreme! The editor-publishers Brenda Bowen (Simon & Schuster) and Elise Howard (Avon) both told *Publishers Weekly* in 1999 that they were finding a new receptivity to hardcovers on the part of the chains (Maughan 1999, 93), and a year later, Andrew Smith, then vice president of marketing for Random House, agreed: "We're selling more hardcovers to teens than we have in the past. The format and price point don't seem to be a problem for them" (Maughan 2000, 28).[1] Apparently not—five years later, the Association of American Publishers reported in 2005 that children's and young adult hardcover sales in 2005 were up an amazing 59.6 percent over the previous year (2006).

YA Imprints Arrive

Although publishers' children's divisions had previously released young adult books, it is small wonder—considering this robust market—that as early as 1999, publishers were starting to launch separate young adult imprints, many specializing in reader-friendly (i.e., commercial) fiction. At least a baker's dozen would emerge between 1999 and 2007. In chronological order, they are

1999: Avon (later Harper) Tempest and Simon & Schuster Pulse

2002: Scholastic Push, TOR Starscape, Penguin Speak, Penguin Firebird

2004: Penguin Razorbill, Houghton Mifflin Graphia

2005: Abrams Amulet

2006: Llewellyn Flux

2007: Aladdin Mix (aimed at tween readers), Harlequin
       Kimani Tru

A measure of their success is found in a startling statistic from the Book Industry Study Group, which found that, in 2006, retail sales accounted for roughly 60 percent of all domestic children's hardcover sales and 90 percent of children's paperback sales (Brown 2006, 24).

In addition to the thirteen new YA imprints, two new adult imprints— Pocket Books' MTV Books (1995) and Simon & Schuster's Spotlight Entertainment (2004)—were aimed directly at the newly emerging crossover audience: eighteen- to twenty-five-year-olds. Though MTV Books publications were notably edgy and clearly aimed at the upper end of the MTV demographic (eighteen- to thirty-four-year-olds), many of its titles could easily have been released as YA and—in one notable case—should have been. I refer to Stephen Chbosky's *Perks of Being a Wallflower*, an extraordinary epistolary novel with a haunting sensibility, an unforgettable protagonist, and an absolutely exquisite narrative voice. Published in 1999, it became an instant YA classic and—had it been published as YA—surely would have been a strong contender for the Michael L. Printz Award.

Not every commercial effort to reach teens was successful, however. One of the most notable failures was the Teen People Book Club, launched in March 2000 by the magazine of the same name in cooperation with the Book of the Month Club. Sadly, this promising effort, which initially brought in four to five times more new members than expected (Maughan and Milliot 2001, 12), lasted only a year before it fell victim not so much to disappointing sales as to the fraught merger of its owner Time Warner with AOL. In the meantime, the self-described categories of books offered by the club and deemed especially attractive to teens are instructive. For those interested in the equation between teens and popular reading, here they are from the club's website, which—sadly—is no longer available:

Amazing books about real teens and real issues

Great novels that will make you laugh or make you cry or make
       your heart pound with fear

Star-studded books on today's hottest celebrities

Useful guides with advice that's truly relevant to your life

And all the new, new, NEW stuff you just won't hear about anywhere else. It's also worth noting that—in a further effort to establish credibility with young adults—titles for the club's catalog were selected with the advice and counsel of a panel of teenagers recruited from across the country called the Review Crew.

Mean Girls Materialize

Ironically or not, the emergence of teens as überconsumers influenced the emergence, a year later, of a new chick lit subgenre that was quickly dubbed both "mean girl" books and "privileged chick lit." A *New York Times* article about this new subgenre with its relentless focus on designer labels and other consumables was amusingly titled "Poor Little Rich Girls Throbbing to Shop" (Bellafante 2003). The chief exemplar of this new subgenre was, of course, Cecily von Ziegesar's Gossip Girl series, which retails the designer-label-ridden lives of fabulously wealthy girls like Blair Waldorf and Serena van der Woodsen, both of whom attend the exclusive Constance Billard School on Manhattan's Upper East Side. Although loosely based on the author's own teenage experience of being a student at the tony Nightingale-Bamford School, these are books in which—the *New York Times* dryly noted—"No cliché of Upper East Side privilege goes unnoticed" (Bellafante 2003, F1).

The genesis of the series was an outline proposal that von Ziegesar wrote when she was working as an editor at the book packager 17th Street Productions (later part of Alloy Entertainment). One of the first such proposals to be shopped around by e-mail, the project was quickly snapped up by the Little, Brown editor Cynthia Eagen, and the rest is literary history—of a sort. Within two years, the incipient series had sold 1.3 million copies and spawned a companion spin-off series, The A List, which was set on the other coast—in Hollywood. The only difference between the two cultures under examination was that the kids in the A List titles didn't attend a private school; instead, they were students at Beverly Hills High, a milieu that irresistibly recalls the once-popular television series *Beverly Hills 90210* and underscores the growing symbiosis between commercial fiction and its electronic counterpart, motion pictures and television.

There would ultimately be a dozen Gossip Girl titles that, through June 2009, had sold upward of 5.5 million copies in the United States and had spawned at least two other spin-off series from von Ziegesar: The It Girl (which has sold 1 million copies since its 2005 launch) and the Carlyles. The latter, which debuted in 2008 with a two-hundred-thousand-copy first printing (Lodge 2008), features triplet sisters who, newcomers to Manhattan, happen to move into the penthouse that Blair Waldorf's family had previously occupied (precisely why von Ziegesar names her characters for hotels is one of the more tantalizing imponderables of these series; perhaps it's for the same reason that Antonio Pagliarulo's the Celebutantes, another recent series starring wealthy triplets, names its protagonists after fashionable Manhattan streets: Madison, Lexington, and Park!).[2]

Gossip Girl publisher Little, Brown found the holy grail of synergy in 2007 when the books inspired a highly touted television series on the CW network. Interestingly enough, it was an earlier television series, *Sex and the City*, that has often been cited as the source of inspiration for the whole burgeoning mean-girl movement. "I give you Sex and the City as told by Carrie Bradshaw's kid sister," the *Manchester Guardian* wrote when the Gossip Girl books debuted in Britain in 2003 (Cooke 2003).

Sex—casual and otherwise—is certainly a fixture in many of these books, but it is couture that might be their most deliciously meretricious aspect. The *New York Times* education columnist Michael Winerip (himself an author of fiction for middle school readers) wrote an interesting piece about this in July 2008. "In Novels for Girls, Fashion Trumps Romance" quotes an academic study of Gossip Girl and two of the series it spawned—Clique and the A List—that found 1,553 brand-name references in the books' collective 1,431 pages—slightly more than one commercial per page (though none was actually paid placement, Winerip decides after some reportorial digging) (Winerip 2008).

It's hard, thus, to disagree with the cultural observer Naomi Wolf (2006), who concludes that in these books, "success and failure are entirely signaled by material possessions—specifically by brands. Sex and shopping take their place on a barren stage, as though, even for teenagers, these are the only dramas left."

Given this commercial patina, it's no surprise that many of these series—though published by all the major houses, including Little, Brown, Simon & Schuster, HarperCollins, Delacorte Press, and others—are created by book packagers, the most successful of which is Alloy Entertainment, which produces some forty books a year and is responsible not only for Gossip Girl and the A-List but also the Clique, the Au Pairs, Pretty Little Liars, Privilege, Luxe, and the more benign Sisterhood of the Traveling Pants. Alloy Entertainment is a division of the larger Alloy Media + Marketing, which describes itself as "one of the largest and most successful marketers and merchandisers to the youth market."[3]

The goal in this still-burgeoning field is to create an instantly recognizable brand or franchise that can be spun off into a variety of economic opportunities—books, television series, movies, products—and then promoted through interactive websites, contests, and social networks.

Typically published as trade paperbacks (though some—Luxe, Traveling Pants, etc.—may also appear in hardcover editions), the books are targeted at the retail market, their covers replete with references to the *New York Times* Best-Seller List and to contests ("Win Shopping Spree—Details Inside"). Their sophisticated cover art, usually featuring photographs of drop-dead gorgeous girls (and boys), is designed to appeal to a broad age range. "Though 'Gossip Girl' was originally published as a YA novel," its editor Cynthia Eagen told *Publishers Weekly*, "we thought the book would have crossover appeal and we specifically designed the cover to have an older, cosmopolitan look. Pretty soon we discovered that women and gay men in their 20s and 30s were buying a ton of these books. Our first Gossip Girl 'Win a Trip to New York' contest winner was actually a 32-year-old woman" (Alderdice 2004, 26).

Genre fiction of all sorts has always had considerable crossover potential, though it has traditionally manifested as teens reading adult titles. The discovery of YA books by adult readers is a new—and fascinating—development that we will examine in greater detail a bit later. In the meantime, it should be noted that, just as the lines of demarcation dividing adult and young adult readers has increasingly blurred since the late 1990s, so have the lines separating genres. Nowhere is this more evident than in the field of romance fiction, where genre bending and blending have become commonplace. In addition to the chick lit, Brit lit, mean girl, and privileged chick lit we've been discussing, there are historical romances (Libba Bray's Gemma Doyle trilogy and the Luxe novels of Anna Godbersen); mystery-suspense romances (virtually anything by Joan Lowery Nixon); gay and lesbian romances (Annie on My Mind, Boy Meets Boy); and the myriad marriages of science fiction, paranormal, fantasy, horror, and speculative fiction with romance (think Melissa Marr and Stephenie Meyer).

Contemporary romance (which includes chick lit) continues to lead the other subgenres in terms of reader popularity, however, and it's here that we find many of the most popular contemporary YA authors—writers like Anne Brashares, Kate Brian, Meg Cabot, Zoey Dean, Melissa De La Cruz, Megan McCafferty, Lurleen McDaniel (all hail the uncrowned queen of the weepies!), and the more mainstream writers who tend to combine romance and realistic fiction—Sarah Dessen, Maureen Johnson, Lauren Myracle, Catherine Gilbert Murdock, and others.

What Harry Hath Wrought

No matter how successful the many-splendored subgenres of romance fiction have been in the twenty-first century, they are all eclipsed by the jaw-dropping success of the fantasy field, this in the wake of one of the most extraordinary phenomena in the history of publishing: the international success of the Harry Potter series. From the 1997 British publication of the first volume, *Harry Potter and the Philosopher's Stone* (retitled *Harry Potter and the Sorcerer's Stone* when the American edition was published in 1998) to the seventh and final volume, *Harry Potter and the Deathly Hallows*, published in 2007, the series broke record after record while dramatically—some might say seismically—changing the world of publishing for young readers.

Although no one could have predicted the ultimate enormity of the phenomenon when the first book was published, the seeds of that success were already sown. It didn't hurt, for example, that the book arrived with an irresistible backstory: its previously unpublished author, J. K. Rowling, was an attractive, divorced, unemployed single mother who was on the dole and living in an unheated Edinburgh flat while writing the book. To keep warm, she reportedly wheeled her baby daughter into cafés and coffee shops, where she wrote the book in longhand (the story varies in its details, of course; according to *Time* magazine she would "sometimes jot down Harry Potter ideas on napkins" [Gray 1999, 71]). That its British publisher then paid £100,000 for the first novel added a fairy-tale patina to the story, which was further burnished when Scholastic ponied up $100,000 for the U.S. rights, an unprecedented sum for an American children's book. Sales more than met expectations as the book became a best seller in both the United Kingdom and the United States, where it appeared on the *New York Times* Bestseller List within three months of its publication. A mere year and a half later, the top three hardcover slots were held by Potter titles, and a fourth was on its way, with a first printing of 3.8 million copies, the largest for any book ever.[4]

Harry had appeared on the cover of *Time* magazine (September 20, 1999), Warner Brothers had acquired film rights (the first film was released in 2001), and Harry Potter was now more than a series of enchanting books; it was a full-fledged publishing phenomenon. Ultimately, of course, there would be seven novels that, together, sold more than 375 million copies and were translated into sixty-five languages. By 2004 the *New York Times* had received enough complaints from adult publishers about the Potter books taking so many slots on its best-seller list that it responded by inaugurating a new—and separate—children's best-seller list!

This was only one of the significant changes that the Potter books would visit on the worlds of publishing and bookselling. Their international success also encouraged the more widespread publication in the United States (and in the United Kingdom) of books first published in other countries, while international cooperation was served when Bloomsbury and Scholastic quickly agreed that each new Potter book should be released simultaneously in the United Kingdom and the United States (typically the U.S. release would have followed the British publication by a year or so). Each new Potter release subsequently became an event—no, an EVENT! The books were embargoed until their official publication date: no advance reading or review copies were released prior to publication, and bookstores put them on sale at precisely one minute after midnight on the official publication date, staying open until the wee hours to accommodate the hordes of overstimulated children (most of them dressed as Potter characters) and their bleary-eyed parents (some also in costume), all waiting in serpentine lines to purchase their anxiously awaited copies.

The normally book-shy mass media ate all this up and hyped Harry relentlessly. Rapturous headlines greeted each new printing or sales record, and when the motion picture versions of the books began appearing, the hoopla approached hysteria. In the meantime, the Internet came alive with fan sites and fan fiction; there were fan gatherings (à la Star Trek conventions), promotional tours, rock bands, and more—enough more that Melissa Anelli, webmaster of the Leaky Cauldron, the premiere Potter fan site, wrote a fascinating account of it all in *Harry: A History* (Pocket, 2008), a book that will be of interest not only to Potter fans but also to future literary historians and cultural anthropologists alike.

The books themselves soon became almost lost in the larger phenomenon that was Pottermania. And that's a pity because they remain extraordinary works of fantasy and J. K. Rowling, a brilliant writer. My personal feelings about the Potter titles has not changed since I gave a starred review in *Booklist* to the very first one in 1998, calling it "brilliantly imagined, beautifully written, and utterly captivating."

These dozen years later, I would still use the same words to describe the books that followed, as well. Rowling has proved a gifted storyteller with a remarkable ability to create a detailed alternative world that coexists with ours. Yet, having read all seven volumes, I believe it is the characters and their interrelationships that will remain with me longest, in part because Rowling permitted them to grow up with their readers over the course of the series (Harry is a year older in each new volume). Thus, though the first several titles were clearly aimed at middle school readers (I recommended the first for fifth to eighth grades, and the literary historian Leonard Marcus [2008] regards the early titles as for eight- to twelve-year-old tweens), each volume thereafter became increasingly sophisticated and, frankly, darker. The final three—*Order of the Phoenix*, *Half-Blood Prince*, and *Deathly Hallows*—are clearly young adult titles. Thus, the changes that Harry Potter visited on publishing affected not only children's books but YA ones, as well. At this writing, only three years have passed since the publication of the seventh volume, and another decade or two must flow under the bridge of history before one can, with any validity, assess the series' lasting place in world literature (or describe them as "classic").

That said, it is indisputably clear that they will command a very large place in all future histories of publishing, for their impact there is already abundantly evident. The international success of the series helped turn young adult literature into an increasingly global phenomenon and sparked a new interest in fantasy as a genre not only for children but also—and perhaps more important—for young adults. It is hard to argue with Holly Koelling's (2007, 64) flat declaration: "Plain and simple, fantasy is a predominant trend in current teen literature." Not only did Harry's success stimulate an amazing outpouring of new fantasy titles (that virtually every one of these must now be part of an ongoing series may be a less salutary trend), it also spurred readers to discover other long-established fantasists whose work had not previously received its due—Diana Wynne Jones, Eva Ibbotson, Margaret Mahy, Diane Duane, and others.

Meanwhile the multigenerational appeal of the Potter books spurred a rush to publish crossover titles and began attracting record numbers of established adult authors to the newly profitable field of books for young readers. The books revived an interest in family reading, too, and demonstrated that, given something they actually wanted to read, boys would embrace books as enthusiastically as girls. The increasing length of the individual volumes (three of the last four exceeded seven hundred pages) also proved that, contrary to traditional wisdom, contemporary young readers would welcome books more than two hundred pages in length. As a result, YA novels have now routinely become many hundreds of pages longer—whether or not they need to be.

One of the less benign aspects of the Potter books was their introduction into the children's field of event publishing, which had long been a fixture of the adult world. Indeed, the runaway financial success of the Rowling series seems to have accelerated a trend that had already begun: the transformation of children's publishing into its adult counterpart, with its relentless focus on the next big, high-concept thing and its corollary shrinking of the backlist and its neglect—benign or otherwise—of the more modest-selling midlist title.

Fangs for the Memories

No surprise that publishing became relentlessly—some might say obsessively—focused on finding the next Harry Potter. To date, the closest it has come is probably Stephenie Meyer's fevered Twilight series, the four-volume saga of teenage Bella's love for the exotically beautiful vegetarian vampire Edward Cullen, a boy who has been seventeen since 1918 (I'm not making this up).

The first volume of the series, *Twilight*, was published in 2005, the same year as *Harry Potter and the Half-Blood Prince*. It, too, came with an interesting—and highly marketable—backstory. Its previously unpublished author, Stephenie Meyer, was an attractive, thirty-one-year-old Phoenix housewife who reportedly found the inspiration for her series in a dream so vivid that she felt compelled to write it down. Three months later it had become a 498-page novel. Over the next three years, it would sell 1.5 million copies. Three more volumes quickly followed, each one more successful—and longer—than the previous ones. *New Moon*, which introduced Edward's rival Jacob—a werewolf no less—appeared in 2006 and weighed in at 564 pages; *Eclipse* (640 pages) followed in 2007; and *Breaking Dawn* (768 pages) came along in 2008 and sold 1.3 million copies in its first twenty-four hours of publication, a record for its publisher Little, Brown/Hachette.

To the unbridled delight of the media, some of the same promotional hoopla that had surrounded the publication of the various Harry Potter titles quickly began to gather around the Twilight titles. "Yes," the *Washington Post* observed, "the creation of Stephenie Meyer's 'Twilight Saga' series, and its subsequent arc toward fame, recall J. K. Rowling's 'Harry Potter' success story to no small extent" (Yao 2008). "Stephanie Meyer: A New J. K. Rowling?" *Time* trumpeted; "Harry Potter and the Rival Teen Franchise" the *Wall Street Journal* chorused; *Entertainment Weekly* hailed "the second coming of J. K. Rowling" (Valby 2008).

Meyer herself has generously acknowledged her debt. "J. K. Rowling, we owe her so much," she told Associated Press reporter Hillel Italie. "First of all, she got publishers to believe that millions of people will pick up an 800-page book. She also got adults reading YA literature. What a gift: she got kids reading and she got adults reading" (Italie 2008).

The similarities between the two as publishing phenomena were startling: once again, each new title was embargoed until one minute after midnight on the official publication date, when it would go on sale to hordes of costume-wearing fans (many of whom call themselves either Twilighters or Twihards); no advance review copies were released; there were a plethora of Internet sites (including one for adult fans called Twilight Moms), fan fiction, Twilight-themed rock bands, and more. As a result, Meyer—with 22 million sales—became *USA Today*'s best-selling author of 2008. The next year she was named to *Forbes*'s Celebrity 100 List of the world's most powerful celebrities, her annual earnings being estimated at more than $50 million (cited in Wikipedia entry).

There were—and are—differences between the two series, however. Unlike Rowling, Meyer launched hers with an implicit fan base. According to the Romance Writers of America, 71 percent of the 58.1 million American romance readers opened their first adult romance novel when they were sixteen (Engberg 2004). The runaway success of Meyer's series is surely at least partly responsible for making the genre the biggest fiction category in 2007 (Hesse 2009). As for the vampire romance subgenre: thanks to Anne Rice it, too, was already a hugely popular genre with an established crossover readership (Google the term and you'll get 2 million hits!). Ironically, its hallmark is often steamy sex, though the hallmark of the first three Twilight volumes was sexual abstinence. This changed dramatically with the fourth volume, however, when Bella and Edward finally married. As Sonya Bolle wryly wrote in her *Los Angeles Times* article "Why 'Twilight' Isn't for Everybody," "The fourth book answers the burning question about what vampires do with all their free time, since they don't sleep. It turns out that married vampires have a lot of sex" (Bolle 2008).

There's no gainsaying the sex appeal of the books and the part it has played in their popularity with pubescent teens, a popularity reinforced by the November 2008 release of the film *Twilight*, which grossed more than $382 million worldwide (Schuker 2009). The second film was released exactly a year later in November 2009 to similar heavy breathing. As for Harry Potter, sex was always a secondary consideration, though as the boy wizard and his friends grew into adolescence in the later books, romantic attraction certainly became a subtext, which then became a major marketing point for the sixth Potter film. "As the new Harry Potter movie opens next week," the *Wall Street Journal* reported, "the bespectacled wizard faces a new challenge: how to compete for the attention of a young audience that has been growing up—and is starting to prefer the angsty teen romances and cooler, edgier characters of the 'Twilight' books and movies" (Schuker 2009).

Perhaps. But there is one area where there is no competition between the rival franchises, and that is literary quality. There Rowling is clearly the superior—and more serious—writer. Meyer, though a natural storyteller with a thorough understanding of her readers' interests, is no stylist, and her four-volume saga shows little promise of ever becoming part of any literary canon. This is as much the genre's fault as it is hers, however. It's hard to take books that focus on "sculpted, incandescent chests," "scintillating arms," and "glistening pale lavender lids" very seriously (quotes from *Twilight*, p. 260), although Annette Curtis Klause did a quite memorable job with the vampire romance in her YA novel *Silver Kiss* (and later served the werewolf romance well, too, with *Blood and Chocolate*).

Nevertheless, romance and horror fiction (including the latter's vampire subgenre) have long and honorable histories. Some, in fact, trace romance back to the very genesis of the novel and such classic titles as Richardson's *Pamela*, Defoe's *Moll Flanders*, and—somewhat later—the Brontë sisters' *Jane Eyre* and *Wuthering Heights*. Similarly, horror had its origins in Horace Walpole's 1764 novel *The Castle of Otranto* and Mary Shelley's 1818 classic *Frankenstein; or, the Modern Prometheus*, while the vampire novel traces its beginnings to Bram Stoker's *Dracula*, published in 1897. When written for young adult readers, however, the two genres typically find their expression not in stand-alone titles but in series, some disposable (like the Sweet Valley High romances and the horror fictions of R. L. Stine and Christopher Pike) and others with perhaps slightly more substance (those by Amelia Atwater-Rhodes and the pseudonymous Darren Shan come to mind). Too, a few memorable individual titles have appeared: think M. T. Anderson's first novel *Thirsty* and some of the later work of Neil Gaiman, notably *Coraline* and his Newbery Medal–winning *The Graveyard Book* (though Gaiman told *Booklist*'s Ray Olsen (2002, 1949), "Do I think of myself as a horror writer? No, I don't except that I love horror"). While not always easy to classify, some of the novels of William Sleator may also be regarded as horror (but none as romance!), and his 2004 novel *The Boy Who Couldn't Die* (Amulet) helped usher in a minitrend in zombie books; this subsequently merged with chick lit to give us such books as Carrie Ryan's *The Forest of Hands and Teeth* (Delacorte); *Zombie Blondes* by Brian James (Feiwel and Friends); *Generation Dead* by Daniel Waters (Hyperion), and more.

Speculative Fiction

As is the case with Sleator's work, much of contemporary imaginative fiction—like romance—has become an interesting exercise in bending and blending, in shape-shifting and morphing. In the second edition of her standard work *Teen Genreflecting*, for example, Diana Tixier Herald has no separate section for horror, assigning it to the more amorphous category "paranormal." Science fiction, though still a separate category, has never matched the popularity of fantasy; indeed, only 5 percent of the titles on BBYA lists since 2000 (no more than twenty-eight in all) can be classed as science fiction, and many observers see it morphing with fantasy into something called speculative fiction.

Interestingly enough, however, this youngest of the genres—often regarded as a twentieth-century phenomenon (though rooted in the mid- to late-nineteenth-century work of Jules Verne and H. G. Wells)—is represented by three winners of the prestigious Margaret A. Edwards Award for Lifetime Achievement in Young Adult Literature: Anne McCaffrey, Ursula K. LeGuin, and Orson Scott Card. Even here, though, there is some room for ambiguity.

McCaffrey's most celebrated work—her Pern novels—are often regarded as fantasy, for example, because they feature dragons; similarly, LeGuin's books also operate on the cusp between traditional science fiction and fantasy, and Card—though more clearly a science fiction practitioner—has never been published for young adults, though he is widely read by them. (The only other genre writer to have won the Edwards is mystery-suspense writer Lois Duncan.)

Of all the genres, however, it is classic fantasy that has produced the most serious works of literature, perhaps because it is the oldest category. In fact, a case could be made that it originated as early as the eighth century with Beowulf (the writer Harlan Ellison dates it even earlier, to the Epic of Gilgamesh!). As a form it also incorporates timeless folklore and fairy tale, though the most memorable codifications of these stories date only to the early nineteenth century, and what we regard as modern fantasy fiction didn't appear until 1865, with *Alice in Wonderland*. And like *Alice,* much of classic fantasy is regarded as children's literature. In fact, very little successful work of the imagination has been published specifically for young adults, perhaps because the field—with its narrow focus on realistic fiction—has been regarded as inhospitable. This is not to say that fantasy hasn't been published, but established gatekeepers have generally failed to recognize it, and its fans have long been critical of the annual Best Books for Young Adults lists, which, in the past, conspicuously lacked such genre titles.

But times change. According to Holly Koelling (2007, 64), "Fantasy accounts for almost fifteen percent of the 577 books on BBYA lists since 2000, the same share as nonfiction and exceeded only by general fiction." The critic and former publisher Anita Silvey (2006, 47) seems to agree: "Instead of craving realistic stories about people like themselves, today's teens are crazy about characters (and scenarios) that have little in common with their everyday lives. Today's adolescents are flocking to fantasy, suspense, and mystery."

Is this all due to the success of Harry Potter? Not entirely, I think. One of fantasy's most attractive features has always been its implicit invitation to escape this careworn world for a visit to a more appealing one, if only in one's imagination. Some need this escape more than others. As the fantasist Tamora Pierce has eloquently stated, "Fantasy is also important to a group that I deeply hope is small: those whose lives are so grim that they cling to everything that takes them completely away for *any* length of time." In the wake of the 9/11 tragedy, the wars in Afghanistan and Iraq, worldwide economic distress, and the specter of global warming, this invitation to escape has surely became increasingly attractive and the group accepting it, ever larger. "Fantasy," Pierce (1993, 51) rightly notes, "creates hope and optimism in readers. It is the pure stuff of wonder."

Or is it dread, instead? One of the most interesting trends in recent specu-lative fiction is the rise of the dystopian novel, a literary form that imagines—sometimes satirically, sometimes somberly—a future world made even worse than the present one by the logical extension of current or threatened societal ills. In M. T. Anderson's *Feed*, for example, the problem is consumerism gone mad; in Nancy Farmer's *House of the Scorpion*, it is human cloning; in Scott Westerfeld's *Uglies* quartet, it is the evergreen adolescent obsession with appearance and celebrity; in Susan Collins's *The Hunger Games*, it is an intriguing combination of dictatorial central government and the current passion for television reality shows. Sometimes the dystopia is the product of technology gone wrong, as in Jeanne Du Prau's Books of Ember series or Mary Pearson's *Adoration of Jenna Fox*, or it might be the result of rampant abuse of the environment (David Klass's *The Caretaker Trilogy*) or another kind of abuse—that of civil liberties as in Cory Doctorow's *Little Brother*. Occasionally, though, the awfulness is not humans' doing at all but an aster-oid's, as in Susan Beth Pfeffer's *Life as We Knew It* and its companion novel *The Dead and the Gone*. Regardless of the cause, all of these books have in common the bleakness of their vision of the future. What kind of escape does the reading of them provide an angst-ridden adolescent? Probably the same kind of release and relief that reading horror fiction provides: the luxury of being scared out of one's wits while thinking, "It's only a book; it's only a book." But as cautionary stories, such dystopian fiction can also serve a larger purpose, inviting idealistic teens to examine the logical consequences of illogical human behavior and to consider how their own actions—or failures to act—might affect the future of the planet and humanity. And therein lies reason for hope, or at least cautious optimism.

The two writers whose work offers—in my estimation—the richest infu-sion of the imaginative into assessments of what can only be called the human condition are David Almond and Philip Pullman. Almond's first book to appear in the United States, *Skellig*, was a Printz honor book, and his second—*Kit's Wilderness*—won the Printz outright (in England, *Skellig* won the Carnegie Medal, and *Kit's Wilderness* was shortlisted for the same prize). These two haunting books, as well as those that have followed—*Heaven Eyes, Secret Heart, The Fire Eaters, Clay,* and *Raven Summer* among them—are nearly impossible to classify but abound in wonders and challenges to their readers' imaginations. As a character in his 2002 novel *Secret Heart* aptly puts it, "The most important things are the most mysterious." The character might well be speaking for Almond himself, and as a result, his books are filled with magical realism and exquisite examinations of light and dark, good and evil, finding magic, metaphor, and larger meaning in their northern England settings that provide the quotidian foundation for so many of his books.

Like Almond, Pullman is also interested in the large issues that generally find expression in high fantasy. In his most ambitious work, the three-volume His Dark Materials series, this is clearly the same dialectic between good and evil that inspired Milton's *Paradise Lost*. Though Pullman writes prose, not poetry, his language—like Almond's—is often soaring, and even majestic, resulting in a style that matches the richness and complexity of his thematic material. The final volume of the trilogy, *The Amber Spyglass*, received the 2001 Whitbread Prize for best children's book of the year in England and was then named Whitbread Book of the Year, the first time a children's book had ever won this prestigious prize. This speaks not only to the intrinsic excellence of the book but also to the coming of age of books for young readers as literature. And, it should be noted, that though published as a children's book, *Amber Spyglass* is very clearly a young adult novel. Just as each succeeding volume of the Harry Potter series became more sophisticated, so did each volume in Pullman's trilogy.

Unlike the Harry Potter books, which stimulated numerous challenges from religious conservatives, Pullman's have excited relatively little controversy in the United States. This is ironic, as Pullman's are by far the more subversive books. Though he is hardly "the most dangerous author in Britain," as one conservative columnist dubbed him, he does have serious reservations about organized religion and one of his characters calls Christianity "a very powerful and convincing mistake" (Miller 2005/2006, 52).

Nevertheless, Pullman is a passionate believer in the moral authority—or perhaps *capacity* would be a better word—of fiction, remarking in a lecture, "We can learn what's good and what's bad, what's generous and unselfish, what's cruel and mean from fiction." Or, as he has also noted, "'Thou shalt not' might reach the head, but it takes 'Once upon a time' to reach the heart" (Miller 2005/2006, 54). His stories—and Almond's, too—bear eloquent witness to the truth of that.

Other Genre Fiction

Historical Fiction

Like fantasy, historical fiction has a long and distinguished—uh—history, beginning with Sir Walter Scott's 1814 novel *Waverly*. But like fantasy, it, too, was not a terribly significant presence in young adult literature until recently. The belief among publishers and adult gatekeepers alike was that young readers were too interested in themselves to embrace stories of the long ago and far away. "'Children only want to read about people like themselves,' teachers assure me," the distinguished novelist Katherine Paterson (1999, 1430) has lamented. The historical novelist Ann Rinaldi (2009) agrees. "When I wrote my first historical 27 years ago [c. 1982] all the publishers said much the same thing. 'We can't give children history. No bookstore will carry it, no child will read it.'"

This belief seems to have become even more firmly entrenched when applied to notoriously solipsistic young adults who, it was believed, would read only realistic fiction with contemporary settings. "In my experience," Jen Hubert wrote at her popular website Reading Rants, "most teens won't even look at hist. fic. unless they have to read it for a school assignment."[5]

This began to change as YA literature became ever more expansive starting in the mid-1990s. Indeed, by the end of the decade, historical fiction had become a significant new category of young adult literature. In 2000 when I assembled my annual list of the best young adult books of the year, I was startled to see that fully twenty-one of the sixty-one works of fiction on my list fell into the historical fiction category, and twenty-seven then appeared on my 2001 list.

A major catalyst for the rise of historical fiction in the 1990s was Scholastic's introduction, in 1996, of its hugely popular Dear America series. These fictional girls' diaries, set in various significant periods of American history, rapidly became enormously popular. Within two years, there were 3.5 million copies of the first twelve titles in print. A companion series for boys, My Name Is America, soon followed, as did two others: the Royal Diaries and My America.

The immediacy of the diary form may well have been part of the series' appeal but so was its innovative format: Scholastic's Jean Feiwel told *Publishers Weekly*, "Our intention was to create a book that was a replica of an actual diary" (Lodge 1998, 31). This meant publication in hardcover (a novelty for series fiction at the time) and in a trim size that was slightly smaller than the standard. The price, a low $9.95, was also unusual and, as it turned out, unusually attractive to booksellers. So once again, the retail market became instrumental in developing a new YA trend.

The hardcover format itself lent a certain patina of respectability to this new exercise in series fiction, but so, too, did the extraordinary roster of distinguished authors whom Scholastic commissioned to write for its new series: Joseph Bruchac, Karen Hesse, Carolyn Meyer, Jim Murphy, Walter

Dean Myers, Ann Rinaldi, and still more. (Interestingly, though, to maintain the polite fiction that the books were actual diaries, the authors' names—no matter how celebrated—did not appear on the books' covers.)

Like the other genres we have explored, historical fiction also lends itself to genre bending and blending. Indeed, "blending with other genres is the most conspicuous trend in historical fiction," expert reader's advisor Joyce Saricks (2008, 33) wrote. There are, for example, historical romances, historical mysteries, historical adventures, and even—in the form of alternative histories—historical fantasies. Saricks also noted one more interesting trend: "Books that combine historical elements with contemporary story lines have become enormously popular." Two excellent YA examples of this are Aidan Chambers's *Postcards from No Man's Land* and Mal Peet's *Tamar*, both of which find meaning for contemporary lives by revisiting World War II. (The routine injection of lengthy flashbacks is another fairly recent innovation in YA fiction.)

All of these disparate elements have conspired to turn historical fiction from required reading to pleasure reading. As the hip (and always engaging!) Hubert noted, in presenting teens with her own list, Historical Fiction for Hipsters: Stories from the Past That Won't Make You Snore, "Sure, you may not know much about history, but learning it from these juicy fictional accounts is way more fun than memorizing any old, dry textbook."[6]

The growing popularity of historical fiction expanded the genre's portfolio well beyond series fiction. Like the entire field of YA, historical fiction has, since the end of the nineties, become home to significant works of literature. Indeed, I would argue that four of the best young adult novels of the past quarter century are historical novels: Aidan Chambers's *Postcards from No Man's Land*, Mildred Taylor's *The Land*, Markus Zusak's *The Book Thief,* and M. T. Anderson's two-volume *The Astonishing Life of Octavian Nothing*. All brilliantly conceived and written, these four titles are further enriched by the very largeness and complexity of their themes, which include war, slavery, and the Holocaust. Each invites us to reexamine our understanding of the human condition and to expand our moral sensibility. One can hardly ask or expect more from literature.

The world embraced by the term *historical fiction* is, of course, a bit of a moving target as today constantly confounds us by turning into yesterday. Time is notable for its passage (or winged flight, as we used to say), and so today's contemporary novel will inevitably turn into tomorrow's historical fiction. A good example of this is Walter Dean Myers's singular novel of the Vietnam War, *Fallen Angels*. When it was first published in 1988, only thirteen years had passed since the end of the Vietnam War, which would, thus, have been within the lived experience of at least its oldest YA readers and was unequivocally a huge part of the lives of those readers' parents and grand-parents. As this is written, however, another twenty-two years have passed, and the war's end has now receded to a point thirty-five years in the past. Those old enough to have fought in Vietnam are now old enough to be the grandparents of contemporary teens, which means that *Fallen Angels* has inarguably turned from a novel of current events into a work of historical fiction.

Literature is inherently dynamic and never more so than when it is young adult literature. Trends come and go, and so it is no surprise that the boom in young adult historical fiction may well have peaked, though I would not go so far as Ann Rinaldi (2009), who lamented, "Now, all of a sudden, the whole ball game seems to be over. We're back where we began. Things have come full circle. Historical novels for teens seem to be chopped liver again." I daresay Richard Peck—for one—would disagree with her; his genial novels of the past—books like *A Year Down Yonder*, *A Long Way from Chicago*, *On the Wings of Heroes*, and last year's *A Season of Gifts*—remain hugely popular. But he might be the exception. Time, as always, will tell.[7]

Meanwhile what has changed, it seems to me, is the routine presence of realistic fiction set—now and without any fanfare—not in the present but in the decades of the sixties, seventies, and eighties. As a reviewer, I've been bemused by the number of these books that don't even mention the precise date of their setting, leaving that to the reader to puzzle out from cultural and other topical references in the text. I don't know that there are any signifi-cant lessons to be learned here except that younger authors are increasingly writing about their own adolescent years, but perhaps today's teens will also find evidence in these books of the truth of the old saying, "The more things change, the more they stay the same," for—no matter how much settings and circumstances change—human beings remain human.

Mystery and Suspense

For many years, mystery and suspense offered the fewest titles published specifically for young adults—and those that were all seemed to be written by either Lois Duncan or Joan Lowery Nixon. But like every other aspect of the YA field, this, too, has changed. One evidence of the new significance of YA mystery-suspense was the 1989 establishment of a young adult category among the annual Mystery Writers of America Edgar Awards.

Perhaps as a consequence a host of new writers have begun experimenting with this form—writers like Carol Plum-Ucci, whose *The Body of Christopher Creed* received a Printz Honor Award in 2001; Nancy Werlin, whose work often evokes that of Robert Cormier; and Kevin Brooks, a British writer whose publisher, the Chicken House, specializes in mystery and speculative fiction and whose books are distributed in the United States by Scholastic. Other notable names include Joyce Armstrong, Willo Davis Roberts, Chap Reaver, Gail Giles, Alex Flinn, Canadian writer Graham McNamee, and more.

As is the case with other genres, there is no shortage of newly popular mystery series, among them Wendelin Van Draanen's already established Sammy Keyes series; Alex Horowitz's hugely popular Alex Rider novels (and a seeming myriad of other new series by him); Julia Golding's promising Cat Royal series of historical mysteries; and Dorothy and Thomas Hoobler's Samurai mysteries set in eighteenth-century Japan. None of these, it is safe to predict, will ever match the enduring popularity—or influence—of the indefatigable girl sleuth Nancy Drew, whose name was once again in the news in 2009 when Supreme Court nominee Sonia Sotomayor acknowledged her early passion for the series, a passion that had earlier been acknowledged by sitting Justice Ruth Bader Ginsburg and retired Justice Sandra Day O'Connor. Such other movers and shakers as Hillary Clinton, Laura Bush, Oprah Winfrey, and the *Washington Post* columnist Kathleen Parker have also publicly pledged their own undying allegiance to Nancy.

Last, the crossover phenomenon has also visited this genre. Among the established adult authors who have begun writing mysteries for young readers are Peter Abrahams, John Feinstein, Michael Winerip, and—most notably—Carl Hiaasen and James Patterson. And in the old-is-new-again department, the British writer Charlie Higson has begun writing a series of thrillers about Ian Fleming's James Bond as a teenager.

Notes

1. My own personal affirmation of this came when, in the fall of 2000, I was browsing in the YA section of the Barnes & Noble store in Chico, California, and—to my absolute astonishment—came across several hardcover copies of my then newly published book *Tomorrowland*.
2. It should be noted, at least in passing, that starting with the ninth volume, the Gossip Girl books—and the later spin-off series—were all ghostwritten, though they continued to bear von Ziegesar's name as author.
3. Alloy Media + Marketing, "Alloy Entertainment," www.alloymarketing.com/entertainment/index.html.
4. By the time the seventh title was published in 2007, the first printing had grown to 12 million copies, and the book sold an unbelievable 8.3 million copies in the first twenty-four hours of publication—that's 50,000 copies per minute!
5. www.readingrants.org/category/historical-fiction-for-hipsters/.

6. www.readingrants.org/category/historical-fiction-for-hipsters/.
7. Five months after Rinaldi's dire evaluation, her next historical novel, *Leigh Ann's Civil War* (Harcourt, 2009), was published.

8

so, how adult is young adult?

The Crossover Conundrum

Though crossover books is a relatively new term, at least one aspect of the phenomenon it contemplates—the notion that young people will read books published for adults—is scarcely a new one. Three hundred years ago, for example, children were avidly reading *Robinson Crusoe* and *Gulliver's Travels*, so many, in fact, that over the years those classics have come to be regarded as children's books. More recently, so many teens have read and embraced *Seventeenth Summer*, *The Catcher in the Rye*, *A Separate Peace*, *To Kill a Mockingbird*, and *The Lord of the Flies* that it is now commonplace to say that, if these books were published today, they'd be released as YA literature. Nevertheless, until recently publishers seemed oddly unwilling to capitalize on this.

Only twenty years ago, for example, Betty Carter (1988, 60), who had chaired the 1986 Best Books for Young Adults Committee, wrote a fascinating article for *School Library Journal* in which she wryly noted that the *New York Times*, in its review of Marianne Gingher's newly published short story collection *Teen Angel*, had stated, "It is perhaps even more damaging to the author's reputation as a writer for grown ups that the American Library Association named Ms. Gingher's novel 'Bobby Rex's Greatest Hit' one of its Best Books for Young Adults for 1986."

I had a similar experience in 1990 when I interviewed the author Mark Childress, who told me that his publisher, Knopf, was refusing to publicize the fact that his adult novel *V for Victor* had just been named to that year's BBYA list. Clearly there was a feeling abroad that an appeal to teen readers somehow tainted an adult title.

That situation was about to change. In fact, it already had changed in another category of publishing: that of picture books for children.

Picture Book Crossovers

"Say 'crossover book' to most people in the industry," Sally Lodge (1992, 38) wrote in 1992, "and they immediately focus on the picture book that appeals to adults as well as kids." This new interest in a form that previously had been targeted at kids in the kindergarten–third grade group had begun in the late 1980s with the publication of Jon Scieszka and Lane Smith's *The True Story of the Three Little Pigs* (Viking, 1989). The instant success of this wackily irreverent, ironic, sophisticated, and offbeat retelling of a classic story quickly attracted the attention of other innovative author-artists such as William Joyce, J. Otto Sebold, Maira Kalman, and Istvan Banyai. When Scieszka and Smith's second collaboration, *The Stinky Cheese Man* (Viking, 1992), received both a Caldecott Medal and a spot on the Best Books for Young Adults list in 1993, the success of the new crossover form was cemented.

When I subsequently spoke with Viking's president and publisher Regina Hayes about this, she acknowledged the sophistication of these picture books but argued, "There's very little that escapes kids. They're growing up in a highly visual age and because they are subject to influences that are so much broader than they used to be—sophisticated graphics, TV, comics, magazines, and so forth—they grow up with a sense of parody that wasn't part of kids' consciousness before." Hayes also saluted the earlier, seminal influence of the late James Marshall (creator of the Stupids, George and Martha, the Cutups, Miss Nelson, and so on). "When I first saw Jim's books, I said 'This is something really new.' I began to realize," she continued, "in part because my own kids responded so strongly to his books and never seemed to outgrow them, that his humor appealed on many different levels" (Cart 1995b, 695).

Another artist who shook up the storytelling strategies and design conventions of the picture book while expanding its audience to older readers was David Macaulay, whose groundbreaking *Black and White* received the Caldecott Medal in 1989 and inspired Eliza Dresang's pioneering critical work *Radical Change: Books for Youth in a Digital Age* (Wilson, 1999) a decade later. Macaulay, of course, is notable for his interest in the architecture not only of the picture book but also that of cathedrals, castles, pyramids, mosques, and even the human body, all subjects of his continuing series of nonfiction picture books that examine, in extraordinarily detailed drawings, how things are built and the way they work. In book after book, Macaulay (1991, 419) has shown, as he stated in his Caldecott acceptance speech, "that it is essential to see, not merely to look, that words and pictures can support each other; that it isn't necessary to think in a straight line to make sense; and, finally, that risk can be rewarded."

Still other risk-taking artists have followed, all of them creating unconventional picture books that challenge expectations and excite the attention of older readers. Chief among them is Peter Sis, the Czech American artist, whose sometimes autobiographical books like *The Wall, Tibet: Inside the Red Box*, and *The Three Golden Keys* are marvels of creative energy, thematic subtlety, and visual imagination. Both his picture book biography of Charles Darwin, *The Tree of Life* (Farrar, Straus & Giroux, 2003) and his autobiographical book *The Wall* (Farrar, Straus & Giroux, 2007) were selected as Best Books for Young Adults.

The Marketing and Maturing of the Crossover

With the ice of a multigenerational market broken, publishers began cautiously experimenting with promoting YA books to adults, helped along by the word-of-mouth discovery by twenty- and thirty-something readers of Francesca Lia Block's five Weetzie Bat books. These were collected and published in an omnibus volume in 1998 with the title *Dangerous Angels*.

"We're giving it an adult trade trim with an adult look and a quote from 'Spin' magazine," its publisher Joanna Cotler explained, adding, "We're also giving it a reading group brochure like our adult books" (Rosen 1997, 29). To further its cross-market appeal, the book was also listed in both Harper's adult and children's catalogs.

Robert Cormier was another author who had always demonstrated potential crossover appeal, never more so than with his most ambitious novel *Fade*, which Delacorte published as a YA title in 1988 and then released as a mass-market adult paperback the following year. Two years after that, the book was reissued as a YA trade paperback. Similarly, Scholastic first issued Walter Dean Myers's Vietnam War novel *Fallen Angels* as a YA hardcover and then as a mass-market adult paperback. The same thing would happen with A. M. Homes's novel *Jack* and Philip Pullman's *Golden Compass*.

Pullman's extremely sophisticated literary-metaphysical fantasy would probably have excited adult interest without any particular help from its American publisher, Knopf. But Knopf's parent company, Random House, pulled out all the promotional stops, giving the 1996 book a $250,000 marketing budget and offering a classic case study of how a children's book could cut across the lines implicitly dividing the myriad imprints that comprise a major publishing house. Thus, Del Ray, Random's adult fantasy and science fiction imprint, quickly acquired paperback rights to *Compass* and its two projected sequels, while Random House Audio Books acquired its own rights, making *Compass* the first children's book that Random House had ever put on tape. Carl Lennertz, director of marketing for the Knopf Group, ordered a thousand advance reading copies and sent them to independent booksellers and wholesalers with a note saying (rather patronizingly, it now seems), "Dear Bookseller: Be a kid again" (Alderdice 1996, 24). Subsequently, seven thousand copies of a more lavish advance reader's copy were distributed to librarians, reviewers, and booksellers. Both the Book of the Month Club and the Children's Book of the Month Club then chose *Compass* as an alternate selection.

Two years later, the first Harry Potter book appeared in the United States, and a year after that (1999), another wildly successful crossover series debuted with the publication of *The Bad Beginning*, the first volume of the mock-gothic Lemony Snicket Series of Unfortunate Events. It was followed, over the next seven years, by twelve more titles (and the obligatory movie, starring Jim Carrey).

In the years since, the crossover book has become such an engrained publishing phenomenon that it is hard to believe that, as recently as 1992, Sally Lodge (1992, 38) wrote, "They [adults] seem to shun the idea of reading a novel published as a young adult book. One of the key barriers appears to be adults' lack of interest in reading about a young protagonist." Or that *Bobby Rex's Greatest Hit* could ever have been called "one of the relatively rare books that transcends age as a criterion for potential readership" (Carter 1988, 60).

If Block, Cormier, Pullman, and Rowling demonstrated that adults would, indeed, read about young protagonists in books published (at least initially) for young readers, two other books clearly evidenced the coming of age of the crossover phenomenon and the increased blurring of the line that divided adult books from young adults (and vice versa): the first was the British writer Mark Haddon's *The Curious Incident of the Dog in the Nighttime* (Doubleday, 2003) and the second was the American author Curtis Sittenfeld's *Prep* (Random House, 2004).

Perhaps because Haddon was already an established writer for children in England, *Curious Incident,* a haunting story of a teenage boy with Asperger's syndrome, was published there in simultaneous children's and adult editions. When it was subsequently released in the United States, however, it appeared only as an adult title, though it immediately became hugely popular with young adult readers. A similar thing happened with the Canadian author Yann Martel's exquisitely inventive novel *Life of Pi,* which was also published in the United States as an adult title. In this case, however, Harcourt, its publisher, recognized the title's crossover appeal and subsequently issued a YA paperback edition.

Why American publishers cannot simply replicate the sensible British model of simultaneity has been much discussed and debated in the years since. Meg Rosoff, an American-born author living in London whose three books to date (including her Printz Award–winning *How I Live Now*) have all been published there in both YA and adult editions, has said "there's less of a stigma against young adult literature" in Britain (Rabb 2008, 23).

Be that as it may, the crossover phenomenon has excited as much interest in the United Kingdom as it has in the United States. Indeed, five of the six books shortlisted for the 2004 Carnegie Medal (Britain's equivalent to the Newbery) were crossover titles. Four years later, Amanda Craig, the children's critic of the *London Times,* wrote, "Crossover books—novels that appeal to adults as much as they do to children—are the publishing phenomenon of the past decade." Craig (2008) attributes the success of the crossover book to the plodding dullness of contemporary adult literary fiction. "It is the power of story-telling which, however, lies at the heart of the crossover novel's rise."

Perhaps so, though the Canadian academic Jeffrey Canton credits marketing, not story, and believes the origins of the phenomenon can be traced to the Land Down Under. "This whole notion of cross-marketing is really, in fact, an Australian notion. They've done it very successfully with a number of writers" (MacDonald 2005, 20). Of course, some English observers credit the Aussies with having introduced YA fiction to England in the first place. "In the UK, fiction for 'young adults' has grown hugely over the past decade," Rachel Cooke wrote in 2003, "we got the idea from Australia"—and the United States, I would hasten to add (Cooke 2003).

Be that as it may, Australia does seem to have developed an extraordinary cadre of gifted, homegrown YA authors, whose work is often both cross-marketed and cross-published there. Brilliant writers like Markus Zusak, Margo Lanagan, and Sonya Harnett belong in this category, though all are published only as YA in the United States, where their work has regularly—

and deservedly—received Printz Award recognition and attracted growing legions of adult readers.

Nevertheless, a certain sense of stigma about being published as YA lingers, at least in the United States. Consider that Sittenfeld's hugely successful first novel, *Prep*, was reportedly rejected by fourteen American publishers before Random House accepted it; "and at least half of them said no because they thought it was YA," Sittenfeld told fellow author Margo Rabb. Rabb, whose own first novel, *Cures for Heartbreak*, was written for adults but published by Delacorte as YA, also had firsthand experience of this. When she told another writer at the MacDowell Colony, a prestigious writer's retreat in New Hampshire, that her first novel was being published as young adult, the other's response was a sniffy "Oh, God. That's such a shame" (Rabb 2008, 23).

The rampant confusion—in England, Australia, Canada, and America—over precisely what constitutes the difference between adult and YA has captured the attention of both the professional and the mass media and has made the crossover book one of the most buzzed about phenomena in today's publishing world. Consider this sampling of articles that have appeared since 2002:

"Trend in Books: Tales Aimed at All Ages," by Phil Kloer, Cox News Service, October 6, 2002

"Crossing Over: A Materials Selector Looks at Adult Books for Teen Readers," by Angelina Benedetti, *School Library Journal*, January 2003

"YA Lit—Not Just for Kids Anymore," by Steve Sherman, *Bookselling This Week*, March 25, 2003

"What Exactly Is a Children's Book?" by Nicolette Jones, *London Times*, April 30, 2004

"YA for Everybody," by Steve MacDonald, *Quill & Quire*, February 2005

"Growing Up," by Judith Rosen, *Publishers Weekly*, February 21, 2005

"Why YA and Why Not," by Sue Corbett, *Publishers Weekly*, September 5, 2005

"Crossover Books for Teens and Twentysomethings," by Gillian Engberg, *Booklist*, November 15, 2005

"The Quest for Crossover Books," by Scott Jaschik, insidehighered.com, May 22 2006[1]

"Crossover Books—Time Out," by Amanda Craig, amandacraig
.com, 2006

"Redefining the Young Adult Novel," by Jonathan Hunt, *Horn
Book*, March 2007

"Teen Fiction Not Just for Teens Anymore," by Tina Kapinos,
Chicago Tribune, June 27, 2007

"Identity Crisis? Not Really," by Meg Rosoff, *Publishers Weekly*,
October 22, 2007

"The Grand Tradition of Crossover Novels," by Meg Rosoff,
Manchester Guardian, 2008

"An Author Looks beyond Age Limits," by Motoko Rich, *New
York Times*, February 20, 2008

"Patterson Aplenty," by Matthew Thornton, *Publishers Weekly*,
May 5, 2008

"'Madapple': What Is a Crossover Book?" by Christina Meldrum,
freshfiction.com, April 7, 2008

"Young Adult Literature: Not Just for Teens Anymore," by
Stephanie A. Squicciarni and Susan Person, *VOYA*, June
2008

"I'm Y.A. and I'm O.K.," by Margo Rabb, *New York Times Book
Review*, July 20 2008

"Guilty Pleasures," by Misty Harris, *Ottawa Citizen*, October 26,
2008

"Crossovers," by Michael Cart, *Booklist*, February 15, 2009

The Invasion of Adult Authors

Further confusing the distinction between adult and young adult is the increasing presence of established adult authors among the ranks of those now writing
and being published for young adults. Attracted by the increasing profitability
of writing for young adults and encouraged by publishers who seek to capitalize on these authors' already established readerships, the list of these grows
longer every day. Some of them—writers like Dave Barry, Ridley Pearson,
Clive Barker, Isabel Allende, Chitra Banerjee Divakaruni, John Feinstein, Carl
Hiaasen, Jacquelyn Mitchard, Robert B. Parker, Michael Winerip, and James

Patterson—are writing commercial or genre fiction. Others, however, attracted by the newly expansive artistic possibilities of the field, are writing literary fiction for young adults. In this category are the likes of Sherman Alexie, Julia Alvarez, Michael Chabon, Francine Prose, Joyce Carol Oates, Joyce Maynard, Cynthia Kadohata, Nick Hornby, Peter Cameron, Alice Hoffman, Ariel Dorfman, Terry Pratchett, and more.

Viking has recently published, for young adults, a selection of T. C. Boyle's previously published adult stories. How does the Pulitzer Prize–winning writer feel about this? "I hope that my publisher will want to do a follow-up collection," he told *Publishers Weekly*, adding, "I'd like to see some of the wilder, more whimsical stories in it" (Rosen 2005, 80). Similarly, Blake Nelson's 1994 adult novel *Girl* was reissued in 2007 as a YA trade paperback by Simon Pulse after Nelson had become a popular author for teens.

How significant—and sometimes confusing—crossover publishing, marketing, and selling have become is epitomized by the case of mega-best-selling author James Patterson (thirty-nine of his adult thrillers have made the *New York Times* Best-Seller List, and in 2007 one of every fifteen hardcover novels sold in America was by Patterson). His entry into the YA field in 2005 with a new series, Maximum Ride (coauthored by an uncredited Gabrielle Charbonnet), was, accordingly, big news and an even bigger success. By early 2008 there were reportedly 4.8 million copies of the first three series titles in print. Nevertheless, when the sales failed to match those of the adult titles, Patterson and his publisher, Little, Brown, decided to reposition the fourth volume, *The Final Warning*, marketing it as an adult title, redesigning the cover art, and raising the price from $16.99 to $20.00. So as not to lose the still-lucrative YA market, the new book was branded "A James Patterson Pageturner" and billed as suitable "for readers from ten to a hundred and ten." (The phrase was, reportedly, coined by Patterson himself, who—before he became an author—was chair of the legendary J. Walter Thompson Advertising Agency.) Even more dramatic was Patterson's insistence that all of the Maximum Ride books—and another new YA series, the Dangerous Days of Daniel X—be displayed at the front of bookstores instead of in the children's or YA section and remain there for as long as any of his adult titles would. Subsequently, the hardcovers would be shelved with adult fiction. As a concession to younger fans, the new titles will be reissued, six months after the hardcovers, as YA trade paperbacks (Rich 2008).

Civilization will probably survive this, but the Patterson brouhaha is the clearest evidence yet that it is not necessarily readers but revenue that is driving the crossover phenomenon, and that explains why it is not necessarily the editorial staff that determines whether a new book will be published as adult or as YA; instead, it is often the sales and marketing staff. Which brings us back to Sittenfeld's *Prep* and Rabb's *Cures for Heartbreak*, both of which—though written as adult titles—could have been published as YA, though only Rabb's was.

What Do You Mean "Young Adult"?

All of this conversation raises another question: what on earth do we mean by the term *young adult*? Surely the term no longer embraces only twelve- to eighteen-year-olds—it must now also include nineteen- to twenty-five-year-olds (or even older, as the twelve-to-thirty-four MTV demographic has become an increasingly desirable market in publishing). Indeed, over the course of the past five or so years, coming of age itself has become a significantly more attenuated process, and as a result a new category of human development has begun to appear that is being called, variously, kiddult, adultescents, twixters, and boomerangers.

This category started to show up when, because of economic hard times, more and more twenty-something Americans began returning home to live with their parents, delaying commitments—to professions and partners alike—until their early thirties. And why not, as many of them—given increasing life expectancies and continuing economic hard times—are looking at living into their nineties and working until they're in their seventies. Who can blame them for not rushing to accept adult responsibilities? How to market to them and—if you're a librarian—how to serve them, however, remains a continuing conundrum.

Further confusing the issue is new research that confounds our long-held belief that the human brain is fully wired by the age of twelve. Scientists have demonstrated that the brain continues to grow until the early or mid-twenties and that the last part to mature is the prefrontal cortex, which is responsible for such adult behavior as impulse control, regulation of emotions, and moral reasoning (Raeburn 2004, 26).

"The age at which Americans reach adulthood is increasing," the psychologist Robert Epstein told *Psychology Today* in 2007—"30 is the new 20," he continued, "and most Americans now believe a person isn't an adult until age 26" (Marano 2007).

"Most Americans" now includes the medical community, too. Between 1994 and 2005 nearly one thousand doctors were certified in a new subspecialty: adolescent medicine. As Kantrowitz and Springen (2005, 65) write, "The old view of adolescence was that it ended at 18 or 19. Now, with many young adults in their early 20s still struggling to find their foothold in the world, doctors call the years from 18 to 28 the second decade of adolescence."

These are all complicated issues, but one way to begin addressing them is, as I mentioned earlier, to consider redefining *young adult*. As it now stands, the term—at least as applied to literature—includes books for readers as young as ten (the category includes middle school literature for ten- to fourteen-year-olds) and as old as twenty-five. My suggestion would be to leave the middle school age range as is but to be scrupulously careful to call it middle school and not YA.

Literature for twelve- to eighteen-year-olds (or thirteen- to nineteen-year-olds) could officially be described as "teen" (a descriptor that more public libraries are using anyway for what had formerly been called young adult services); and books for eighteen- (or even sixteen-) to twenty-five-year-olds could be categorized as "young adult." Granted, there's a good deal of over-lapping among these categories, but the folks they contemplate don't fall into rigidly defined demographics—they are all individuals who grow and mature at different rates and, accordingly, have different individual needs, interests, and appetites. And they should be encouraged to range freely among the three groupings, reading up or down as their needs and interests dictate.

I don't offer this suggestion whimsically, fully recognizing that—as I wrote in my January 2005 "Carte Blanche" column—"the biggest impediment to making this change a practical reality is that it contemplates creating a new area [or areas] in libraries and bookstores; it might also mean reorganizing publishing or, at the very least, encouraging the children's and adult sides of publishing houses to communicate and publish cooperatively" (always the starry-eyed dreamer, I) (838).

According to *Publishers Weekly*, a few independent bookstores have already started cautiously experimenting with adding new sections for titles with appeal to older adolescents (or younger "adultescents"!) (Rosen 2008). And the YALSA board, at its 2009 annual meeting, approved the Serving New Adults Interest Group and charged it with "discuss[ing] issues relating to serving young adults in their late teens and early twenties. We seek to develop and exchange ideas," the conveners continued, "on how libraries can continue to best serve these 'new adults' as they navigate life after the high school years."

Meanwhile, so many books are appearing, willy-nilly, with reader appeal that crosses over from sixteen to twenty-five (and up) that, since 2004, I've been reviewing them for *Booklist* as a separate category of adult books (Cart 2009). Significantly, *Prep* was one of the first I reviewed.

These books typically have several features in common: many are first novels by writers who, themselves, are often in their twenties, and their novels typically feature protagonists in their late teens or early twenties, characters who are—like Holden Caulfield before them—coming of age with various degrees of grace and success. Perhaps most significant, though published as adult books, almost all of the titles could easily have been published as YA had someone not determined they would be more advantageously (read "profitably") published as adult.

The Alex Awards

Speaking of adult books for young adults brings us to YALSA's Alex Awards, a list of the ten best adult books for young adults that has been assembled annually since 1998. In light of our lengthy discussion of the ongoing blurring of the boundary between adult and young adult books, this category-driven list might seem, at first blush, a bit regressive. But as Betty Carter notes, "Alex winners put more books on the table for librarians to read and use for readers advisory. And that's what Margaret Edwards [the legendary YA librarian for whom the awards are named] was about: wide reading and solid recommending in order to create lifetime readers of thousands of young adults" (Carter 2008, 22).

Spearheaded by Deborah D. Taylor, the former YALSA president, and funded by the Margaret Alexander Edwards Trust, the Alex Awards began in 1997 as a five-year YALSA project designed to investigate the use of adult books with young adult readers. It was the ad hoc committee appointed to administer this project that recommended the creation of both an annual list of best books and the presentation of a program at each annual ALA conference that would focus on some aspect of adult books for young adults. Thus, it was that the first program, held in 1998, featured a lecture titled "Back to the Future with Adult Books for the Teenage Reader." Presented by Richard F. Abrahamson, professor of literature for children and young adults at the University of Houston, it offered a retrospective view of the historic importance to young adults and their reading of adult books; it also examined the continuing importance of nonfiction in stimulating teens' interest in reading adult books (Abrahamson is the coauthor with Betty Carter of the important book *Nonfiction for Young Adults from Delight to Wisdom* [Oryx Press, 1990] now sadly out of print) and called for more future research on the relationship of adult books and teen readers while stressing the importance of providing teens with enhanced opportunities for free reading—of both YA and adult books.

The Alex Awards ultimately became a permanent YALSA fixture in 2002 when the five-year project concluded and the board voted to perpetuate the list under the cosponsorship of *Booklist* magazine, which for a number of years has been adding four categories of repeat notes to adult titles to identify those with special interest to general readers, mature teens, teens with special interest in specific subjects, and those books with particular curriculum value.

As a result, 120 adult books have been named Alex winners. Viewed retrospectively, they are remarkable for the diversity of reading interests they represent, ranging from commercial and genre fiction to serious investigations of race, ethnicity, and civil rights, and from sports to memoirs to science. But they also have some important elements in common: one is the large number of nonfiction titles, particularly in the categories of biography, science, and narrative accounts of adventure; a second is the large number of first novels; and a third is the increasingly large number of what we would now call cross-over books (e.g., *Over and Under, The Year of Ice, The Curious Incident of the Dog in the Night-Time, Black Swan Green, The Thirteenth Tale, Upstate, Anansi Boys, As Simple as Snow, Swimming to Antarctica, My Sister's Keeper, Project X, The Kite Runner, The Fall of Rome, 10th Grade, Imani All Mine, What Girls Learn,* and more).

And so it would seem that the Alex Awards themselves, while continuing to acknowledge the historical propensity of teens for reading adult books, have inevitably reflected the changing nature of those adult books. One imagines that the redoubtable Margaret A. Edwards, who always had one eye firmly fixed on the future of teens and of reading, would be pleased.

And in the larger context of the many changes that continue to visit young adult literature, one thing that Abrahamson said in his Edwards lecture remains singularly apposite: "If we truly cared about creating lifetime readers," he noted, "we wouldn't be talking about either young adult books or adult books, we'd be discussing the need to use both" (Abrahamson 1998, 383).

Notes

1. This interesting article demonstrates the ubiquity of the crossover phenomenon, which has invaded academic publishing where the term describes the attempt to find books with crossover appeal to the mainstream market.

back in the real world

Immigration, Mixed Race, and Other New Realities of Teen Life

Not only was the face of young adult literature changing in the 1990s; so was the face of the American population. For as the 2000 census would reveal, the previous decade had seen the largest influx of immigrants to this country since the end of the nineteenth century.

Because of this surge in immigration, 80 percent of the 1990s population growth consisted of racial and ethnic minorities, growing America's minority populations to a record 87 million, 43 percent more than in 1990 and 90 percent more than in 1980.

"The nation is much more diverse in 2000 than it was in 1990," John Long of the Census Bureau's Population Division told the *Sacramento Bee*, "and that diversity is more complex than before" (Westphal 2001, 1).

Contributing to that complexity was the fact that the 2000 census was the first to allow respondents to self-identify as of more than one race. This new opportunity was bracketed by the publication of two significant young adult novels featuring mixed-race protagonists: William Bell's *Zach* in 1999 and Chris Crutcher's *Whale Talk* in 2001. Further raising adolescent awareness of the changing face of race in America were two nonfiction titles that also appeared in 1999: Pearl Fuyo Gaskins's collection of interviews with mixed-race teens *What Are You?* (Holt) and Gary B. Nash's *Forbidden Love: The Secret History of Mixed-Race America* (Holt).

The census offered its new mixed-race option in the form of six categories from which respondents could choose (white, black, American Indian or Alaska Native, Asian, Native Hawaiian or Other Pacific Islander, and some other race), an option that—statisticians pointed out—could yield a total of sixty-three mixed-race combinations. Two minimum categories for ethnicity—Hispanic or Latino and not Hispanic or Latino—were also included, though persons who chose either of these categories were then asked to select one of the racial categories as well. (Because Hispanics can be of any race, the Census Bureau regards them as an ethnicity.) Forty-eight percent identified themselves as white, and 2 percent as black. However, another 42 percent of the Latino respondents chose, instead, the box labeled "some other race." As Mireya Navarro (2003, 21) explained in the *New York Times,* "While there are clearly white Hispanics and black Hispanics, many more come from racially mixed stock, with white, black, and American Indian or other indigenous strains" (some respondents, for example, wrote in such identities as Mayan, Tejano, and mestizo).

Ultimately, a total of 6.8 million respondents—42 percent of them under the age of eighteen—identified themselves as of more than one race. In addition, 3.1 million reported being partners in a mixed-race marriage (up from 500,000 in 1970), and 13–15 percent of unmarried households were also of mixed race (Navarro 2003).

This trend to diversity has continued in the years since the census. Between 2000 and 2006, the mixed-race population grew by about 25 percent, whereas the overall population grew only 7 percent. By 2008 the number of multiracials had grown to 7.3 million, or 3 percent of the population (Hendricks 2008). The cultural implications of this are predictable: as early as 2004, the *New York Times* was reporting that "[ethnic] ambiguity is chic" and "using faces that are ethnically ambiguous is the latest youth marketing trend" (LaFeria 2004, E1).

Accelerating this trend to acceptance is the increasing number of public figures now offering mixed-race role models—Tiger Woods, Keanu Reeves, Norah Jones, Halle Berry, Mariah Carey, and—not least—President Barack Obama! Small wonder that by 2008, the University of Illinois sociologist Jorge Chapa was telling the *San Francisco Chronicle* that biologically, race is a fiction.

But, of course, race in America still matters and remains a highly sensitive issue, as the firestorm of controversy that followed the 2009 arrest by a white police officer of black Harvard professor Henry Louis Gates in his own home evidenced. The editor-author Marc Aronson—who published the Gaskins and Nash titles while he was still at Holt—has offered his own timely and thoughtful take on this complex issue in his young adult book *Race: A History beyond Black and White* (Seo/Atheneum, 2007).

Nevertheless, interest in ethnicity continues to increase as Hispanics (an ethnicity, not a race, according to the census) now are the largest and fastest-growing demographic group in the United States. They are, in fact, the country's largest minority, having surpassed blacks in that category in 2002. By 2008 their numbers had grown to 47 million, and, as those of mixed race, Hispanics were younger than the general population; in 2009 they accounted for 22 percent of all those under the age of eighteen, a 13 percent increase since 1980 (Fry 2009).

It is estimated that by 2050, minorities will constitute 54 percent of the American population. Hispanics, numbering 133 million, will account for 30 percent. The Asian population, growing from 16 million in 2009 to 41 million in 2050, will account for another 9 percent, and blacks will grow in number from 41 million to 66 million and from 13 percent to 15 percent of the population.

A Literature of Diversity?

Given these extraordinary statistics and the sweeping post-1980s social changes they represent, are we any closer to offering young readers a viable literature of similar diversity and complexity? It is very difficult to marshal reliable numbers, but the Cooperative Children's Book Center (CCBC) at the University of Wisconsin, Madison, has been making a heroic effort since 1985. That was when it began tracking the number of books being published by and about African Americans, but it soon expanded that purview. As the staff explain, "Because of the great interest in these statistics and with the increasing concern for accurate and authentic portrayals of people of color in literature for children, in 1994 we began keeping statistics for the numbers of books 'by and about' American Indians, Asian/Pacific Americans, and Latinos, as well [as African Americans]."[1]

Since then, the staff note that while they have seen the actual numbers of individual titles ebb and flow over the years, they have yet to see what they continue to call multicultural literature make up more than 10 percent of the new books being published. That percentage drops to less than 5 percent when it includes only titles written and/or illustrated by people of color (i.e., people working from within their experience).

In terms of actual numbers, the CCBC estimates that some three thousand trade hardcover books for youths were published in 2008.[2] Of that number, 172 featured African Americans, 98 featured Asian Pacific Americans,

79 featured Latinos, and 40 featured American Indians. No need to reach for your pocket calculators: in 2008 a grand total of 389 books were published to give faces to how many tens of millions of young people who have been—and still are—regarded by too many as the "other." The situation is even worse if you limit the number of books to those created by authors and artists working from within the culture. In that case, the totals for African American books shrink from 172 to 83; for Native Americans, from 40 to 9; for Asian Pacific Americans, from 98 to 77; and for Latinos, from 79 to 48.

Why such miniscule numbers? There are many reasons, most of which we've already articulated: there still aren't enough editors of color, there still aren't enough writers of color, there still isn't enough of this, there isn't enough of that—but most of all, the sale of multicultural books simply isn't generating enough dollars to entice publishers to significantly expand their offerings. Consider that over the course of its five years of existence, YALSA's annual Teens' Top Ten List—books nominated and chosen by teens themselves—has included only a single multicultural title, *Gangsta Rap* by the British writer Benjamin Zephaniah. This benign neglect may be due in part to a lack of worthy titles, but it also says something significant about the equation of popularity with teens and sales, something significant that has not escaped the attention of publishers that are at pains to package multicultural books in any way that might enhance their appeal. Sometimes this strategy is effective; sometimes it is not. Consider the case of Justine Larbalestier's *Liar*, published in 2009. Its publisher, Bloomsbury, inadvertently sparked a firestorm of controversy when word reached the blogosphere that this novel about an African American girl with "nappy" hair was being packaged with a dust jacket featuring the photo of a white girl with long, straight hair. The author herself was among those complaining, telling *Publishers Weekly* that "the problem is longstanding and industry-wide. Whitewashing of covers, ghettoizing of books by people of color, and low expectations (reflected in the lack of marketing push behind the majority of these books) are not new things" (Springen 2009).

Bloomsbury quickly decided to redesign the jacket, saying—in a very convoluted press release—"We regret that our original creative direction for 'Liar'—which was intended to symbolically reflect the narrator's complex psychological makeup—has been interpreted by some as a calculated decision to mask the character's ethnicity" (Springen 2009).

Well, yes, but . . . If this still seems a bit outrageous, it is also a vivid reminder that publishing and bookselling are profit-driven businesses, and—as we have seen—since the late eighties, they have become gigantic businesses, most of them—ironically—multinational. I say "ironically," for if multicultural literature is a celebration of diversity, multinational corporations are a celebration of commonality: a single-minded focus on the bottom line. This is compounded by the fact that, since the mid-nineties or thereabouts, the traditional market for multicultural books—libraries and schools—has taken a backseat to the retail market, which means Barnes & Noble and Borders, Amazon, and increasingly big-box stores like Wal-Mart, Kmart, and Target.

Larbalestier herself seemed to acknowledge this when she told *Publishers Weekly*, "However, we consumers have to play our part, too. If you've never bought a book with someone who isn't white on the cover, go do so now. Start buying and reading books by people of color" (Springen, 2009). Otherwise, one suspects, these markets will continue to homogenize output and, in pursuit of sales, turn children's book publishing (including YA) into what we earlier called event publishing. No wonder one editorial director glumly observed to me recently, "They only let me publish big books now."

As a result, it becomes ever more difficult for new writers—of any color—to break into print, especially if their work is perceived as midlist. This unfortunate phenomenon underscores the growing importance of small independent publishers like Lee & Low, Children's Book Press, Cinco Puntos Press, Arte Público, and others that remain committed to publishing multicultural literature. (You can find and download a five-page list of these presses at the CCBC website, www.education.wisc.edu/ccbc.)

Though I'm sometimes concerned about the proliferation of awards and prizes—like adding too much water to the soup, it tends to dilute the broth—there's no gainsaying their importance to the evolution of multicultural literature. I've already mentioned the Coretta Scott King Awards, but let me also note—in the context of my earlier jeremiad about the difficulty of breaking into print—that the King awards have done a great service by adding a category for new talent, which encourages publishers to give new voices a chance to be heard. And let's acknowledge, too, the recently created William Morris First Book Award from YALSA that will, we hope, further encourage publishers to take a chance on new and previously untested creative voices.

Meanwhile, such other prizes as the Pura Belpré, Americas, and Tomás Rivera remain hugely important, too, in focusing attention on Latino writers. In the field of young adult literature, the Margaret Edwards Award has—to date—gone to two black writers, Walter Dean Myers and Jacqueline Woodson, though it has yet to go to either a Latino or Asian writer (though Gary Soto and Laurence Yep, respectively, would be natural choices).

As someone who was involved with the creation of the Michael L. Printz Award, I'm delighted to note that this youngest of the major prizes seems to have the best record of diversity. Its first recipient, in 2000, was Walter Dean

Myers, for his memorable novel *Monster*. In 2004 it was Angela Johnson's turn for her novel *The First Part Last*. In 2002 An Na was the recipient for her first novel, *A Step from Heaven*. And Marilyn Nelson was a Printz honor recipient in 2006 for her book *A Wreath for Emmett Till*.

The name of the 2007 recipient offers a natural segue to another newly emergent literature that is giving faces—literally—to the formerly invisible. I'm referring to Gene Luen Yang, who in 2007 became the first person to receive the Printz for a graphic novel, *American Born Chinese*, published by First Second Books (this was also the first graphic novel to be shortlisted for the National Book Award).

Other graphic novel imprints are also expanding our understanding of the world. Pantheon, for example, is the publisher of the Iranian artist Marjane Satrapi's hugely successful two-volume memoir of her rebellious childhood in Iran, *Persepolis* and *Persepolis 2*, and Knopf has given us Mark Alan Stamaty's *Alia's Mission: Saving the Books of Iraq*.

As continuing tensions in the Middle East have captured American readers' attention, a handful of traditional print books—virtually all of them published as adult titles with strong crossover appeal—have also appeared to address conditions of being there. Several of the most popular—Azadeh Moaveni's *Lipstick Jihad* and Azar Nafisi's *Reading Lolita in Tehran*—deal with Iran, and Khaled Hosseini's *The Kite Runner* (an Alex Award winner) is a coming-of-age novel set in Afghanistan in the 1970s. A crossover nonfiction book about that same country is Said Hyder Akbar's *Come Back to Afghanistan: A California Teenager's Story*. Virtually the only author writing about the Middle East for children and young adults, however, is the Palestinian American poet and novelist Naomi Shihab Nye.

Another people of color who have been almost equally overlooked—at least in terms of authentic representations of their culture—are Native Americans. Only a handful of authors are currently writing from within that experience, among them Sherman Alexie, Joseph Bruchac, Louise Erdrich, Linda Hogan, Leslie Marmon Silko, and Cynthia Leitich Smith.

Like YALSA, the International Reading Association sponsors an annual booklist selected by teens. Called Young Adults' Choices, the list has been around since 1986 and involves the participation of seventh- through twelfth-grade students in selected school districts around the country. Perhaps because a book, to be eligible, must have received two positive reviews in professional journals, the resulting Choices lists do offer a slightly better representation of multicultural books than YALSA's. Of the 270 titles selected since 2000, nearly 10 percent (26) could be called multicultural. In terms of races, cultures, and ethnicities represented, the titles group as follows: 15 are about African

Americans; 5, about Asians; 4, about Hispanics; 1, about Native Americans; and 1, about a Black and Hispanic mixed-race couple. The authors represented are, for the most part, well-established names like Walter Dean Myers, Sharon M. Draper, Sharon G. Flake, Angela Johnson, Janet McDonald, Lensey Namioka, Gary Soto, and Pam Munoz Ryan.

Ultimately, one wonders how many authors and how many books might be sufficient to represent the variety and richness of America's new racial, cultural, and ethnic experiences? There is no answer to this question, of course, but it certainly invites discussion and the observation that it is not only quantity but also quality of content that will drive such conversations.

My earlier introduction of the visual format also invites some discussion of the beautifully illustrated nonfiction that is now being published about the multicultural realities of American life, but that discussion will have to wait for a later chapter. Let me conclude this discussion by reiterating my belief that fiction remains essential to understanding our human condition in all its complexities. The heart has its reasons that the mind cannot know, which means we come to understanding not only through our head but also through our heart. It is fiction—the best fiction—that offers us essential opportunities for cultivating empathy, for feeling sympathy and emotional engagement with others. This leads me to another essential point: multicultural literature is indispensable because it enables us not only to see ourselves in the pages of good books but also to see others, to eavesdrop on their hearts, to come to understanding and to what I can only call commonality.

The world is changing apace—for good or for ill. But change has always visited our lives whether or not we're ready. And it remains literature that can help us cope with this sometimes-vexing and often-perplexing fact of life.

Another Diversity: Risky Behaviors

According to the National Longitudinal Study on Adolescent Health (Add Health, for short), "The main threats to adolescents' health are the risky behaviors they choose" (Resnick et al. 1997). Unfortunately, such behaviors continue to be every bit as diverse as adolescents' ethnic and racial identities (and are sometimes related to them, though the Add Health study found that performance in school and the amount of unsupervised time spent with peers were more reliable predictors of risky behavior than race or income) (Stepp 2000).

Ranging from physical and emotional violence to drug and alcohol abuse, from risky sexual behavior resulting in sexually transmitted diseases and unintended pregnancies to driving recklessly and carrying weapons to school, risky behaviors remain very real factors in the daily lives of twenty-first-century teens, even though the incidence of specific, individual dubious behaviors waxes and wanes.[3]

No matter how much things change, however, one thing remains constant: "You have to realize that all adolescents are going to take risks," Lynn Ponton (1999, 55), the author of *The Romance of Risk: Why Teenagers Do the Things They Do*, asserts. "Adolescents define themselves," she continues, "through rebellion and anger at parents or other adults, engaging in high-risk behaviors including drinking, smoking, drug use, reckless driving, unsafe sexual activity, disordered eating, self-mutilation, stealing, gang activity, and violence." And the company of "a toxic best friend or group of friends can escalate bad behavior," she concludes.

The incidence and magnitude of such behavior can be exaggerated, however, and often is by the sometimes-sensational media attention it receives. Researchers who continue searching for the source of teen behavior that is inarguably risky are giving these circumstances more serious consideration. Are the teens themselves the cause, or is it their parents—or could it be the absence of their parents? One of the most interesting things that author Patricia Hersch found in researching her book *A Tribe Apart* was that while teenagers may claim they want privacy, they also crave and need attention. "Every kid I talked to at length," Hersch told *Newsweek* magazine, "eventually came around to saying without my asking that they wished they had more adults in their lives, especially their parents" (Kantrowitz and Wingert 1999, 38–39).

What impact this might or should have on the long-standing tendency of young adult authors to exclude significant adult characters from their books is moot. But it gives pause that so often the adults who do appear—be they parents or teachers—are presented as the cause of rather than the solution to the problem plaguing a teen protagonist.[4] Or that, in the interest of empowerment, teens are shown as having to resolve their problems by themselves without adult interference.

But perhaps the tide is turning even here, for in recent years, some salutary (even exemplary) titles have finally begun appearing, books showing meaningful, supportive relationships between teens and caring adults—books like E. R. Frank's *America*, Joan Bauer's *Hope Was Here*, and Benjamin Alire Saenz's *Last Night I Sang to the Monster*, to name but a few.

I say "caring adults" instead of "parents," by the way, because diversity has clearly visited this area of adolescent lives as well. As social circumstances have continued to change, the old definition of *family* has changed dramatically, too. The rapid growth of fractured, nontraditional, blended, and in-transition families poses its own set of challenges, wrenching adjustments, and new risks to today's young adults. The challenge to authors, editors, and publishers of young adult books is how to keep pace with these changes and how to artfully incorporate them into the literature of realism for the twenty-first century. Meanwhile the opportunity for young adult librarians and teachers to provide a caring adult presence in teen lives has increased exponentially.

Violence and Its Consequences

The riskiest of teen behavior involves violence and related injury, which remain the leading causes of death among all youths ages five to nineteen—67 percent from injury, 16 percent from homicide, and 14 percent from suicide (FindYouthInfo.gov 2008).[5]

These are startling—and sometimes shattering—statistics. According to the Centers for Disease Control and Prevention, "a number of factors can increase the risk of a youth engaging in violence. Among them: a prior history of violence; drug, alcohol, or tobacco use; poor family functioning; poor grades in school; poverty in the community; and association with delinquent peers."[6] (The Department of Justice has reported a steady resurgence of gang problems in recent years; see Egley and O'Donnell 2009.)

It is hard not to think that growing up in a violence-ridden world—the Oklahoma City bombing, the Columbine shootings, 9/11, international terrorism, the Iraq War, the war in Afghanistan, and so on—and imagined but powerfully visualized (and sometimes glamorized) violence in movies, on television, on the Internet, and in video games (*Grand Theft Auto*, anyone?) has some impact, as well. According to the University of Michigan Health System, "Literally thousands of studies since the 1950s have asked whether there is a link between exposure to media violence and violent behavior. All but eighteen have answered 'yes.'"[7]

Accordingly, the exponential growth of a media presence in adolescent lives may give one pause. In his fascinating recent book *Guyland: The Perilous World Where Boys Become Men*, the sociologist Michael Kimmel (2008, 145) writes, "Today's young people—from little kids to adults in their late twenties and early thirties—represent the most technologically sophisticated and media savvy generation in our history. The average American home has three TVs, two VCRs, three radios, two tape players, two CD players, more than one video game console and more than one computer. American kids 8 to 18 spend about 7 hours a day interacting with some form of electronic media; the average 13-to-18-year-old spends two hours a day just playing video games."

Kimmel—who teaches at State University of New York, Stony Brook—chillingly continues, "The dominant emotion in all these forms of entertainment is anger. From violent computer games to extreme sports, from racist and misogynistic radio show content to furious rap and heavy metal music, from the X-rated to the Xbox, the amount of rage and sensory violence to which guys have become accustomed is overwhelming. It doesn't even occur to them that all this media consumption might be extreme" (149). Extreme and extremely desensitizing and ultimately dehumanizing, perhaps?

The American Academy of Pediatrics agrees, pointing out that "extensive research evidence indicates that media violence can contribute to aggressive behavior, desensitization to violence, nightmares, and fear of being harmed."[8]

As we have seen, young people have good reason to fear being harmed, and it doesn't help that, as Kimmel notes, "The most avid consumers of this new media are young men 16 to 26. It's the demographic group most prized by advertisers" (145), who, needless to say, cheerfully stoke the fires of that young male avidity.

A Literature of Risk

Does it seem counterintuitive to argue that we need more—not less—literature that addresses these same issues honestly and realistically? In the wake of the tsunami of violence inundating today's young adults, do we really need books that embrace violence, too? I believe we do.

After all, the great gift literature can give its readers that new—and old—media can't is the experience of empathy and sympathy. Books can take their readers into the interior lives of characters in ways that television and video can't. They not only can show what is happening to characters but also can powerfully convey how what is happening feels. Interactive games and media can, doubtless, improve hand-to-eye coordination. But books can improve heart-to-eye coordination and even can create it when—as increasingly seems the case—it is altogether absent.

The shocking absence of empathy in today's adolescent lives is nowhere more powerfully evidenced than in the epidemic of bullying that is plaguing America's schools, playgrounds, parks, and neighborhoods.

Bullying

Bullying is hardly new, but the newly minted attention it has been given increased dramatically in the wake of the Columbine High School shootings.

The perception created by media coverage of the tragedy was that the two teen-age boys who killed one of their teachers and twelve of their classmates were seeking revenge for having been bullied. A decade later, thanks to the pains-taking research of the Denver journalist Dave Cullen for his book *Columbine* (Twelve, 2009), we know that wasn't true, but it certainly could have been.

As Kimmel (2008, 57) reports, "For the past five years I've conducted a research study of all the cases of random school shootings in the United States. One factor seems to stand out: Nearly all the boys who committed these tragic acts have stories of being constantly bullied, beaten up and gay baited." Not, Kimmel adds, because they were necessarily gay, but because "they were *different* from the other boys"—or girls, as bullying is no respecter of gender. Indeed, according to the CDC an estimated 30 percent of all kids between sixth and tenth grade (i.e., more than 5.7 million) report having been involved in bullying.[9]

"Bullying takes on different forms in male and female youth," accord-ing to the National Youth Violence Prevention Resource Center (NYVPRC), which was created by the federal government in the wake of Columbine to serve as a single point of access to information about youth violence.[10] Accord-ing to the NYVPRC's informative fact sheet "Bullying Facts and Statistics," "While both male and female youth say that others bully them by making fun of the way they look or talk, males are more likely to report being hit, slapped, or pushed. Female youth are more likely than males to report being the targets of rumors and sexual comments."[11] As for the bullies themselves, the NYVPRC tellingly notes, "Bullies have a strong need to dominate others and usually have little empathy for their targets."

If any good thing came out of Columbine, it was the elevation of attention given to this epidemic problem and the very rapid emergence of a subgenre of young adult literature that continues to explore the many aspects of this issue with insight and empathy. Arguably the first book to emerge in this category was Todd Strasser's chilling documentary novel *Give a Boy a Gun* (Simon & Schuster, 2000). Strasser charts the growing disaffection of two teenage boys, Gary and Brenden, who first dream of taking revenge on the people who have bullied them (principally members of the school's football team) and then transform that dream into reality. In my starred *Booklist* review of this important title, I compared it to the work of the late John dos Passos, for Strasser, like dos Passos, spices his narrative with a contrapuntal collection of quotations, facts, and statistics about real-life school and gun violence. He concludes his book with appended lists of shootings and other incidents of school violence that occurred while he was writing *Give a Boy*.

A number of other novels dealing with school violence have appeared in the decade since Strasser's; among them are Ron Koertge's verse novel *The*

Brimstone Journals (Candlewick, 2001); Nancy Garden's *Endgame* (Houghton Mifflin, 2006); Diane Tullson's *Lockdown*, a novel from Canada (Orca, 2008); C. J. Watson's *Quad* (Razorbill, 2007); and Jennifer Brown's *Hate List* (Little, Brown, 2009). At least two excellent crossover titles have also appeared: Jim Shepard's *Project X* (Knopf, 2004) and Jodi Picoult's *Nineteen Minutes* (Atria, 2007).

Not all violent responses to bullying are directed at the bullies; sometimes the target is the victim him- or herself. One of the most common ways teen girls punish themselves for being different is by cutting. Shelley Stoehr's 1991 novel *Crosses* is the first YA novel to examine this growing phenomenon, which has since become a fixture in teen fiction. Another gravely misguided strategy for coping with bullying is suicide, a topic that was taboo in YA literature for many years (for fear of creating a copycat effect among young readers). This has recently begun to change, since the enormous success of Jay Asher's 2007 novel *Thirteen Reasons Why* (Razorbill), a book in which a teenage girl named Hannah kills herself, leaving a package of cassette tapes articulating her reasons. Laurie Halse Anderson also addresses this issue in *Twisted*, her novel in which a teen boy contemplates killing himself in response to intolerable bullying.

Fortunately, not all bullying results in apocalyptic violence. Arguably the best-known book on how the targets of bullying can find a creative way to respond is James Howe's *The Misfits* (Atheneum, 2001), the story of four middle school students who are misfits and, accordingly, the targets of painful bullying. Instead of getting even, the four resolve to change their school's climate of abuse by running for class office on a no-name-calling platform. Clearly, Howe's novel touched a nerve; its huge popularity has inspired national No Name Calling Week, which middle and elementary schools observe all across the country.

That bullying is a universal experience was demonstrated by the U.S. publication of Tullson's *Lockdown* from Canada and the Australian Palestinian author Randa Abedel-Fattah's novel *Does My Head Look Big in This?* This story of a teenage girl, Amah, who decides to begin wearing a hijab to her prep school in Sydney, is an eye-opening examination of universal considerations of faith and intolerance.

The newest kind of bullying also has international ramifications thanks to the ubiquity of the Internet. I'm referring here, of course, to cyberbullying, the posting of innuendo, put-downs, gossip, lies, and—perhaps worst of all—compromising photos online.

"Cyberbullying is the fastest-growing form of bullying happening around the world," according to C. J. Bott (2008, 120), a retired English teacher and author of two books about the subject: *The Bully in the Book and in the Classroom* and *More Bullies in More Books* (Scarecrow, 2004 and 2009, respectively). One of the attractions of this technique is that it allows the bully both anonymity and the ability to inflict pain without being forced to see its effects, which "also seems to incite a deeper level of meanness" (Harmon 2004, A1). Perhaps worst of all, there is no escaping this type of bullying; it spreads virally and follows the victim everywhere. Cyberbullies can be both boys and girls, but the latter tend to predominate. A few recent books about this invidious phenomenon are Laura Ruby's *Good Girls* (HarperCollins, 2006), Shana Norris's *Something to Blog About* (Amulet/Abrams, 2008), and Laurie Halse Anderson's *Twisted* (Viking, 2007).

Perhaps because of these books, a new anti-bullying technique has begun gaining favor. In an April 5, 2009, front-page article in the *New York Times*, the reporter Winnie Hu wrote, "The emphasis on empathy here and in schools nationwide is the latest front in a decade-long campaign against bullying and violence." According to Hu (2009, A1), "The Character Education Partnership, a nonprofit group in Washington, said 18 states—including New York, Florida, Illinois, Nebraska, and California—require programs to foster core values such as empathy, respect, responsibility, and integrity."

Not all violence is related to bullying, of course. On September 11, 2001—scarcely two years after Columbine—the attack on Manhattan's World Trade Center brought the specter of international terrorism and the threat of violent death to the forefront of American teens' consciousness. Within a year, a dozen or more books—virtually all of them nonfiction—had appeared with the goal of helping young readers of all ages cope with this new fear factor in their lives. Though short fiction was included in *911: The Book of Help*, the anthology that Marc Aronson, Marianna Carus, and I coedited (Marcato/Cricket, 2002), full-length fiction about this terrible event has been slower to surface. Joyce Maynard's crossover novel *The Usual Rules* (St. Martin's) appeared in 2003 and Francine Prose's YA title *Bullyville* (HarperCollins) followed in 2007. Finally, in 2009, David Levithan's *Love Is the Higher Law* (Knopf, 2009) appeared. In an eloquent letter to the reader, Levithan explained his reasons for taking us back to that terrible event: "As time goes by, it's really easy to remember 9/11 and the days afterward as a time of tragedy, fear, grief, and loss. Less easy to remember—and even harder to convey—is that it was amazing not just for the depth of that loss, but also for the heights of humanity that occurred. The kindness. The feeling of community. The deepening of love and friendship" (Levithan 2009, 1).

This, it seems to me, is the most compelling argument one can offer for writing fiction about even the most unpleasant realities of teens' lives, the kinds of realities we have been confronting in this chapter. For life, even at its darkest, can hold the promise of hope and positive change—especially when we read about it with open minds and hearts, with intellectual attention and emotional empathy. I would be remiss if I ended this chapter without acknowledging three authors whose work gives us that opportunity and experience.

Three Exemplary Authors

Walter Dean Myers

Over the course of his long career (his first book for young readers, *Fast Sam, Cool Clyde, and Stuff* was published in 1975), Myers has built a reputation as one of a handful of the most important young adult writers in the history of the genre. He has done this by trusting his growing legions of readers with the difficult truth about the real world in which they must live their lives. Poverty, violence, drugs, guns—none is stranger to his young adult fiction.

In his Margaret A. Edwards acceptance speech, Myers (2008, 99) said, "There are always children that need to be rescued from some obscure hell, to be brought into the light of recognition so that we can no longer avoid looking at their suffering." "What I can do," he continued, "is help make all our children and all our young adults visible again. I can help begin the process of peeling away labels they have been burdened with, that diminish their humanity."

This is what he does to such good effect in his novel *Monster*, but a similar commitment to humanity, to the humane, is central to all of Myers's work, whether it is written for children or for young adults. A prolific writer (he's published nearly one hundred books), Myers has worked for all ages and in a variety of different forms, ranging from picture books to chapter books to nonfiction and from poetry to memoir to hard-edged young adult fiction. In the process he has become one of our most honored writers for youths; he is, for example, the only author to have received both the Margaret A. Edwards Award and the Michael L. Printz Award; he is a five-time recipient of the Coretta Scott King Award and a four-time recipient of a King Honor; he has twice received a Newbery Honor and has twice been a National Book Award finalist.

It's worth noting, too, that he was one of the first to give faces to young soldiers fighting in two American wars, those in Vietnam (*Fallen Angels*) and Iraq (*Sunrise in Fallujah*) and in that process invited his readers to examine not only their own personal values but also those of the nation in which they live.

"If we do not write about all our children," Myers (2008, 101) has said, "write about them with hard truths and a harder compassion, then we have, in a very significant way, failed our own futures." Reflecting on his career as a writer, on the future, and on his legacy, Myers once wrote, "I would like to be remembered as giving something back to the world" (Gallo 1990, 149). There is absolutely no question that he will be.

Chris Crutcher

Chris Crutcher, a Margaret A. Edwards Award–winning author, has been writing intelligent and heartfelt fiction for young adults since 1983 (*Running Loose*). His dozen or so novels are distinguished by their authentic and artful depiction of the fact that—as one of his characters memorably puts it— "Human beings are connected by the ghastly as well as the glorious" (*Chinese Handcuffs*). Because Crutcher has been fearless in depicting the ghastly aspect, those who feel young adults can't be trusted with the truth have often challenged and censored his work. Crutcher begs to differ, and each of his novels is an eloquent argument for the imperative importance of honest, candid books in helping young readers navigate that perilous passage known as adolescence.

"If, as an author, I can make an emotional connection with my reader, I have already started to help him or her heal," Crutcher writes. "I have never met a depressed person, or an anxious person, or a fearful person who was not encouraged by the knowledge that others feel the same way they do" (Davis 1997, 314).

In making this point, Crutcher writes with the authority of one who has worked as a teacher, school director, and child and family therapist. His youthful protagonists are routinely challenged by physical, emotional, and family problems, among them abuse, suicide, and anger that can erupt in violence (Crutcher's novels and Kimmel's nonfiction *Guyland* make wonderfully complementary reading!). Crutcher's work is also distinguished by his inclusion of not always admirable but always fully realized adult characters. In light of what we have discovered about the importance of caring adults in adolescent lives, it is particularly noteworthy that in virtually every one of Crucher's novels, an adult mentor figure is present.

Crutcher's work is not flawless; he has a tendency to overload his work with thematic issues, and his treatment of them is sometimes didactic but never perfunctory and never less than completely honest. And in the integrity of their treatment of the pain that is endemic to teenage life, they are all invitations to empathy. As his biographer and fellow novelist Terry Davis (1997, 313) has said, "He believes that stories have the power to heal and . . . he knows what a great need there is for healing."

Adam Rapp

A successful playwright like Paul Zindel before him, Adam Rapp began
writing for young adults in the 1990s; his first novel, *Missing the Piano,* was
published in 1994 and helped usher in the new golden age of YA literature.
In the half dozen novels that have appeared since, Rapp has written some of
the most harrowing—and haunting—young adult novels in the history of the
field. The protagonists of his unsparingly realistic novels—Blacky Brown
(*Little Chicago*), Steve Nugent (*Under the Wolf, Under the Dog*), Custis (*33
Snowfish*), Jamie (*Punkzilla*), and others—live lives in extremis. Victimized,
incarcerated, bullied, sexually abused, mentally ill—they all struggle to survive the worst a seemingly sociopathic, or perhaps sadistic, world can throw
at them. If these sound like the worst of the problem novels of the 1970s,
know now—right now—that they are not. Though the circumstances they
reveal are often ugly, so ugly the reader may want to look away, the books
themselves are beautiful in their compassion and caring and—thanks to his
gifts as a dramatist—lyrical in the unconventional, unforgettable voices Rapp
creates for his characters.

> So my name is Steve Nugent. I'm just seventeen. It was my birth-
> day last month, in November. Now it's the middle of December,
> and the trees around here are caked in ice and sort of silvery in that
> creepy, wintry way, so right now seventeen seems like a hundred
> years off. (Rapp 2004, 1)

> At night the sky glows purple like the light from a TV when a
> VCR movie is done playing. And the stars get so big they look like
> knives coming at you. Some of them stars look like spaceships,
> too. Especially them blue ones.
>   It would be cool if one of them blue stars came and a spaceman
> lit up his insides and showed us his moon bones. . . . Them space-
> men probably got stronger hearts than humans, too, cuz they don't
> got no pit bull worries or no money suit worries or no Bob Motley
> worries. All them worries make your heart small, and the smaller
> your heart the less it glows. (Rapp 2003, 96)

> There's a new subdivision going up and the rain makes the houses
> look like they were dropped out of the sky.
>   Nobody lives here yet. It's all piles of bricks and skeleton wood.
>   From the cab of the bulldozer I can see into the half-made
> house. It's all skinny wood and chicken wire. I think that houses
> have bones too.

> I wonder when they put the walls in cause the walls are skin.
>
> I wonder how electricity works cause electricity's like veins.
>
> Trying to figure this out makes me sleepy. (Rapp 2002, 89)

In a wonderful way, Adam Rapp resembles Maurice Sendak in his outrage at a world that often fails, abuses, and exploits its young. In his recent appreciation of Sendak, *Making Mischief,* Gregory Maguire (2009, 68) identifies the artist's "steady and unflagging creed: The weak and lowly are not to be abused."

As was Sendak, Rapp is an inveterate risk taker and fearless truth teller in dramatizing this creed, and so his work is controversial and no stranger to the censor. But anyone who cares about kids—whether they're named Jack and Guy or Blacky or Steve—needs to be a champion for this work, just as Rapp (and Sendak) are champions for their characters.

Attention must be paid; truth must be told. And that is Rapp's creed:

> Ma always says, No matter how hard it is you gotta tell the truth, Blacky. No matter how hard. (Rapp 2002, 75)

> I don't mean to be weird P but in your letter you said how you wanted the truth about stuff even if it's ugly and trust me it's going to get a little ugly. (Rapp 2009, 3)

The truth can be ugly, but the unflagging love that Rapp shows again and again for his characters, inviting his readers to love them, too, even if the world sometimes doesn't, is beautiful.

In *Punkzilla,* Rapp's eponymous protagonist receives a letter from a girl named Jenny. In it she writes of her boyfriend Branson, "He cries sometimes when nobody's looking, like when he's in the bathroom or hiding behind a car, and that's why I know his soul has gold in it. And your's [*sic*] does too, Zilla. Your's has gold and silver."

And so, I venture to say, has Rapp's.

If only there were more space, I would give attention to other writers whose unsparing honesty and courageous convictions have given faces and stories to young adults in jeopardy—writers like Laurie Halse Anderson, Brock Cole, Carolyn Coman, E. R. Frank, Chris Lynch, and Han Nolan. But for now, I can only acknowledge their considerable contributions with appreciation and admiration and move on to our next chapter.

Notes

1. CCBC, "The Cooperative Children's Book Center," www.education.wisc.edu/ccbc.
2. The CCBC does not include paperback or other series books targeted at the mass market in its statistics. Otherwise, these numbers would be much larger.
3. Every two years, the Centers for Disease Control and Prevention conduct the National Risk Behavior survey, which monitors health-risk behaviors among ninth- to twelfth-grade students. For specifics, see www.cdc.gov/yrbss.
4. Not so many years ago, after I had finished booktalking nearly one hundred new YA novels to an audience of librarians and teachers, one of the few men present asked an agonized question: "Aren't there *any* YA books that present positive father figures?" It was, I acknowledged, a very good question.
5. In 2006 nearly six thousand young people ages ten to twenty-four were murdered, an average of sixteen each day.
6. National Center for Injury and Control, www.cdc.gov/injury.
7. University of Michigan Health System, www.med.umich.edu.
8. AAP Policy, "Policy Statement," http://aappolicy.aappublications.org/cgi/content/full/pediatrics;108/5/1222.
9. Centers for Disease Control and Prevention, "Injury Prevention and Control: Violence Prevention," www.cdc.gov/violenceprevention.
10. It remains an excellent source; its website is at www.safeyouth.org.
11. National Youth Violence Prevention Resource Center, "Bullying Facts and Statistics," www.safeyouth.org/scripts/faq/bullying.asp.

sex and other shibboleths

YA Comes of Age—and Not a Moment Too Soon

It's possible to view the history of young adult literature as a series of inspired exercises in iconoclasm—of envelope pushing, taboo busting, shibboleth shattering—Hinton's acknowledgment of teen class warfare, Childress's of heroin abuse, Cormier's of evil's ascendancy, and so on.

The one area of life that has most stubbornly resisted such taboo breaking is, however, human sexuality. This is hardly press-stopping news. Puritans invented America, after all, who viewed sexual expression as something to be denied and suppressed. And this attitude has been a hardy perennial ever since. The former *New York Times* television critic John J. O'Connor (1994, B5) put it a bit more acerbically: "It's hardly news," he wrote, "that America is inhabited by large numbers of Puritanical hysterics."

Whether hysterical or more reasoned, such Puritanism has long flowered in the garden of young adult literature. Margaret A. Edwards (1969, 72) herself acknowledged this, writing in her book *The Fair Garden and the Swarm of Beasts*, "Many adults seem to think that if sex is not mentioned to adolescents, it will go away. On the contrary it is here to stay and teenagers are avidly interested in it. There are excellent factual books on the market, but the best novels on the subject go beyond the facts to the emotional implications of love."

Having made that point, Edwards proceeded to discuss what she regarded as eight "exemplary" novels involving sexuality.[1] That all eight are adult titles says something, I think, about the near-total lack of YA titles on the subject even as late as 1969; that the preceding decade had been one of sexual liberation and revolution seems to have escaped the notice of young adult authors and publishers! At any rate, of the exemplary eight, Edwards (1969, 72) writes, "All of these have something to say about love that cannot be learned from informational books. Too many adults wish to protect teen-agers when they should be stimulating them to read of life as it is lived."

Such reticence assumed life-and-death proportions in the 1980s with the appearance of AIDS and its nearly incomprehensible lesson that love can kill. Before we talk about AIDS—and other sexually transmitted diseases—however, we need to look at the cautious and halting evolution of young adult literature's attitude toward and treatment of sex.

The first important novel to deal with teenage sexuality was Henry Gregor Felsen's *Two and the Town* (Scribner's, 1952). Though simplistic and cautious by today's standards, the novel was, nevertheless, fifteen years ahead of its time in its treatment of premarital sex, pregnancy, and forced marriage.

The high school football star Buff Cody gets the dark-haired loner Elaine Truro pregnant, and they are forced by Elaine's father to marry. When a baby, little Buff, is born, big Buff enlists in the Marine Corps to escape this new burden. Happily, in the corps, he learns how to be a real man and take responsibility for his family. He returns home—after a high school football injury conveniently provides a deus ex machina reason for early separation from the service—determined to be "happy with his wife and little Buff." Although the possibility of a happy ending is, thus, held out to the reader, it comes only after a censorious community has thoroughly punished the two teens for their indiscretion. And the implication remains that Buff will probably never get to be the coach he always dreamed of becoming. Such "punishment" for sexual activity was, of course, a de rigueur staple of popular culture at the time.

Despite its carefully cautionary element, Felsen's book was quite controversial. Edwards (1969, 82) recalls that "the book came off the press in the fifties, a few weeks before the American Library Association met in New York City. There was to be a preconference on young adult work in the public library, and I was to sit on a panel where I expected the book to be questioned. Sure enough [the book] came up for discussion and the panel seemed agreed it 'was not up to Felsen [a reference, I presume, to his usual standards], which simply meant they thought it too hot to handle. I came to the book's defense saying we had no other book that dealt honestly with this problem . . . and asked what they would give to a young person who wanted a book on the subject. One of the true-blue ladies drew herself up and announced, 'I would give him' "The Scarlet Letter."'"

Those Puritans had little to fret about for the next fifteen years, until 1967 brought a second important milestone on the road to YA literature's sexual liberation: Ann Head's *Mr. and Mrs. Bo Jo Jones* (Putnam). At that, there was no cause for immediate alarm, as the book was published in hardcover as an adult novel. However, within a year, it "was offered to high school students through paperback teenage book clubs" (Cart 1996, 192) and quickly became a harbinger, along with *The Outsiders* and *The Contender*, of more realistic fiction to come. Its lingering influence and enormous popularity are evidenced by the fact that it has appeared on two of YALSA's four retrospective best-of-the-best lists.

Bo Jo is not dissimilar to *Two and the Town* in its bare plot outline. Once again, two teenagers, July and Bo Jo (Bo Jo is the boy) are swept away by passion; July becomes pregnant and they elope. This time, however, the couple's families attempt to break up the marriage. Her father runs the local bank, and Bo's works as a construction foreman. Parental interference is the least of July and Bo Jo's problems, however. They quarrel over money and friends, and their baby dies; they break up, but in the end they are reunited and go off to college together. In the context of what has preceded it, the happy ending may be more author imposed than inevitable; nevertheless, as a work of fiction, the book is a more fully realized effort than *Two and the Town*, and its popularity spurred a number of imitators. Witness the fact that only three years later in 1970, "four of the five top books sold through the Xerox Educational Publications' teenage book clubs were about sex and pregnancy" (Kraus 1975, 19).

The same year *Bo Jo* was published for adults, Zoa Sherburne's *Too Bad about the Haines Girl* (Morrow) was published for young adults. This time the teenage girl who becomes pregnant does not marry the father but actually turns, instead, to her parents for help with her problem, one of the rare instances of this happening in early YA books.

A year before that, in 1966, Jeanette Eyerly's *A Girl Like Me* (Lippincott) appeared. In this one, it's not the protagonist but a friend, Cass Carter, who brings shame on her family and is sent off to a Dickensian home for unwed mothers. At the twelfth hour, the baby's father, the wealthy Brewster Bailey Winfield III (you can't make this stuff up), appears and volunteers to make Cass an honest woman, but she nobly refuses, having decided to give the baby up for adoption "by somebody who'll love him, even if it turns out to be a girl—a girl like me" (Kraus 1975, 21).

Abortion as an option in resolving an unwanted teenage pregnancy was not offered until Paul Zindel's 1969 novel *My Darling, My Hamburger*

(Harper). The indefatigable Jeanette Eyerly wasn't far behind, though. Her take on the topic, *Bonnie Jo, Go Home* (Lippincott) appeared in 1972 and presented, the author Norma Klein (1991, 24) noted, "such a negative, dark view of abortion that it would scare the wits out of almost anyone."

For good or for ill, all these books had one thing in common: they were primarily concerned not with the sexual act but with the (usually dire) consequences. Not so Judy Blume's revolutionary *Forever*, which was published in 1975 as a celebration of the sexual act itself. Not only do Blume's protagonists, high school seniors Katherine and Michael, have sex, they (shudder) enjoy it, and the reader gets to watch the explicit action!

"This time Michael made it last much, much longer, and I got so carried away I grabbed his backside with both hands, trying to push him deeper and deeper into me—and I spread my legs as far apart as I could—and I raised my hips off the bed—and I moved with him, again and again and again—and at last I came." Whew!

The late Norma Klein (1991, 23), whose own novels offered a similar cinema verité take on teenage sexuality, notes that "'Forever' was the first—I hope not the last—book to show teenagers it was all right to have sexual feelings, to be unashamed of this very natural physical and emotional reality. It showed them that love [Blume's title is ironic, of course], even when it doesn't last forever, is still an important part of growing up."

The only trouble with this is that it's not love that Blume writes about; it's sex as a rite of passage that Katherine can't wait to experience and have done with. As a result, it too often seems that Blume has written not a novel but a scarcely dramatized sex manual, including a chapter-long account of Katherine's visit to a Planned Parenthood clinic (after she has read "a whole bunch of pamphlets" her grandmother has sent her from the organization). However courageous and wonderfully well intentioned it was, *Forever* remains more tract than novel (though a tract probably wouldn't name a boy's penis Ralph as Michael dubs his, providing an occasion for nervous giggling by readers in the years since).

I'm reluctant to offer such harsh-sounding criticism of *Forever*, because it earned Blume a Margaret Edwards Award in 1996 (it was the only one of her titles the selection committee cited) and because I wholeheartedly agree with Norma Klein's (1991, 25) assertion, "I would like more, not less, explicit sex in books for teenagers."

Not to include sex in books for contemporary young adults—48 percent of whom have had sexual intercourse[2]—is to agree to a de facto conspiracy of silence, to imply to young readers that sex is so awful, so traumatic, so dirty that we can't even write about it. That's why I applaud Blume's candor, because it shattered the prevailing conspiracy of silence and made it possible for the writers who came after her to deal more maturely with one of the most important aspects of life. Well, if not of life then certainly to life, as it wouldn't exist without the sexual act. Until Blume spoke out, most teenage readers might have been forgiven for continuing to believe that the stork brought babies.

I think *Forever* also made it possible for young women to consider questions of choice—not about abortion, to which the word *choice* has now been inextricably linked, but about having sex. They can choose—despite all the wheedling, pleading, and importuning of their male partner—not to be physically intimate, a theme that would inform Norma Fox Mazer's later novel *Up in Seth's Room* (Delacorte, 1979).

It is also thanks to Blume that other writers have had the liberty of beginning the important work of investigating other, less savory aspects of sex—notably its perversion by the interjection of violence in the form of rape and sexual abuse. Thus, in 1976, a year after *Forever* was published, another important pioneering novel, this one by Richard Peck, appeared. *Are You in the House Alone?* was arguably the first YA title to deal with rape, not sensationally or exploitatively, but with Peck's signature sense, sensitivity, and insight. Not surprisingly, it was named an ALA Best Book for Young Adults.

Perhaps the last taboo to fall in the literary sexual arena was not rape but another form of sexual abuse, incest, which—according to the National Center for Victims of Crime—"has been cited as the most common form of child abuse."[3]

This sensitive subject was first addressed in the pseudonymous Hadley Irwin's 1985 novel *Abby, My Love* (McElderry), a title that was also chosen as a Best Book for Young Adults. (As mentioned earlier, Scott Bunn's 1982 novel *Just Hold On* had also addressed the subject but only peripherally.) Seven and eight years later, respectively, Ruth White dealt with the subject in *Weeping Willow* (Farrar, Straus & Giroux 1992) and in 1993 it was Cynthia D. Grant's turn in "Uncle Vampire" (Atheneum, 1993). In 1994 three of the best books, in terms of literary quality, about this issue were published: Francesca Lia Block's *The Hanged Man* (Harper), Cynthia Voigt's *When She Hollers* (Scholastic), and Jacqueline Woodson's *I Hadn't Meant to Tell You This* (Delacorte) (*Lena*, a sequel to this last novel, was published in 1998).

Though these books are quite different from one another in their treatment of sexual abuse, all have in common the art their gifted authors employ in transforming what could have been a simple journalistic reporting of the facts of this excruciatingly painful problem into powerfully artful literature—

literature that is beautiful in its passion and in its righteous anger at the horrors the world sometimes visits on young women.

Incest is defined by the National Center for Victims of Crime as "sexual contact between persons who are so closely related that their marriage is illegal (i.e., parents and children, uncles/aunts and nieces/nephews, etc.). This usually takes the form of an older family member sexually abusing a child or adolescent."

In many cases, the perpetrator is portrayed in YA books as a stepfather or a mother's live-in boyfriend (as in the Voigt novel); but more often it is the biological father (Irwin, Block, Woodson), a reflection of real-world circumstance. One expert with the National Center for Victims of Crime, for example, has estimated that 1 million Americans are victims of father-daughter incest, and the number grows by some sixteen thousand each year.

The perpetrator need not be a father, however; he may also be an uncle (*Uncle Vampire*) or an older brother, as in Carolyn Coman's *Bee and Jackie* (V. C. Andrews's lurid and histrionic *Flowers in the Attic*, which features a similar "forbidden" relationship, was published as an adult book but has attracted generations of young adult readers).

Not all of these cases are so clear cut, however. Meg Rosoff's Printz Award–winning novel *How I Live Now* features a physical relationship between cousins, and not a relationship that is forced on the girl protagonist, but one she enters willingly, having fallen in love with her male cousin. Though Rosoff delicately and sensitively handles the relationship, some adult readers were outraged, and others—who weren't—pointed out that such relationships are perfectly legal in many states.

Most YA novels that have featured incest portray a girl as the victim, a reflection of real-world circumstance. However, boys are not immune from such victimization, as Stephen Chbosky dramatizes in his extraordinary novel *The Perks of Being a Wallflower* (MTV/Pocket, 1999). His emotionally disturbed, fifteen-year-old protagonist, Charlie, is revealed to have been victimized by a favorite aunt, whom he movingly forgives near the book's end. Alex Sanchez's later novel *Bait* features a boy who has been abused by his stepfather.

Regardless of the relative involved, sexual violence of all sorts—assault, rape, incest—typically strikes close to home. According to the 2007 National Crime Victimization Survey (NCVS), "approximately two-thirds of victims were attacked by a non-stranger (generally an acquaintance or family member)" (www.rainn.org).

Sadly, sexual assault remains one of the least reported of crimes, well below the rates for robbery or aggravated assault. This suggests that many of the statistics may underreport the incidence of such violence. Even without allowing for that factor, the numbers are alarming. The Department of Justice reports an estimated 248,300 sexual assaults against victims twelve and older in 2007.[4] Unfortunately, the Justice Department doesn't offer demographic subcategories, so we don't know how many of the twelve and older are teenagers. Other earlier studies, however, suggest that some 15 percent of victims are younger than twelve; 29 percent, twelve to seventeen; and 80 percent, younger than thirty. The highest-risk years are twelve to thirty-four, and girls ages sixteen to nineteen are four times more likely than the general population to be victims. Seven percent of girls in grades 5–8 and 12 percent of girls in grades 9–12 report being sexually abused, whereas 3 percent of boys in grades 5–8 and 5 percent of boys in grades 9–12 report being victims.

As in the case with incest, few books deal with the sexual abuse of boys, and those that do are often not altogether successful. One of the first to do so was Catherine Atkins's 1999 novel *When Jeff Comes Home* (Putnam), the story of a fifteen-year-old boy who is kidnapped by a stranger. Held captive for two and a half years, the boy is routinely forced to have sex with his kidnapper, a man named Ray, who also photographs the boy naked. When Ray rather improbably returns Jeff to his home and the circumstances of the boy's captivity become public, most people believe the boy is gay (he isn't) and subject him to horrible verbal and emotional abuse, which only heightens Jeff's already virulent feelings of self-hatred. The book too often strays into the melodramatic and never clarifies Ray's sexual identity, leaving the reader with the impression that he is gay and that, as one character puts it, "These faggots that prey on our kids, they should be strung up, electrocuted, tortured."

A second book is Katherine Jeffrie Johnson's *Target* (Roaring Brook, 2003), in which a sixteen-year-old boy is violently (and graphically) raped by two men, an experience that leaves him so badly traumatized he is virtually catatonic. The motives of his attackers are never clearly delineated, though the author does make the point that most such acts are not sexually motivated but are exercises in power and domination. Nevertheless, the boy, Grady—like Jeff—is left self-hating and agonizingly questioning his own sexual identity (he wonders why he didn't fight back, a question that plagues Jeff, too). Further muddying the waters are Grady's flashback memories of being abused as a child by the man next door.

Given the incendiary nature of the offenses committed in these books, it does seem that ambiguities need to be very carefully handled, lest they perpetuate stereotypical thinking, and the authors need to be equally careful to ground their material in clinically sound research and to avoid any temptations to melodramatic or even gothic treatment of situation and characterization.

There is, however, no ambiguity at all about the fact that, "although it involves forced sex, rape is not about sex or passion. Rape has nothing to do with love. Rape is an act of aggression and violence."[5] An excellent novel that offers a dramatic example of this is Jaira Placide's *Fresh Girl*, in which opposition soldiers in Haiti rape the female protagonist, Mardi, during a political coup.

Nevertheless, one understands why teens may be confused about this subject, as rape and other sexual violence too often take place in the context of a presumed romantic relationship. Indeed, according to the CDC, "1 in 4 adolescents reports being a victim of verbal, physical, emotional, or sexual abuse from a dating partner each year."[6]

The CDC explains, "Dating violence is a type of intimate partner violence. It occurs between two people in a close relationship. There are three common types of dating violence: physical (when a partner is pinched, hit, shoved, or kicked), emotional (name calling, teasing, threats, bullying, etc.), and sexual (forcing a partner to engage in a sex act when he or she does not or cannot consent)." According to the CDC, one in four adolescents in 2007 reported verbal, physical, emotional, or sexual abuse from a dating partner each year.

Compounding the problem, Stanford University reports, is the fact that "controlling and abusive relationships can be very difficult situations to deal with, usually because by the time a person realizes that they are in (such a relationship), it has already gotten to the point where it is extremely difficult to break free (physically, emotionally, psychologically, etc.) and seek help."[7]

Unfortunately, when seeking help or reporting incidents of violence, 86 percent of female high school students in one study said they would "confide in a friend," and only 7 percent said they "would talk to police" (American Bar Association 2006, 3). Why the reluctance to go to the authorities? Because the consequences of going to authorities can sometimes be dire, a reality that has never been better dramatized than in Laurie Halse Anderson's Printz Honor Award novel *Speak*, about which I have written earlier. Nevertheless, it's important to note that when Anderson's protagonist, incoming high school freshman Melinda, calls 911 to report that she has been raped at an end-of-summer party, she winds up a virtual outcast, because her assailant was one of the most popular boys in school. Melinda is finally vindicated when the boy attempts to assault her again and is discovered in the act.

As with Melinda, the point of view offered in books about rape is typically that of the victim; a notable exception is Chris Lynch's 2005 *Inexcusable* (Atheneum/Seo). In this gritty National Book Award finalist, the narrator is a teenage boy who has date-raped the girl on whom he has a crush. He professes his innocence to readers, but as he tells them more about his life it becomes increasingly obvious that he is self-delusional and that his view of his actions and himself is far different from reality. One of the more interesting aspects of this novel is the boy's depiction (and understanding) of his relationship with his heavy-drinking father, a single parent.

Speaking of parents, the survey mentioned earlier does not indicate how many teen respondents would actually confide in a parent, but in another study 83 percent of tenth graders surveyed said they would sooner turn to a friend than to a teacher, counselor, parent, or other caring adult (ABA 2006).

Perhaps it's no wonder, then, that in a 2004 survey, 81 percent of parents said they "either believe teen dating violence is not an issue or admit they don't know if it's an issue" (ABA 2006, 3).

This might be because, like Melinda's parents, they simply don't recognize the symptoms of abuse or, like Caitlin's parents in Sarah Dessen's *Dreamland*—another superb novel about this subject—they are distracted: Caitlin's "perfect" older sister has run away with her boyfriend. In the wake of this trauma, Caitlin's life begins to unravel as she experiments with drugs and begins dating wealthy Rogerson Briscoe, forming a relationship that quickly turns violently abusive. Or it might be because the parent, him- or herself, is abusive, as in the case of Alex Flinn's first novel *Breathing Underwater* (HarperCollins, 2001). In this one, protagonist Nick's father's pattern of abusive behavior has influenced the boy's own understanding of how to behave in a relationship. Accordingly, he soon becomes an abuser of his girlfriend, Caitlin. Fortunately, a court-mandated anger management class will help disabuse him of his unhealthy ideas and habits.

A different—and unspeakably worse—example of parental abuse is depicted in Lori Aurelia Williams's *When Kambia Elaine Flew in from Neptune* (Simon & Schuster, 2000), a book in which a twelve-year-old girl's mother has prostituted her for money. (In Adam Rapp's *33 Snowfish*, thirteen-year-old Custis has also been prostituted, not by a parent but by "the man who owns me," as the boy heartbreakingly puts it).

These are all deeply disquieting stories, but as I have attempted to show with my lengthy survey of statistical evidence, they do represent the actual life circumstances of an alarming number of adolescents. And perhaps, one hopes, making their stories available will foster understanding and promote positive change. As before, I've focused on empathy-inducing fictional treatments, but there is also a growing body of nonfiction that provides material to foster intellectual understanding of the problem, as well. In some cases, this nonfiction gives voices and faces to those who have been victims. An excellent example is Carolyn Lehman's *Strong at the Heart: How It Feels to Heal from Sexual Abuse* (Farrar, Straus & Giroux, 2005), a book that gathers the personal stories of eleven young men and women who are survivors of such abuse.

How teens themselves view the sex act is subject—like everything else in their dynamic lives—to never-ending change. Sometimes, when the media are involved, this takes on a frustratingly chicken-or-egg aspect. Consider the case of oral sex, an activity that for years remained little discussed and seldom studied. No wonder most of Oprah Winfrey's viewers were shocked to hear her announce on a 2002 edition of her talk show that "there's an oral sex epidemic" (Flanagan 2006). A year later, Oprah revisited the issue, this time devoting an entire program to the question, "Do you know what your teen is really doing?" (Daum 2006). Apparently, a whole lot of them were engaged in giving or receiving oral sex. Or were they?

A year after Oprah's second pronouncement on the subject, a *New York Times Magazine* cover story titled "Whatever Happened to Teen Romance?" stirred the pot of still-simmering discussion. The contributing writer Benoit Denizet-Lewis (2004, 32) reported that "oral sex is common by eighth or ninth grade" and "hooking up is more common than dating." He continued, "To a generation raised on MTV, AIDS, Britney Spears, Internet porn, Monica Lewinsky and 'Sex and the City,' oral sex is definitely not sex (it's just oral) and hooking up [getting together for the express purpose of having sexual activity] is definitely not a big deal" (33). "The trend toward 'hooking up' and 'friends with benefits' [basically friends you hook up with regularly] has trickled down from campuses into high schools and junior highs" (32).

Were these new phenomena real, or were they simply anecdotes that sensational media overstatement might actually turn into trends? These questions were answered a year later in a 2005 study from the National Center for Health Statistics, which revealed—according to the government's "most comprehensive survey of American sexual practices"—that more than half of America's fifteen- to nineteen-year-olds reported having had oral sex. This is slightly more than the number who reported having had actual intercourse (55 percent of boys and 54 percent of girls reported having either given or received oral sex, whereas 49 percent of boys and 53 percent of girls reported having experienced intercourse) (Lewin 2005a, A11).

Again, one wonders if this had been happening all along, or if Oprah and the *New York Times* pronouncements turned it into a self-fulfilling prophecy? We'll probably never know, but we do know that Bethany Buck, editorial director for Simon & Schuster's teen imprint Simon Pulse, was watching Oprah's 2003 program—and recognized book possibilities in the topic (see Lewin 2005a, E6; Flanagan 2006). She contacted the author Paul Ruditis, and together the two came up with the idea and characters for a trade paperback original titled *Rainbow Party*, which—in due course—set off a firestorm of controversy.

The plot of this latter-day problem novel involves a sexually active tenth-grade girl named Gin who decides to hold a rainbow party, which—readers soon learn—is a party at which girls, each one wearing a different color lipstick, perform fellatio on each of the boys present. By party's end, the boys all have rainbow-colored penises.

Published as a trade paperback original in 2005, the book was one of the rare few that the major chain bookstores refused to carry, thanks to prepublication controversy. As Tamar Lewin (2005b, E1) wrote, "While 'Rainbow Party' by Paul Ruditis has received a less-than-enthusiastic reception from booksellers, it has won plenty of attention from bloggers and conservative columnists and prompted lots of talk among teenagers, parents and school officials." Lewin (2005b, E1) quotes Ruditis as telling her, "We knew it would be controversial. But everyone involved felt it was an issue worth exploring in a fictional setting. And I don't think anyone who reads the book could come out wanting to have a rainbow party."

In fact, the party never happens. Though a dozen of the school's most popular teens agree to attend, second thoughts soon begin to set in, and by book's end, only two kids show up—both of them boys who have already been revealed to be something less than models of morality. And even they are out of luck, because Gin's father comes home unexpectedly early and nips his daughter's plans in the bud.

Though the book's premise is certainly provocative, its execution is pedestrian and predictable, ultimately more cautionary than crass. Ruditis is at pains, for example, to make several didactic points about the risks of sexual behavior and the importance of sex education. He does this by creating a popular health-issues teacher, Ms. Barrett, whom a nervous administration has ordered to teach an abstinence-only curriculum. As a result, she is unable to share essential information about sexually transmitted diseases with her students. And, wouldn't you know it, more than three dozen sophomores contract oral gonorrhea as a consequence. Not surprisingly—and to her credit—the teacher resigns in protest.

The information she might have shared, had those abstinence-only strictures not constrained her, could have included some alarming statistics from the CDC: (1) After decreasing annually since 1999, gonorrhea infection rates among adolescents ages fifteen to nineteen increased 2 percent from 2004 to 2005 and then increased an additional 6 percent from 2005 to 2006; (2) similarly, the number of HIV/AIDS cases diagnosed among fifteen- to seventeen-year-olds increased by 34 percent in 2006; and (3) birthrates among fifteen- to nineteen-year-olds also increased in 2006 for the first time since 1991 and then increased again in 2007; the rate of increase from 2005 to 2007 was 4 percent.[8] Clearly, unprotected sexual activity remains a part of too many adolescent lives.

At the risk of redundancy, I will say that statistics alone are informative, essential, and—in the cases we've been discussing—perhaps even life saving. Most kids, however, find them boring (I know I did!); worse, they may suspect they're overstated to scare them if not straight then celibate.

Accordingly, we really do need more unapologetically candid and well-crafted fiction about these issues. And it is a very positive thing, I think, that since the turn of the twenty-first century, young adult literature has truly come of age in its willingness to address some of the darker aspects of the human experience with honesty. A measure of how far the literature has come since the problem novels of the 1970s is Elizabeth Scott's *Living Dead Girl* (Simon Pulse, 2008), the horrifying and harrowing story of the abduction of ten-year-old Alice by a pedophile who—for the next five years—batters her physically, starves her, and abuses her sexually on what seems to be a daily basis. As a result, Alice has become what she herself calls "a living dead girl." Her emaciated and battered body stubbornly continues to live though her spirit, her psyche, and her ability to feel or empathize have all been dead for a very, very long time. At fifteen, Alice knows that she is too old to sat-isfy pedophile Ray's hungers much longer, and she is resigned to the fate of the first "Alice," her predecessor whom Ray murdered when that girl turned fifteen. And, sure enough, the day comes when Ray orders Alice to find her replacement, in exchange promising that she can then continue living with him and his new "little girl."

There is worse to come, much worse as it happens. What saves this extremely difficult book from lapsing into melodrama or genre horror fiction is, first, the numbly affectless—but pitch-perfect—voice that Stone has cre-ated for Alice to use in telling the reader her own story. In a sense, it recalls the voice of Brock Cole's Linda, who lets "the facts speak for themselves" in recounting her own tortured story (*The Facts Speak for Themselves*, Front Street, 1997). Second, Stone is brilliant at creating a sense of verisimilitude. I find it hard to imagine a reader who would seriously doubt the reality of Alice's circumstances or the viability of the characters the author has created to populate her increasingly bleak setting. And third, she allows her story's logic to drive it to its inevitable conclusion. There is no possibility of redemp-tion for either Ray or Alice, and so there is no false sense of optimism or hope layered on the inevitable endings of their respective lives.

The most important thing that Stone has done, however, is to posit and then prove, in the bitter events of Alice's existence, the truth of the girl's own formulation of her "three life lessons," which are "1. No one will see you. 2. No one will say anything. 3. No one will save you."

One hopes that young readers who meet the Alice that Stone has made visible in the pages of this searing book will make it their mission to change the world of their futures to ensure that in it there will be no more Alices.

Notes

1. *Of Human Bondage, Wuthering Heights, The Cruel Sea, Love Is Eternal, Winter Wheat, Gone with the Wind, Bridge to the Sun,* and *Three Came Home.*
2. Centers for Disease Control and Prevention, "YRBSS: Youth Risk Behavior Surveillance System," www.cdc.gov/yrbss.
3. National Center for Victims of Crime, "National Center News," www.ncvc.org.
4. Rape, Abuse and Incest National Network, www.rainn.org.
5. KidsHealth, http://kidshealth.org.
6. Centers for Disease Control and Prevention, www.cdc.gov/ncipc/pub-res/DatingAbuse FactSheet.pdf.
7. Sexual Assault and Relationship Abuse Prevention and Support, "A Resource for the Stanford Community," www.stanford.edu/group/svab/.
8. Centers for Disease Control and Prevention, www.cdc.gov/mmwr/preview/mmwrhtml/ mm5926a1.htm?s_cid=mm5730a1_e.

lesbian, gay, bisexual, and transgender literature

The Controversies Continue

Though John Donovan's *I'll Get There, It Better Be Worth the Trip* (Harper), the first YA novel to treat the subject of homosexuality, may have appeared in 1969, only two years after *The Outsiders* and *The Contender*, no more than eight others about this subject followed over the next eleven years. Worse than their paucity, however, was the fact that, though well intentioned like *I'll Get There*, they were equally riddled with stereotypes, a subject that is addressed at some length in *The Heart Has Its Reasons*, a critical history of young adult literature with gay, lesbian, and queer content that I coauthored with Christine A. Jenkins (Scarecrow, 2006). Suffice it to say that these early efforts perpetuated the stereotypical view of homosexual lives as unrelievedly bleak, lonely, danger filled, and—as often as not—doomed to a tragically early end, usually in a car wreck, because all these books were crowded with the worst drivers this side of my grandmother.

It should also be mentioned that virtually every one of the central characters in these books was white and middle class. The first black character, Rosa Guy's eponymous Ruby, had appeared as early as 1976, but no other blacks would appear until the 1991 publication of Jacqueline Woodson's *The Dear One* and no Latinos until 1995.

Though the world of GLBT teens remained an all-white one, an otherwise more realistic—and positive—picture of homosexuality did begin emerging in the eighties, starting with Nancy Garden's classic *Annie on My Mind* (Farrar, Straus & Giroux, 1982), the first YA novel to acknowledge that homosexuality was about more than sex(uality): it was also about love, a love that should dare to speak its name.

A year after the publication of *Annie*, another first expanded and enriched the field: the first literary novel with gay content, Aidan Chambers's *Dance on My Grave* (Harper, 1983), appeared; this was also the first of many gay-themed novels from Great Britain that would be published in the United States.

Other notable firsts from the eighties include Norma Klein's *Breaking Up* (Random House, 1980), the first to include a gay parent; then Gary W. Bargar's *What Happened to Mr. Forster?* (Clarion, 1981) became the first to include a working gay teacher (I say "working" because Isabel Holland's Justin McLeod, in *The Man without a Face* [1972], was also a teacher but a retired one). Unfortunately, the eponymous Mr. Forster established a new stereotype, the self-sacrificial gay teacher who quietly gives up his job rather than cause distress to his students. An exceptionally important first appeared in 1986, M. E. Kerr's *Night Kites*, the first YA novel about AIDS. Even though the pandemic, which in its early years principally affected gay men, had been around since 1981, nervous publishers had been notably reluctant to address the subject in books for teens. Indeed, Kerr, in her Margaret A. Edwards acceptance speech, acknowledged that she felt she might have committed a form of professional suicide in writing the book, especially because her AIDS sufferer is a young gay man. She explained: "It seemed to me that *not* to have a homosexual be the AIDS sufferer would be a way of recognizing the illness but not those who have it . . . a sort of don't ask/don't tell proposition, where the reader can know the nature of the plague, without having to deal with those personalities who threaten the status quo" (Cart and Jenkins 2006, 63).

Unfortunately, in the years since there have been only a handful of other YA novels dealing with this issue, even though more than 45,400 persons between the ages of thirteen and twenty-four have been infected since 1981 and AIDS continues to be a major cause of medical concern in America. As noted earlier, the number of cases among fifteen- to seventeen-year-olds increased 34 percent in 2006, and in 2007 a total of 2,462 new cases were diagnosed among thirteen- to twenty-four-year-olds.[1]

And yet, other than *Night Kites*, only two other novels addressed the issue in the eighties—thirteen were added to that number in the nineties, but since the millennium, there have been only four or five more. One that addressed the pandemic in Africa—Alan Stratton's *Chanda's Secrets* (Annic Press, 2004)—was selected as a Printz honor title in 2005.

In addition to being a decade of firsts, the 1980s also saw a significant increase in the number of GLBT novels: forty titles compared to a mere eight in the seventies. However, only half a dozen would prove to be of enduring literary value. In addition to *Annie on My Mind, Dance on My Grave,* and *Night Kites*—all mentioned already—three others offered notable contributions to the gradually emerging field: Ron Koertge's *Arizona Kid* (Joy Street, Little, Brown, 1988), A. M. Homes's *Jack* (Macmillan, 1989), and Francesca Lia Block's *Weetzie Bat* (Harper, 1989).

Koertge's story of the memorable summer a teenage boy spends with his gay Uncle Wes in Arizona is significant not only because it includes the issue of AIDS but also—and even more significant—because it is the first gay-themed novel since M. E. Kerr's *I'll Love You When You're More Like Me* (Harper, 1977) to include humor, a refreshing change in a field more given to the tragic than the comic. Homes's novel about a boy who discovers his father is gay is notable not only for its wryly humorous voice but also for its realistic depiction of a teen's journey from anger to acceptance. Block's novel is notable, like Koertge's, for its inclusion of AIDS but also—and more significant—for its lyrical celebration and openhearted embrace of love as both an aspect of homosexuality and an ingredient essential to the human experience.

The field of GLBT literature for young adults continued to expand in the nineties, the number of titles being published—seventy-five—nearly doubling the forty that appeared in the eighties. Unfortunately, once again, advances were more statistical than aesthetic. Too many of the novels in the new decade (fifty-one of seventy-five) continued to focus narrowly on the coming-out experience, and too few dealt with the realities of living as an out teen. Also, the literature's gender imbalance, a problem since its beginnings, continued apace. Thus, in the eighties 73 percent of the books featured gay males and only 27 percent lesbians. The numbers in the nineties were, if anything, even more skewed, with 69 percent dealing with gays and only 26 percent with lesbians. The remaining 5 percent included both gay and lesbian characters, a notable advance for a literature that had previously been so rigidly divided between genders. Another interesting—but dubious—trend of the nineties was the movement of the gay or lesbian character from the central role of protagonist to that of secondary character. In the eighties 40 percent of gay characters had been protagonists and 60 percent secondary characters. But in the nineties only 27 percent remained protagonists, and 73 percent had become secondary characters. This may have made the books more accessible to nongay readers (like the earlier practice of making the narrator straight even when the central character was gay), but demoting the characters to often one-dimensional supporting roles tended to rob them of their individuality, make them token gay characters, and invite the danger of lazy stereotyping.

Nevertheless, there were a number of 1990s books—at least twenty of the seventy-five—that remain significant either for their literary quality or for the advances they introduced into the field. Sometimes they offered both, as in the case of Jacqueline Woodson's novels *The Dear One*, *From the Notebooks of Melanin Sun*, and *The House You Pass on the Way*, which variously featured characters of color, a mixed-race relationship, fully realized adult lesbian characters, and more. Less successful literarily but equally important in terms of innovation were the two Pride Pack novels of R. J. Hamilton (*Who Framed Lorenzo Garcia* and *The Case of the Missing Mother* [Alyson, 1995], a miniseries that introduced gay Latino characters to the field (a nonseries novel that did the same was Gloria Velasquez's *Tommy Stands Alone* [Arte Público, 1995]).

Francesca Lia Block added three novels to her Weetzie Bat cycle in the 1990s: *Witch Baby*; *Missing Angel Juan*; and—most notably—*Baby Bebop*, which gave readers the backstory of Weetzie's gay best friend Dirk.

The nineties also saw the publication in the United States of important novels from Australia (*Peter* by Kate Walker) and New Zealand (Paula Boock's *Dare Truth or Promise* and William Taylor's *The Blue Lawn*), confirming, for American readers, the universality of the homosexual experience.

One of the best written and most emotionally satisfying of the novels about AIDS, Theresa Nelson's *Earthshine*, was published in this decade (by Orchard, in 1994), and Robert Paul Walker's *The Method* (Harcourt) made history by being the first YA novel to include a gay pride parade, acknowledging—in the process—that gay and lesbian teens did not have to live in hermetically sealed isolation but could be part of a larger—and even companionable—culture. As for M. E. Kerr, she continued her long-standing habit of innovation by giving readers the first novel to deal with bisexuality: *Hello, I Lied* (HarperCollins, 1997), and a second novel by her, *Deliver Us from Evie* (HarperCollins, 1994), offered an unusual take on stereotyping by offering perhaps the most fully realized lesbian character to date, the titular Evie, who resembles Elvis Presley and enjoys fixing farm machinery, telling her mother, "Some of us look it, Mom! I know you so-called normal people would like it better if we looked as much like all of you as possible, but some of us don't, can't, and never will!"

Important short stories with gay or lesbian content also appeared in this decade: Marion Dane Bauer's *Am I Blue?* (HarperCollins, 1994) was a landmark collection entirely devoted to gay or lesbian characters and themes. And two of the most memorable stories in Chris Crutcher's *Athletic Shorts* (Greenwillow, 1991) addressed gay themes: *In the Time I Get* featured a character with AIDS, and the unforgettable *A Brief Moment in the Life of Angus Bethune* gave us a teenage boy with not one, but two, sets of homosexual parents!

Both the growing literary importance of fiction with homosexual content and its increasingly widespread acceptance were evidenced by the 1999 publication of Ellen Wittlinger's *Hard Love*, a book that became one of the first Printz Honor Award recipients, setting the stage for significant progress in this field in the decade to follow.

Sure enough, 2003 would be a singularly important year in the ongoing evolution of GLBT literature. This was the year Aidan Chambers received the Michael L. Printz Award for his extraordinary, gay-themed novel *Postcards from No Man's Land*, which subtly and thought provokingly addressed the complications that visit the nature of sexual identity. That same year Garret Freymann-Weyr received a Printz honor for her novel *My Heartbeat*, which examines two teenage boys' attempts to define their own sexual identities. Also in 2003, the Margaret A. Edwards Award was presented to Nancy Garden. As in the earlier case of Judy Blume, the selection committee—to underscore its importance—mentioned only one of the recipient's books in the award citation. It was, of course, *Annie on My Mind*.

The volume of titles giving faces to lesbian, gay, and bisexual teens also continued to grow significantly in the new century. From 2000 through 2008, no less than 165 GLBT titles were published, an average of more than 16 per year (compared with 1 per year in the 1970s, 4 per year in the 1980s, and 7 per year in the 1990s).

In a positive development, new output also reflected many of the diverse trends that have defined young adult literature for the twenty-first century. Thus, GLBT content began enriching literary fiction; genre fiction; commercial fiction; crossover novels; short stories; poetry; and a growing body of ethnically, racially, and culturally diverse literature. Even better, it has finally begun giving faces to perhaps the last invisible teens, those who are transgender. The first transsexual character had actually appeared in Francesca Lia Block's 1996 short story "Dragons in Manhattan" (published in her anthology *Girl Goddess #9* [HarperCollins]).[2] The first appearance of a transgender character was in Emma Donoghue's *The Welcome*, a story in my 2001 anthology *Love and Sex* (Simon & Schuster). And there are three transgender stories—by Francesca Lia

Block, Jennifer Finney Boylan, and Jacqueline Woodson—in my 2009 collection *How Beautiful the Ordinary* (HarperCollins, 2009). Meanwhile, though, in 2004 a transgender character finally became the focus of an entire novel, Julie Anne Peter's groundbreaking and National Book Award–shortlisted *Luna* (Little, Brown, 2004). A second novel featuring a transgender character, Ellen Wittlinger's *Parrotfish* (Simon & Schuster), followed in 2007.

A significant number of important new writers have emerged in recent years to continue bringing art, innovation, and diversity to GLBT literature. Among them, certainly, are the author-editor David Levithan, whose 2003 novel *Boy Meets Boy* (Knopf) employs a breathtakingly good mixture of realism and fantasy in its creation of an idealized world in which sexual differences are not castigated but celebrated! A second new talent, Alex Sanchez, has explored multiple aspects of the gay and lesbian life experience in his Rainbow Boys trilogy (Simon & Schuster) and, in his 2004 novel *So Hard to Say* (Simon & Schuster), he wrote one of the few gay-themed novels for middle school readers. Other significant new writers include Christian Burch, Nick Burd, Brent Hartinger, Steve Kluger, Brian Malloy, P. E. Ryan, Sara Ryan, Brian Sloane, Bill Konigsberg, and Martin Wilson, among others.

The GLBT literature remains a literature in transition. Despite the many gains in the field, advances still need to be made. For example, too many titles, especially those that remain focused on coming out, continue to treat being homosexual or transgender as a problem or issue. Similarly, not enough novels feature characters whose GLBT identity is simply a given, as it is in stories about heterosexual characters. And in that same connection, more novels are needed that acknowledge that homosexuality is about more than the sex act. Given the increasingly early age at which young people are now coming out, we also need more novels for middle school readers that examine this phenomenon. We continue to need more GLBT novels, too, with characters of color and characters who come from other cultures and ethnicities. Also needed are more novels with same-sex parents. And, last, the genre must continue to come of age as *literature.*

Nevertheless, if ours is not yet the "wonderful world" that a gay character in *Boy Meets Boy* sees when he looks about him, we are getting there—and (pace John Donovan) it will definitely be worth the trip!

Yet the Controversies Continue

No matter how compelling a case one might make for bringing candor to young adult literature, many folks continue to take strenuous exception. The result is not only a great deal of huffing and puffing by the mainstream media but also a cascade of book challenges in America's schools and libraries. No one can say precisely how many of these occur, as the American Library Association's Office of Intellectual Freedom estimates that 70–80 percent of such cases typically go unreported. If so, that would mean there are significantly more than the 3,376 challenges that were reported between 2000 and 2008. Of those, 1,225 challenges were for sexually explicit material; 1,008 for offensive language; 720 for material deemed unsuited to age group; 458 for violence; and 269 for homosexuality.

Although some of these cases involved books published as adult titles, they were all challenged—in 51 percent of the cases by parents—because of their use by or with children and young adults. Indeed, the largest incidence of challenges has taken place in school libraries (35 percent), followed closely by classrooms (33 percent), and, last, by public libraries (25 percent).[3]

For the past three years, the single most challenged book has been the innocuous and charmingly told picture book *And Tango Makes Three*, the true story of Roy and Silo, two male penguins at New York's Central Park Zoo, who having formed a same-sex attachment, were given an egg to hatch and rear. The principal reasons this book has been challenged include, according to the ALA, "anti-family," "homosexuality," and "unsuited to age group." Other picture books featuring same-sex parents (though human ones)—notably *Daddy's Roommate* and *Heather Has Two Mommies*—have also excited numerous challenges over the years; they were, in fact, second and ninth on the list of the hundred most challenged books of the nineties, according to the Office of Intellectual Freedom. More central to our concerns, though, are the YA titles that have excited controversy. Not surprisingly, the Gossip Girl books are among those, along with *The Perks of Being a Wallflower*; the Alice series by Phyllis Reynolds Naylor; Crutcher's *Athletic Shorts*; Cormier's *The Chocolate War*; the TTYL series by Lauren Myracle; the Printz honor title *The Earth, My Butt and Other Big Round Things* by Carolyn Mackler; Myers's *Fallen Angels*; and *Go Ask Alice*.

There is, of course, a great deal of factual information about censorship, ALA being a staple source of much of it. There are a few works of fiction, too, that put a more human face on the issue, including Nancy Garden's *The Year They Burned the Books* and *Places I Never Meant to Be*, a collection of stories edited by Judy Blume and written by often-challenged authors. Reading Blume's introduction to this book is—for me, anyway—a trip down memory lane. Blume recalls that as a junior in high school she went to her local public library in search of a copy of the novelist John O'Hara's *A Rage to Live*. "But I couldn't find it," she explains. "When I asked, the librarian told me THAT book was RESTRICTED. It was kept in a locked closet, and I couldn't take it out without permission from my parents" (Blume 1999, 2).

Today it's not locked closets we need to worry about; it's locked minds—minds that are impervious to alternative points of view and terrified of telling young people the sometimes-thorny truth about the realities of the world. One certainly understands and empathizes with parents and other concerned adults who wish to protect youngsters from the sensationalistic, the meretricious, and the mendacious. I confess that I, myself, worry when I observe the levels of extreme violence my three great-nephews are exposed to in the video games they play for hours at a time (two of the three boys are nine; the third is thirteen). And I certainly believe that parents need to be aware of and responsible for their offspring's reading, viewing, and interacting habits. However, I draw the line when parents unilaterally and adamantly decree that not only their own children but also those of other parents may not have access to materials. Perhaps even more troubling to me is the continuing barrage of sensationalistic articles that appear in the mainstream media—media that are, or so I was taught in journalism school, supposed to be defenders of intellectual freedom and the people's right to know (the blogosphere is another story, an exponentially more visceral place, where anonymous posters condemn and castigate to a fare-thee-well, one reason I avoid its precincts). As was the case in the 1990s, a never-ending stream of over-the-top exposés of books for youth continues to emanate from the fourth estate. Here's a sample collection of twenty-first-century headlines:

"Tales of Raw Misery for Ages Twelve and Up" (*New York Times*, July 20, 2007)

"Young Readers, Harsh Reality" (*New York Times*, June 13, 2002)

"New Book on Children's Sexuality Causes a Furor" (Associated Press wire story, April 3, 2002)

"It Ain't Half Hot, Mum" (Manchester *Guardian*, February 23, 2003—yes, some of these stories appeared in the British press)

"So It's Goodbye to Janet and John" (*London Times*, May 2, 2003)

"City's Ed. Boobs" (*New York Post*, October 13, 2003—the lede for this story is "The three R's in education were almost always racy, raunchy, and risqué")

"What (Sex) Boys (Sex) Think (Sex) About" (*New York Times*, October 7, 2003—this is actually an article about the television series *Life as We Know It*, but the show was adapted from Melvin Burgess's controversial YA novel *Doing It*)

"Teen Playas" (*Entertainment Weekly*, March 7, 2005)

"Racy Books for Teens Pondered" (*Brattleboro [Vermont] Reformer*, July 9, 2005)

"Battle of the Books: The Problem with 'Problem' Young Adult Fiction (*Slate*, June 17, 2005)

"Racy Reads" (*New York Journal News*, July 10, 2005)

"You're Reading . . . What?" (*Wall Street Journal*, June 24, 2005)

"Young Readers Pulled into a Rich, Amoral Teen Universe" (*San Francisco Chronicle*, September 24, 2005)

"Teen Fiction Plots Are Darker and Starker" (*Denver Post*, July 5, 2009)

"It Was Like All Dark and Stormy" (*Wall Street Journal*, June 6, 2009)

"Rape, Abortion, Incest: Is This What CHILDREN Should Read?" (*Daily Mail*, July 9, 2009)

As was the case in the nineties, too many of these articles were written by reporters who had not a clue about young adult literature and had not read the books they decried. In announcing the impending publication of Melvin Burgess's *Doing It*, for example, a reporter for the *Guardian* snarkily wrote, "Apparently it's really filthy" (Cooke 2003). It's not, of course. Provocative, yes, but also a clear-eyed look at three teenage boys' sex lives—or occasional lack thereof. That one of the three is having an affair with his (female) teacher is doubtless responsible for the appearance, in its wake, of several other YA novels dealing with the same sensitive subject: R. A. Nelson's *Teach Me* (Razorbill, 2005) and Barry Lyga's *Boy Toy* (Houghton Mifflin, 2007). Each of these titles must be evaluated on its own merits, but it's worth noting that *Doing It* received the *Los Angeles Times* Book Award as best young adult book of the year.

Because the reporters of these media accounts have no background in YA literature, their pieces oftentimes approach the ludicrous—at least to knowledgeable professionals. Unfortunately, it's not only professionals who are reading them. It's also credulous parents or people who are looking for a cause—célèbre or otherwise—and who, in turn, also fail to read the books but nevertheless head to the barricades or, more probably, the nearest library to file a challenge (I'm speaking here as one who was himself a public library administrator for twenty-five years and served as president of both YALSA and the Assembly on Literature for Adolescents of the National Council of Teachers of English). This explains such odd anomalies as finding *Looking for Alaska*, John Green's superb and Printz Award–winning novel, being lumped together with the pedestrian *Rainbow Party*, simply because both address sexual conduct.

By now it should be clear that the twenty-first century has brought new artistic freedom to both writers and publishers of young adult books. With that new freedom, however, has come new responsibility—not only for them but also for librarians, teachers, and reviewers. That responsibility includes reading widely, receiving a grounding in the history of the literature, developing critical evaluative and thinking skills, being aware of the realities and problems of YA life, and being on the lookout for the truly exploitative and irresponsible—especially because the ongoing process of liberating young adult literature from some of its former restraints continues to redefine not only its audience but also its marketplace.

Who knows what tomorrow may bring, but as for today, this surely remains one of the most exciting periods in the whole history of young adult literature. And to prove that, even more excitement awaits us in the next chapter.

Notes

1. Centers for Disease Control and Prevention, http://www.cdc.gov/mmwr/preview/ mmwrhtml/ss5905a1.htm
2. A transgender person is one who identifies with the opposite sex; a transsexual is a person whose sex has been surgically changed.
3. www.ala.org/oif.

the viz biz

Transforming the Funnies

Beginnings

The comics have long been a staple of American popular culture; in fact, they were one of the seven "lively arts" identified by the cultural critic Gilbert Seldes in his landmark 1924 book of the same title.[1] Nevertheless, they found neither respect nor place in America's school and public libraries, where, for decades, they were considered at best ephemeral and at worst either subliterate or downright subversive. This impoverished attitude began to turn around in the 1980s and 1990s, but it didn't become a certifiable phenomenon until YALSA devoted an entire 2002 preconference to the subject. To widespread surprise, the event was a sellout and was, in fact, the best attended of all the ALA preconferences that year. How the comics came to the library limelight and, almost overnight, turned into must-have staple constituents of library collections is a fascinating story.

It began in the 1890s with the first newspaper comic strips. One of the earliest and most influential of these was R. F. Outcault's *Hogan's Alley*, which debuted on May 5, 1895, in the *New York World*. Not a strip but a single-panel cartoon, the feature introduced the Yellow Kid, who quickly became its signature character. As the comics historian Richard Marschall (1989, 24–25) writes, "It was 'Hogan's Alley' starring the Yellow Kid that truly turned the newspaper world upside down. Every paper had to have its own color comic section and every publisher longed to have its own counterpart of the Yellow Kid."

Among those early counterparts were Rudolph Dirks's *The Katzenjammer Kids*, Frederick Opper's *Happy Hooligan*, and Winsor McKay's gorgeously drawn *Little Nemo*, which would influence generations of children's picture book artists to come, ranging from Maurice Sendak to William Joyce.

Created, frankly, to sell newspapers, the comics quickly attracted huge audiences of eager readers, among them the many new immigrants who were arriving in America as part of the greatest wave of immigration in this country's history. The strips appealed not only because they featured immigrants themselves—especially the tenement dwellers of *Hogan's Alley* and the German Americans in *Katzenjammer Kids*—but also because people who did not have English as a first language embraced visual stories that they could comprehend at a glance.

Though at first confined to a single panel, the new comics quickly became a more kinetic exercise, assuming the form of multipanel strips of sequential images. It didn't take long thereafter for the first spin-offs to appear: book-length compilations of previously published daily strips that, as early as 1902, were being called comic books.

The first comic book to contain all new stories and characters, *New Fun 1*, debuted in 1935, the same year that Walt Disney's first comic book, *Mickey Mouse Magazine*, appeared.

In the meantime, another kind of kinetic reading experience that married words and pictures in a seamless symbiotic unity, the children's picture book, had debuted (Wanda Gag's *Millions of Cats* [Coward McCann, 1928] is often cited as the first of these), and cartoons had begun to move in the form of animated film even earlier. Winsor McKay, for example, produced a hand-colored film of his *Little Nemo* around 1911, and Disney's first sound cartoon, *Steamboat Willie*, came along in 1928. In the decades since, all three of these art forms have continued to maintain a creatively symbiotic relationship, though it is the comic book that has contributed most directly to the emergence of today's library-friendly comics form known as the graphic novel.

In 1938, three years after the first original comic book appeared, the comics made another giant leap forward with the publication in 1938 of *Action Comics #1*, which introduced Jerry Siegel and Joe Shuster's soon-to-be-immortal Superman. A year later, another caped crusader, Bob Kane's Batman, appeared, and within a decade another four hundred superheroes had joined the ranks. America had never been so well protected!

The next two decades saw such an exponential growth in comic book publishing that the period is generally regarded as the golden age of comic books. According to the industry observer Michael R. Lavin, comic book sales were ranging from 500 million to 1.3 billion copies a year by 1953.[2] In the meantime, however, those same comic books had become much edgier in content thanks to the rise of graphically violent horror, crime, and war "comics," especially those published by William Gaines's EC imprint. In 1954 the child psychiatrist Frederick Wertham's controversial book *The Seduction of the Innocent* (Rinehart) appeared. Linking comic book violence to the rise of juvenile crime, Wertham's book created a backlash that resulted in the Comic Book Hearings of the U.S. Senate Subcommittee on Juvenile Delinquency and the creation of the starchy Comics Code Authority. The adverse publicity almost destroyed the comic book industry as sales plummeted and the number of publishers shrank from some three dozen to no more than nine.

Fortunately, the visual has always had an enduring appeal, and by 1956 a new silver age of comics had begun, quickly becoming a more robust revival, with the 1960s debut of two new features from Marvel Comics: *Fantastic Four* and, perhaps more notably in terms of young adult literature, *Spiderman*, who was, in reality, the troubled teen Peter Parker, arguably the first psychologically complex superhero. While this was happening, the counterculture movement of the sixties had begun spawning adult, underground comics created, most notably, by R. Crumb, whose work has, in the years since, become so respectable that it is now regularly featured in the *New Yorker*!

The increasing sophistication of characterization and subject matter came together in 1978 in the pages of veteran cartoonist Will Eisner's ambitious book *A Contract with God, and Other Tenement Stories*. To describe this novel-length collection of four linked literary stories, Eisner used the term *graphic novel*, which has since become identified with him, though it had actually been used two years before in George Metzger's 1976 book *Time and Again*.

The Comics Come of Age

Nearly another decade would pass, however, before three other important, genre-changing works appeared in the same landmark year, 1986, to truly launch a new age of grown-up comics called graphic novels. The three were Art Spiegelman's *Maus*, Frank Miller's *Dark Knight Returns*, and Alan Moore and Dave Gibbons's *Watchmen*. Until that time, comic books had been sold at newsstands or, increasingly, at specialty comic bookstores. As the developments we've been charting began to broaden the comic book audience, however, some publishers like Fantagraphics, Drawn & Quarterly, Viz, and Dark Horse started selling their output through general bookstores. This, in turn, began attracting the attention of librarians. Thus, as early as 1984, the Hawaii State Public Library System began acquiring this form of visual and verbal communication. California's Berkeley Public Library followed suit in 1989. Enough libraries had hopped on the comic book bandwagon by 1994 that *VOYA* magazine launched a regular column, "Graphically Speaking," in which the librarian Kat Kan became one of the first to review graphic novels for a library-based readership. In the meantime, Spiegelman's *Maus* and its sequel *Maus II*, released in a single volume in 1992 by Harper, received the Pulitzer Prize and signaled that the venerable comic book had finally come of age as a newly vibrant and vital art form that deserved a place even on respectable library shelves.

In the wake of *Maus*, established comics publishers like DC, Fantagraphics, Top Shelf, and Drawn & Quarterly began experimenting with similarly serious graphic novels or alternative comics, as they were also called. In fact, DC started two imprints—Vertigo and Paradox Press—to differentiate its darker, more sophisticated efforts from its traditional superhero series. The former imprint, launched in 1993, published such early classics as Alan Moore and David Lloyd's *V for Vendetta* and Neil Gaiman's *Sandman* (an original Sandman graphic novel, *The Sandman: Endless Nights*, published in 2003, became the first graphic novel to make the *New York Times* Best-Seller List). The latter imprint, formed the same year, published both Howard Cruse's novel of the civil rights era, *Stuck Rubber Baby*, and Max Allan Collins and Richard Rayner's *Road to Perdition*, which, some years later, would become a movie starring Tom Hanks and Paul Newman.

The trend to the alternative continued in 1995 when the Canadian publisher Drawn & Quarterly began issuing Adrian Tomine's serially published *Optic Nerve*, while in 1998 Fantagraphics published Daniel Clowes's *Ghost World* and, in 2000, Joe Sacco's innovative exercise in graphic journalism *Safe Area Goradze*.

At the same time, a handful of major trade book publishers began experimenting with what—to them—was still a new form. One of the first was Avon; its imprint Neon Lit debuted in 1994 with a graphic version of Paul Auster's noir novel *City of Glass*. Three years later, Bob Mecoy, who had become vice president and senior editor at Simon & Schuster after launching the Avon imprint, told *Publishers Weekly*, "Basically what we were doing was making paper movies." He continued, "Book publishing now competes with the rest of the entertainment industry and that means finding other viable ways to tell a story, especially at a time when the public seems so interested in multimedia entertainment" (Morales 1997, 49).

Not only was the public interested but so, increasingly, were other traditional book publishers. In 1996 Little, Brown, the longtime American publisher of the Belgian cartoonist Herge's internationally celebrated *Tintin*, published Ben Katchor's critically hailed *Julius Knipl: Real Estate Photographer*, and Pantheon, which has since become the most important trade publisher of literary graphic novels, followed in 1998 with Katchor's next novel, *The Jew of New York*. Pantheon subsequently published Clowes's *David Boring* (2000) and Chris Ware's extraordinary *Jimmy Corrigan: The Smartest Kid on Earth* (2000), which is widely regarded as the field's first masterpiece.

Though avidly read by teens, all of these books were technically published for adults. One of the first titles to be published expressly for young adults was Karen D. Hirsch's original anthology *Mind Riot: Coming of Age in Comix* (Simon & Schuster/Aladdin, 1997), and—in 2000—the Joanna Cotler imprint at HarperCollins launched the Little Lit series, coedited by Art Spiegelman and his wife Francoise Mouly, the art editor of the *New Yorker*. Clearly, as Spiegelman quipped, "Comics aren't just for grownups any more" (Reid and MacDonald 2000, 44–45). And they certainly weren't just for collectors, aging fan boys, or other habitués of specialty comic bookstores. By the time the silver anniversary of the graphic novel arrived in 2003, *Time* magazine had claimed, "Graphic novels have finally reached a point of critical mass in both popular consciousness and sales. Micha Hershman at Borders confirms the trend, saying, 'Over the last four years graphic novels have shown the largest percentage of growth in sales over any other book category'" (Arnold 2003).

As noted earlier, libraries had begun purchasing this vital new art form as early as the mid-eighties; indeed, as Judith Rosen (2003, 52) pointed out, "Initially libraries led the way in embracing comics as a way to get young people to read. And wholesalers that service libraries developed catalogues, e-mailings and Web sites to help with building graphic novel collections."

This hope—that the popularity of comics and graphic novels might lure kids to the library and induce them to read—was a fundamental reason for librarians' initial interest in developing these collections. Other reasons that have stood the test of time include the following:

- Comics' proven capacity to increase visual literacy, an essential skill in a digital age

- Their high visual content, which recommends their use with reluctant readers and English-language learners

- Their established viability as a new—and continuously evolving—art form

- Their indispensable place in popular culture

- And—more pragmatically—their demonstrated capacity for increasing circulation and enhanced use of other library collections

Libraries Enter the Picture

Nevertheless, it wasn't until 2002 that a true turning point arrived; not only did YALSA hold its first graphic novel preconference; its Popular Paperbacks Committee issued a recommended list of graphic novels for teens, and "Get Graphic @ Your Library" was selected as the theme for national Teen Read Week. Just three years later, YALSA launched its annual Great Graphic Novels for Teens list, an act that invited serious consideration of how to review and evaluate the evolving art form. The policies and procedures for the Great Graphic Novels Committee list the following criteria:

- Reflect an integration of images and words

- Exhibit a clarity of visual flow on the page

- Ability of images to convey necessary meaning

- Outstanding quality of the artwork's reproduction

- Narrative enhanced by the artwork

- Narrative dominated by sequential art component

Several years earlier, curious about this same issue of evaluation, I interviewed the two-time Eisner Award–winning graphic novelist Eric Shanower, creator of *The Age of Bronze*, an epic retelling of the Trojan War in comic book form. To my question, "How should librarians go about assessing work like yours?" he replied, "They should ask: Is the artwork engaging? Does it draw a reader into the story? Is the movement of the story from one panel to the next clear? The visual storytelling doesn't necessarily need to be 'easy' or even linear but it does need to be comprehensible. Also, does the artwork serve the story? The evaluation of its technical aspects should be specific to the medium of the comics, but the evaluation of the emotional and intellectual content and impact—the aesthetic experience as a whole—will generally have much more in common with the ways other media are evaluated" (Cart 2002b).[3]

The continuing—and even expanding—library interest in graphic novels spurred a number of trade publishers (among them Abrams Amulet, Random House, Puffin, and Hyperion) to start publishing graphic novels specifically targeted at young readers. In 2005 Scholastic became the first children's book publisher to inaugurate its own graphic novel imprint, which it called, appropriately, Graphix. Though initially focused on books for younger readers—including an ambitious, multivolume colorized release of Jeff Smith's classic Bone series—Graphix published its first YA graphic title, *Breaking Up*, by Aimee Friedman and Christine Norrie in 2007.

That same year, Simon & Schuster children's publishing announced an ambitious division-wide effort to encourage the publication of comics and graphic novels by all of its imprints, and Ginee Seo/Atheneum quickly responded with *Chiggers*, an original graphic novel by the award-winning cartoonist Hope Larsen.

By far the most promising and ambitious new imprint, however, was Roaring Brooks' First Second. Led by the editorial director Mark Siegel, himself a comics artist and book designer, the line launched in the spring of 2006; within a year one of its books had garnered remarkable recognition. *American Born Chinese*, by Gene Luen Yang, became the first graphic novel to receive the Michael L. Printz Award; it was also the first graphic novel to be shortlisted for the National Book Award.

Siegel, who grew up in France, brings a cosmopolitan sensibility to his imprint, which publishes not only American comic artists but also editions of distinguished comic art from all over the world in a high-end, soft-cover format with French flaps and a uniform six-by-eight-and-a-half-inch trim size.

In light of the growing sophistication and aesthetic ambition of the highly visual form, one must ask what, exactly, a graphic novel is these days—is it just, as some have asserted, "a long comic book" (Estrada 2006, C4) or "a comic book that needs a bookmark?" (McGrath 2004a, 26).

Yes and no. The form certainly has its roots in the humble comic book. And in the comic book industry itself, graphic novels are still often called trade comics, and many graphic novelists continue to call themselves cartoonists. That said, graphic novels are, in fact, distinguished from comic books, first, by their greater length and, second, by their sturdier format. Traditional comic books remain a cross between a pamphlet and a magazine; they're single-issue publications that usually appear monthly, are stapled rather than bound, and are seldom longer than thirty-six pages. Graphic novels, however, are square bound, original, never-before-published, book-length stories or collections of (previously unpublished) short stories.

They are a medium, not a genre; a form that combines words, pictures, and iconic language presented in sequential panels to create a whole work that is larger than the sum of its parts. They require the reader to invest creative energy and imagination to supply actions and events implied by breaks between the panels. And before we get too lost in analysis, graphic novels are technically different not only from comic books but also from trade paperbacks, which are book-length compilations of previously published material, usually consecutive issues of an ongoing series. To further confuse the issue, trade paperbacks can be published in either soft or hardcover formats, and graphic novels can also be nonfiction.

Though comics and graphic novels have clearly been a field in flux since the mid-1980s, one thing about them did remain fixed for far too long: the medium's tendency to attract significantly more male readers than females (as evidence, consider that a hallmark of comics has been their unfortunate tendency to objectify women). Which is not to say, of course, that there were no girl-friendly comics. Consider the popularity of two very different classics: *Little Lulu* and *Wonder Woman.*

Little Lulu was the creation of the cartoonist Marjorie Henderson Buell, who signed her work "Marge," but Wonder Woman was the creation of a man, William Moulton Marston, a psychologist who is famous for having been involved in the invention of the polygraph.[4] His superheroine debuted in All Star Comics No. 8 for December 1941 and—immediately popular—has been published, more or less continuously, since. The character's popularity received a boost, of course, with the debut of the television series starring Lynda Carter in 1975 (it remained on the air until 1979). But the comic's popularity gradually waned in the 1980s, and it was actually discontinued for a year in 1986 before being reintroduced in 1987. It was not until 2006, however, that the adventures of the superheroine were, for the first time, written and drawn by a woman, the cartoonist Gail Simone.

Though few women actually worked in the field, *Little Lulu* and *Wonder Woman* weren't the only comics targeted at girl readers. A whole subgenre of romance comics came into existence in the late 1940s (at the same time that romance fiction for teens was the reigning genre in book publishing) and stuck around until the 1970s. With titles like *Young Romance, Falling in Love,* and *Heart Throbs,* they were as full of clichés, stereotypes, and overripe dialogue as a B movie. And, of course, they were all written by men. As the romance comics gradually faded into oblivion in the 1970s, Paul Levitz, the president and publisher of DC Comics, told *Publishers Weekly,* "Publishers essentially abandoned the [female] demographic. Nobody put a lot of effort into trying to reach them for the next couple of decades" (Deahl 2007).

Manga

This situation began to change dramatically with the mid-1990s explosion of manga—Japanese comics. Like *graphic novel*, the term *manga* describes a format, not a genre, because manga can be about any subject and addressed to an audience of virtually any age, though the earliest manga to reach the United States were typically for children, such as *Pokémon*. Despite the diversity of their content—which includes media tie-ins, superheroes, fantasy, science fiction, romance, sports, action-adventure, humor, and more—manga tend to conform to a readily recognizable artistic style: their characters all have enormous eyes and tiny noses; most of the books are done in black and white; and—most challenging to older American readers—they are read from right to left and back to front. Most manga are also part of seemingly endless series (Jason Thompson identifies more than nine hundred of them in his recent book *Manga: A Complete Guide* [Del Rey, 2007]), each of which may fill thirty or more paperback volumes and, like soap operas, run for years. (*Ranma ½*, the first manga to become popular in the United States, is also the longest-running series to date, having lasted thirteen years! The successor to *Ranma* appears to be Masashi Kishimoto's *Naruto*. A total of forty-four volumes of the adventures of this young ninja in training had been published through September 2009.)

There are a prodigious number of manga subcategories, but two of the most prominent are *shojo* and *shonen*; the former—targeted at girl readers—tend to be character driven, and the latter, aimed at boys, are typically plot driven.

Though still a relative newcomer to the U.S. market, manga have been a fixture of Japanese popular culture for more than sixty years.[5] It wasn't until women began writing and drawing manga for the first time in the late 1960s, however, that shojo became an indispensable part of the Japanese comic mix. And even then, they didn't begin to attract an audience of American readers until the late 1980s and 1990s, when Viz and Tokoyopop, which became the two largest publishers of manga in the United States, were founded.

Since that time, manga has become one of the fastest-growing segments of the publishing industry, and girls are among its fastest-growing group of readers; indeed, manga were the first comics that many modern girls ever read. Why them and not American comics? Well, in part because of the diversity of shojo's content. If American comics focused on superheroes, shojo explored a much wider, girl-friendly world ranging from fantasy to fashion and from high school stories to romantic comedy.

Not surprisingly many of the most popular shojo titles are not only written and drawn by women, they also feature female characters and, perhaps accordingly, are sometimes called the chick lit of the graphic novel world (especially *josei*, manga aimed at adult women readers).[6]

Sailor Moon is probably the classic example of shojo. Created by Naoko Takeuchi, it's the story of a fourteen-year-old schoolgirl who is granted magical powers after she meets a talking cat named Luna. (The shojo tradition of female characters having magic powers may derive, the critic Paul Gravett argues, from the Shinto tradition of female deities and priestesses.)

Arguably even more popular than *Sailor Moon* is *Fruits Basket*, by a female artist who works under the pseudonym Natsuki Takaya. *Fruits Basket* is the story of an orphan girl named Tohru who lives in a tent in the woods. There she is befriended by a mysterious family named Sohma, the members of whom, when hugged by a person of the opposite sex, turn into one of the animals of the Chinese zodiac.

Speaking of opposite sex, *Ranma ½*, though drawn and written by the female artist Rumiko Takahashi, is the story of a male teenage martial artist. He's a male some of the time, anyway. It turns out that Ranma is enchanted and turns into a woman whenever he is splashed by cold water. To turn back into a male, he must be splashed by—you guessed it—hot water.

As *Ranma* demonstrates, some shojo feature male characters. Another notable example is Clamp's *xxxHolic*, the story of a teenage boy who goes to work for a witch. Clamp is not a single artist but a four-woman studio that, over the past seventeen years, has produced twenty-two popular manga series, including—in addition to *xxxHolic*—*Chobits, Cardcaptor Sekura, Tsubasa,* and *X*. Finally, another form of shojo that features male protagonists is *shonen-ai*. Translated as "boy love," these books indeed feature idealized romantic relationships between two boys. Shonen-ai are seldom sexually explicit, though a form called *yaoi*, aimed at older readers, often is.

The appeal and influence of manga of all sorts on the U.S. market have been significant. By 2005 the form had even spawned an American version called OEL (original-English-language) manga, comics created for the American market by non-Japanese artists.

But it is manga's role in establishing a female audience for graphic novels that may be its most lasting contribution. As a result, more women are entering the field, and mainstream American graphic novel publishers are beginning to aggressively court girl readers.[7] The publisher NBM, founded in 2005, initially targeted the tween market for young girls by issuing graphic adaptations of the classic Nancy Drew mysteries. In 2006 DC introduced an entire new imprint called Minx, a line of original graphic novels aimed at young female readers.

In reaching out to this new audience, DC took an unusual step for a comics publisher: it joined forces with Alloy Marketing and Media, the packager—as we have seen—responsible for such successful book series as Gossip Girl and Sisterhood of the Traveling Pants. The Minx line debuted in May 2007 with a graphic novel titled *The Plain Janes*. Written by the established YA novelist Cecil Castellucci, the novel had art by Jim Rugg and recounted the doings of a nonconformist art girl gang. Unfortunately, despite significant media attention and the publication of nearly a dozen critically praised graphic novels, DC retired the new imprint barely two years after its 2007 launch.

There is no question, however, that graphic novels by women author-artists have become an important part not only of manga but also of the entire graphic novel scene. A well-attended panel at the 2008 New York Comic Con was devoted to the growing number of comics aimed at girls, and two of the most critically hailed graphic novels of the past ten years are by women: Marjane Satrapi's *Persepolis* and Alison Bechdol's memoir *Fun Home* (Houghton Mifflin, 2006) (Rosen 2009b).

Comic Art—Oxymoron or Appraisal?

Satrapi and Bechdol are distinguished writers as well as artists, and they evidence another trend that has been building in the field since about 2005. The television journalist Rachel J. Allen explains: "Graphic novels have gotten bigger because they're, well, better. The past five years have often been trumpeted by the comic book industry as 'The Golden Age of Writers'" (Allen 2006).

First Second's Mark Siegel agrees: "With the advent of an author-driven market—as opposed to series-driven or merchandising-driven market—creators have a platform and potential to reach a great audience by developing their own personal vision, their own unique voice" (Brill 2006).

As a result, a number of celebrated authors have been drawn to the graphic novel as a new form of self-expression. Such luminaries as Michael Chabon, Jonathan Lethem, Jodi Picoult, Greg Rucka, Brad Meltzer, and Joss Whedon have all tried their hands at writing graphic novels. Even manga have been affected, thanks to the emerging popularity in 2008 and 2009 of *gekiga*, or literary manga, the alternative comics of Japan.

The new popularity of the form with writers has also manifested itself in the appearance of young adult books with protagonists who want to be cartoonists. Some of these books, like Daniel Ehrenhaft's 2006 novel *Drawing a Blank*, Sherman Alexie's 2007 National Book Award–winning *The Absolutely True Diary of a Part-Time Indian*, and Stephen Emond's *Happyface*, include their characters' artwork; others—like Barry Lyga's *The Astonishing Adventures of Fanboy and Goth Girl*—do not (Lyga by the way is the coauthor of a professional volume for teachers titled *Graphic Novels in Your Media Center*). A slightly different take is found in Perry Moore's 2007 novel *Hero* (Hyperion) in which the teenage protagonist is not a cartoonist but the son of one of the greatest superheroes of his time!

The growing aesthetic excellence of the form is further evidenced by Houghton Mifflin's decision to add an annual volume of *Best American Comics* to its acclaimed Best American series; further evidence is Yale University Press's publication of Ivan Brunetti's two-volume *Anthology of Graphic Fiction* as well as *Masters of American Comics*, the catalog of a landmark exhibition of comic art organized jointly by Los Angeles's Hammer Museum and the Museum of Contemporary Art.

The Current Market

The market for alternative comics and graphic novels has grown steadily since the late nineties, which has meant a continuing shift from the traditional comic bookstore as the prime sales outlet to general bookstores, especially the chains. As a result, in 2006 the sales of graphic novels actually exceeded those of comics for the first time ($330 million compared to $310 million). Some 2,800 graphic novels were published that year, according to Milton Griep of ICv2, a pop culture website that tracks the market. A total of 144 of these were targeted at teens and tweens, up from only 64 in 2005. And fully 1,200 of the 2,800 graphic novels were manga, a growing number of them coming not from Japan but from Korea, where they're called *manhwa*. Statistics for 2007 were even more positive: sales rose 12 percent to $375 million and the total number of graphic novels grew to 3,391, of which 1,513 were manga (MacDonald 2008).

Though the growth in the number of teen and tween titles for the same period slowed to only 1 percent and that of literary graphic novels to 2 percent, the library portion of the market remained significant, as demonstrated by the fact that an entire day of the 2006 New York Comic Con was devoted to a conference within a conference. Stackfest, cosponsored by *Library Journal* and the distributors Diamond and BroDart, was targeted specifically at librarians and those who are interested in reaching them. The next year, the 2007 Book Expo America (BEA)—the book trade's leading exposition and trade show—featured a large panel with the topic "The Science, Art, and Magic of

Graphic Novel Selection for Libraries," and the 2009 BEA boasted three such panels (Reid and MacDonald 2009).[12]

Earlier evidence of the importance of the library market had come in 2005, when for the first time, a librarian was added to the panel of judges that select the winners of the annual Eisner Awards, the Oscars of the comic book industry. Kat Kan (a teen services librarian) was the first librarian judge, and she has been followed in years since by such experts as Robin Brenner, Eva Volin, Mike Pawuk, and Francisca Goldsmith, all of whom have worked as YA librarians.

The library market's new prestige also translates into sales: for example, the recent inclusion on YALSA's Alex Awards list of Jeff Lemire's graphic novel *Tales from the Farm* (Top Shelf, 2007) almost immediately generated ten thousand new sales of the book! (MacDonald et al. 2008)

Clearly, there is no question about the growing popularity of the graphic novel form with librarians and teachers. The books are now regularly reviewed by all the professional journals (*Booklist* even publishes an annual "spotlight" on graphic novels), and since 2005 virtually every publisher of series nonfiction—Rosen, Capstone, Stone Arch, World Almanac, Lerner, ABDO, and others—has been releasing titles in this format, too.

Anxious to expand their market, juvenile trade publishers have recently begun mining their backlists for print books—both fiction and nonfiction—that can be adapted as graphic novels. HarperCollins, for example, published a graphic version of Neil Gaiman's *Coraline*, and Simon & Schuster launched ongoing adaptations of its Pendragon and Childhood of Famous Americans series. Scholastic is offering a graphic version of Ann Martin's popular Babysitter's Club series, and Yen Press (the graphic novel division of Hachette Book Group) has launched adaptations of James Patterson's Maximum Ride series and has announced plans to do a graphic novel version of Stephanie Meyer's Twilight series. Meanwhile, the comics publisher Marvel has announced plans to publish graphic novel versions of Margaret Edwards Award–winner Orson Scott Card's *Ender's Game* and *Ender's Shadow*, as well as an adaptation of Stephen King's *The Stand*.

Though sales of graphic novels in both book and comic stores actually dropped approximately 8 percent during the first half of 2009 (thanks to America's dramatic economic downturn), sales nevertheless remain such a strong part of the overall book market that, in the spring of 2009, the *New York Times* launched its first graphic books best-seller list, featuring three categories: hardcover, softcover, and manga. Obviously a once-niche-market phenomenon has entered the mainstream, and all indications are that it is there to stay.

Notes

1. *The Seven Lively Arts* (New York: Harper and Brothers, 1924). For the record, the other six were movies, musical comedy, vaudeville, radio, popular music, and dance.
2. University at Buffalo, "Comic Books of the 1950s," http://libweb.lib.buffalo.edu/comics/index.html.
3. The fundamental introduction to the comics medium remains Scott McCloud's *Understanding Comics* (Kitchen Sink Press, 1993), and a good introduction to library use of the medium is Francisca Goldsmith's *Graphic Novels Now* (American Library Association, 2005).
4. While Buell did the single-panel Lulu cartoons that appeared in the *Saturday Evening Post*, the Lulu comic books were, in large part, also the work of a man, John Stanley, who—along with Carl Barks, who drew Uncle Scrooge for Disney—is regarded as one of the two great creative talents in the history of comic books.
5. A comprehensive and beautifully designed history of manga is Paul Gravett's *Manga: Sixty Years of Japanese Comics* (Harper Design International).
6. Shonen manga for adult men is called *seinen*.
7. The Friends of Lulu, a nonprofit organization, was founded in 1994 to promote female readership and participation in the comics field.

the eyes have it— other visual forms

Photo Essays and the New Nonfiction

Today's children are the first generation to grow up more accustomed to digital screens than the printed page; as wireless devices proliferate, kids increasingly understand and appreciate data that is transmitted to them in visual form.

—James Bickers, "The Young and the Graphic Novel," 2007

In the early 1990s, at about the same time that the crossover picture book was becoming a phenomenon, the author-artist Diane Stanley was beginning to use the traditionally fictional form to limn the real lives of historical figures like Charles Dickens, Shakespeare, Leonardo da Vinci, Cleopatra, and others. As a result, the picture book became another crossover vehicle, this time one to convey information, both textual and visual. Of course, some of the earlier work of David Macaulay and the more contemporaneous work of Peter Sis also enriched this category. Readers interested in pursing this subcategory further are referred to Patricia J. Cianciolo's 1999 book *Informational Picture Books for Children* (American Library Association), which offers a cogent analysis of the form and describes and analyzes more than 250 examples of informational picture books.

The idea that pictures can convey information and understanding as well as or better than text is hardly a new one. Bishop Comenius, the Czech educational reformer whose 1658 visual encyclopedia *Orbis Pictus* is often regarded as the first picture book, once observed, "For it is apparent that children (even from their infancy almost) are delighted with pictures and willingly please their eyes with these sights" (Avery 1995, 7).

Nevertheless, for many years American nonfiction remained earnestly unadorned. And no wonder—from its beginnings in the 1820s work of Samuel Griswold Goodrich (Peter Parley), its purpose was utilitarian and its presentation dryly didactic.

The purpose-driven, curriculum-related nature of nonfiction continued to dominate the field for more than a century, and as a result, most (though not all) nonfiction came in the form of series from institutional publishers. Its appearance was often forbidding, distinguished by pages of dense, pedestrian text unbroken by pictures; when images did appear, they were often small, black and white, and—as often as not—culled from the files of the Bettman Archives.

This finally began to change in the 1950s, when children's publishing entered a period of expansion and Random House launched Landmark Books, its influential and wildly popular series of history and biography titles. In 1958 a Congress worried that America was losing the space race to Russia passed the National Defense Education Act, which generously funded libraries' purchase of books in the sciences; this, in turn, led to the appearance of still more nonfiction series—such as Crowell's Let's Read and Find Out—as well as the debut of such soon-to-be-celebrated writers of nonfiction as Isaac Asimov, Franklyn Branley, Millicent E. Selsam, Herbert S. Zim, and others. The boom years continued through the sixties, thanks in large part to another infusion of federal money, this time from the Elementary and Secondary Education Act, which was part of President Lyndon Johnson's Great Society legislation. Anxious to spend their windfalls quickly, libraries issued a de facto demand to publishers for more new books.

And, the publisher and author James Cross Giblin (1988, 29) recalls, "Publishers scurried to meet [the demand] by launching new series of information books for every age group in every conceivable subject area."

Unfortunately, the well of federal funding abruptly ran dry in 1969, when as a result of its focus on the Vietnam War, the Nixon administration turned its attention from books to bullets, and juvenile nonfiction was one of the first victims.

Publishing being a famously cyclical business, however, the depressed—and depressing—situation of nonfiction began gradually to improve in the mid-seventies, thanks, this time, not to an infusion of funds but to exciting visual content; these visuals were crisply produced photographs offered in the form of what soon came to be called the photo essay. Though pioneered by the *Life* magazine photographers Alfred Eisenstaedt, Margaret Bourke-White, Thomas McAvoy, and Peter Stackpole, it is the editor Norma Jean Sawicki, then at Crown, that Giblin credits with establishing "the photoessay as a genre unto itself. Led by the interest in photoessays," Giblin (1988, 30) continues, "the juvenile nonfiction area made a quiet but steady comeback in the early 1980s."

The texts of these books improved appreciably, too, thanks to the entrance into the field of a new generation of writers, like Brent Ashabranner, Betsy Maestro, Gail Gibbons, Dorothy Hinshaw Patent, Milton Meltzer, Jean Fritz, and Russell Freedman. And when engaging text and captivating, impeccably researched visual content came together in an artistically seamless whole in Freedman's *Lincoln: A Photobiography* (Clarion, 1987), a nonfiction book won the Newbery Medal for the first time in thirty-two years, and a new kind of informational book was born.

Also contributing to that birth was the British publisher Dorling Kindersley, which—in the late 1980s—had launched its revolutionary series Eyewitness Books, which were published in the United States by Knopf. Employing what it called a "lexigraphic approach," DK devised a new way to publish nonfiction. The publisher Peter Kindersley explained, "One of the problems with words is that they're incredibly slow, while pictures are incredibly fast. When you put them together, they work in completely different ways. (*Children's Software Review* 1997).

As I wrote in *Booklist* in 2002, "What DK did—with almost revolutionary panache—was essentially to reinvent nonfiction books by breaking up the solid pages of gray type that had previously been their hallmark, reducing the text to bite-size, nonlinear nuggets and surrounding them with lavish white space and pictures that did more than adorn—they also conveyed information. Usually full-color, they were so crisply reproduced they seemed almost to leap off the page. Carter and Abrahamson, in their essential [book] 'Nonfiction for Young Adults' call the images 'stunning visuals . . . all artfully arranged on the pages for visual appeal'" (Cart 2002a, 399). Kindersley may have best explained the new approach when he then wrote, "Through the picture I see reality and through the word I understand it" (Cart 2002a, 399).

In the Know: Libraries and the New Nonfiction

The word (i.e., the text) was the focus of yet another important YALSA preconference, important because it underscored the growing prominence of nonfiction in libraries. Held in 1990 and called "Just Say Know," this one devoted two days to an exhaustive examination of the newfound importance and allure of nonfiction and information materials for young people. As Linda Waddle (1991, 361) wrote in *Journal of Youth Services in Libraries*, "The sessions were designed to help participants become better evaluators and users of the increasing quantity and variety of nonfiction materials." Presentations ranged from "Booktalking Nonfiction" to "Apartheid in South Africa" and from "Evaluation and Review of Current Self-Help Books" to "Magazine Publishing: The *Sassy* Approach."

The keynote speakers were Betty Carter and Richard Abrahamson, whose book *From Delight to Wisdom: Nonfiction for Young Adults* Oryx Press had published that same year. The coauthors addressed attendees in the presentation "The Role of Nonfiction in Developing Lifetime Readers." Staunch advocates of the form, they asserted that "young adults who want to know about this world, or this planet, or this society don't care to continually extrapolate their ideas from fiction; they want to examine more reliable sources. Only nonfiction responds to this need" (Waddle 1991, 366–67). And what about those who want to know about themselves, instead? "Young adults read for identification. Neither fiction nor nonfiction dictates a reader's stance; the reader always does. Frequently, the reader interacts on a personal level with nonfiction" (366). In other words, nonfiction provides the facts; it is the reader who provides the same kind of emotional response he or she would while reading fiction.

Surprisingly, only one presentation addressed the visual aspect of nonfiction. In it James Cross Giblin and Norma Jean Sawicki offered their answer to the often-heard complaint: "But All They Do Is Look at the Pictures: Illustrations in Nonfiction Books." And clearly they did look, for the impact of those pictures continued to inform the evolution of the informational book as established writers like Freedman, Jim Murphy, Rhoda Blumberg, Kathryn Lasky, and Patricia Lauber were joined by Albert Marrin, Janet Bode, Laurence Pringle, Susan Kuklin, Elizabeth Partridge, and James Cross Giblin himself, who had retired from publishing to devote himself full-time to his career as a writer of award-winning information books. All of these authors were extraordinarily good writers, but they also understood the importance of incorporating significant visual material into their texts.

At the same time, another editor-publisher, Marc Aronson—whose name has been a fixture of these pages—was continuing to develop nonfiction for older young adults at Holt and, later, at Carus Publishing, where he had his own imprint, Marcato Books. However, he, too, retired and has since become not only one of America's most eloquent advocates for nonfiction but also the author of some of its most intellectually challenging and stimulating titles in books like *Sir Walter Raleigh and the Quest for El Dorado* (Clarion, 2000), *The Real Revolution* (Clarion, 2005), *Unsettled: The Problem of Loving Israel* (Seo/Atheneum, 2008), and others.[1]

There is no fictionalizing to be found in any of these fine writers' books— no imagined conversations, no messing with history or chronology to make a better story—all demonstrate the importance of creating a narrative and, to that end, of borrowing techniques from novelists without violating the accuracy or the integrity of their books' content. Freedman (1994, 138–39) has addressed this aspect of his work, saying, "I think of myself first of all as a storyteller, and I do my best to give dramatic shape to my subject whatever it may be. . . . By storytelling, I do not mean making things up, of course. I don't mean invented scenes, or manufactured dialogue, or imaginary characters."

Freedman goes on to discuss the importance of developing character by including telling details (the contents of Lincoln's pockets the night he was assassinated); using anecdotes; creating vivid scenes (including William Herndon's description of the chaos Lincoln's two sons wrought in his law office); and—to give readers a sense of what historical personages actually sounded like—quoting from letters, diaries, journals, speeches, and other written matter. When handled expertly, the result is a compelling narrative that offers the power of story without sacrificing any of the authenticity of fact.

This is, surely, an art, and it is no wonder that since the mid-1970s, award attention has finally begun to be paid to this formerly unregarded form. The Boston Globe–Horn Book Awards, for example, added a category for nonfiction as early as 1976. The Society of Children's Book Writers followed in 1977, and the Book Guild of Washington initiated a body of work award for nonfiction that same year. In 1983 a total of three Newbery honors were presented for nonfiction (to Kathryn Lasky, Rhoda Blumberg, and Patricia Lauber); and in 1988 Freedman received the Newbery itself for *Lincoln*. Two years later, the National Council of Teachers of English initiated its Orbis Pictus Award (the first winner was Jean Fritz, for her *Great Little Madison*), and in 2000 the Association of Library Service for Children, which also presents the Newbery and Caldecott medals, created the Robert F. Sibert Medal to be awarded annually to the author(s) and illustrator(s) of the most distinguished informational book published in English during the preceding year. The first award, presented in 2001, went to Marc Aronson for his *Sir Walter Raleigh and the Quest for El Dorado*, which many considered a young adult book. Interestingly, one of the four honor books that year—Judd Winick's *Pedro and Me*—was also regarded as young adult and was a graphic novel, to boot. In the years since, award and honor recipients have included both children's and YA titles—among the latter being the 2003 winner, James Cross Giblin's *The Life and Death of Adolf Hitler*, and—that same year—an honor to Jack Gantos for his edgy memoir *A Hole in My Life*, which was also the recipient of a Printz Honor Award.

Why YALSA did not immediately follow suit with a similar award for the best informational YA book excited a great deal of discussion. Some pointed to the fact that nonfiction is eligible, after all, for the Printz (witness the Gantos book), but others have pointed out that no informational book has actually won this most prestigious YA award, and only two such books have even received honors—*A Hole in My Life* and Elizabeth Partridge's *John Lennon.*

Still, nonfiction has always been represented on the annual Best Books for Young Adults lists, but even there the news is not altogether salutary. As Betty Carter noted in the first edition of *Best Books for Young Adults*, "Not only has BBYA changed from an almost exclusively adult list to a strongly juvenile one but it has also reversed from including mostly nonfiction books to containing a predominance of fiction titles. . . . In 1993 seventy-five percent of the books were fiction" (Carter 1994, 39–40). In the second edition, Carter again wrote, "Nonfiction fails to appear in representative numbers on BBYA lists. Part of that failure may be because of the reading tastes of the committee, but part is also because of publishing output" (2000, 12). (Though she doesn't specify this, a total of 79 percent of the 1999 list were novels.)

In the third edition of the book, published in 2007, the editor Holly Koelling reported that 20 percent of the titles on the 2001–2007 lists were nonfiction (80 percent, thus, are fiction), but she included poetry in her count (Carter did not), which suggests that the fiction-nonfiction imbalance is even greater than before on both the basic list and the BBYA Top Ten lists. During the period described by Koelling, only five of the seventy titles selected (i.e., 7 percent) for these lists were nonfiction. And when one looks at the six Teens Top Ten lists that YALSA has generated since 2003, the results are even more discouraging: the teens themselves have chosen not a single nonfiction title! The International Reading Association's Young Adults' Choices lists from 2002 to date are slightly but not much better: 9 of 180 titles (5 percent) selected by those teens are nonfiction.

It would seem that teens—and even many librarians—continue to equate nonfiction with textbooks; the fact that the lion's share of nonfiction is still published as curriculum-driven series by institutional publishers surely doesn't help, though even these books have shown marked improvement in recent years. As author Elaine Landau suggested in 2006, "The lines between series and trade nonfiction begin to blur a bit" (Weisman 2006, 59).

Despite all of the extraordinary advances that have been made in the field, nonfiction remains the kitchen-bound Cinderella of young adult literature, while her stepsister—fiction—remains the belle of the ball. But a glass slipper may finally be at hand. In 2009 YALSA finally created the Award for Excellence in Nonfiction for Young Adults. The first award (and honors, if any) will be presented in 2010. Will it make a difference? Will it turn nonfiction from scullery maid to princess? Time will tell. But the latest developments in publishing—as we will see in the next chapter—suggest that if it is the latter, her palace may well be a virtual one.

Note

1. Aronson writes insightfully about nonfiction and many other aspects of young adult literature and publishing in his two collections of essays and speeches: *Exploding the Myths* and *Beyond the Pale* (Scarecrow, 2001 and 2003, respectively).

of books and bytes

Multiple Literacies, the Death of Print, and Other Imponderables

My more culturally aware readers may have already noted that what I've been calling the new golden age of young adult literature coincides almost exactly with what is also widely regarded as the age of irony.[1] I mention this because I find it so wonderfully ironic that the field's renaissance, which has driven the publication of more YA books than ever before, should have occurred during the same period in which many people are also saying that—thanks to a dazzling array of digital distractions—no one is reading books any longer.

Are Young Adults Reading?

The catalyst for much of this dire muttering was a 2004 National Endowment for the Arts study titled *Reading at Risk*, which found that "the percentage of Americans reading literature has dropped dramatically over the past 20 years" (ix). Although this sounds suspiciously like hyperbole, the statistics reported were, indeed, startling, showing that the percentage of U.S. adults reading literature had dropped from 56.9 in 1982 to 46.7 in 2002. More to our point, the most precipitous drop (from 59.8 percent in 1982 to 42.8 percent in 2002) took place among eighteen- to twenty-four-year-olds, which led the report writers to note, "The trends among younger adults warrant special concern, suggesting that unless some effective solution is found, literary culture and literacy in general will continue to worsen" (xiii).

Critics of the report—and there were many—pointed out that the NEA's definition of reading was a very narrow one ("confoundingly narrow," charged Charles McGrath), limited—as it was—to novels, poetry, and plays. Nonfiction was not included, nor were magazines or newspapers or any reading that was done in association with work or study. Even more interesting, though quick to imply it might be partly responsible for the decline, the report did not consider the Internet at all, even though, as McGrath (2004c, WK3) pointed out, "When people surf the Web, what they are doing, for the most part, is reading."

Sensitive to these criticisms, the NEA issued a follow-up report in 2007. Titled "To Read or Not to Read," it expanded its definition of reading to include all kinds of reading, a category that includes reading done online. It also broadened its statistical base to include data from some two dozen other studies by the Education and Labor Departments; the Census Bureau; plus selected academic, foundation, and business surveys. Despite this expansion, the 2007 findings were no more positive than those of 2004, showing a continuing decline in both reading and reading proficiency, especially—now—among those between the ages of nine and seventeen. "These trends," the new study noted, "are concurrent with a falloff in daily pleasure reading among young people as they progress from elementary to high school. In 2006, for example, the data found that 15 to 24-year-olds were spending only 7 to 10 minutes a day voluntarily reading anything at all" (Thompson 2007). This is especially unfortunate, as the new study also showed that students who did read for fun nearly every day performed better in reading tests than did those who reported reading never or hardly at all.

This study, too, excited considerable debate and criticism, ranging from reservations about its data to its perceived lack of nuance.[2] Timothy Shanahan, past president of the International Reading Association, told the *New York Times*, "I don't disagree with the NEA's notion that reading is important, but I'm not as quick to discount the reading that I think young people are really doing" (a reference, according to the *Times*, to reading on the Internet) (Rich 2007).

Marc Aronson concurred, arguing that the problem was not a crisis in reading "but, rather, a problem on the part of adults who idolize a certain kind of fiction reading and have trouble making sense of the mixture of fiction, digital information, nonfiction and assigned reading that make up the diet of the YA reader" (Cart 2007, 42).

Similarly, the educational technology consultant and former YALSA president Linda Braun said, "The more willing adults are to recognize the important role that technology-based reading—blogs, wikis, text messages, and the like—has in teen lives, the more likely it is that teens will start to think of themselves as readers" (Cart 2007, 42).

We will address the role of the Internet in young adult reading in a moment, but first we should acknowledge that reading advocates were surprised by the unheralded release of yet another NEA report in 2009, especially because this one, *Reading on the Rise,* found that after twenty years of decline, "literary reading has risen among adult Americans" (1).

And "best of all," NEA Chair Dana Gioia wrote, "the most significant growth has been among young adults, the group that had shown the largest declines in earlier surveys. The youngest group (ages 18–24) has undergone a particularly inspiring transformation from a 20% decline in 2002 to a 21% increase in 2008" (National Endowment for the Arts 2009, 1).

What on earth caused such a dramatic about-face? "There is no statistical answer to this question," Gioia wrote—a bit coyly, I fear. He then went on to credit "the heightened sense of urgency created by alarming studies like 'Reading at Risk' and 'To Read or Not to Read' [to cite only NEA's own contributions to the genre]."

Certainly some credit is owed the NEA, but might an increase in online reading also have played a part in this rise? Gioia doesn't say, only reiterating earlier equations of reading declines with "an unprecedented large variety of electronic entertainment and communication options" (National Endowment for the Arts 2009, 1–2). Nevertheless, the study did note one positive link in finding that 15 percent of adults surveyed said they do, indeed, read literature on the Internet.

As for children and teens, a separate study—the 2008 Kids and Family Reading Report commissioned by Scholastic and conducted by the Yankelovitch consumer trends research company—found that nearly two in three of nine- to seventeen-year-olds surveyed have extended their reading experience via the Internet (e.g., visited a fan site, visited an author's website, used the Internet to find books by a particular author), and "high frequency Internet users are more likely to read books for fun every day" (Sellers 2008).

All of this discussion, however, begs another, even more basic question.

Can Young Adults Read?

In 2006 the *Washington Post* reported that the Alliance for Excellent Education was estimating that 6 million middle and high school students couldn't read at acceptable levels. "Educators said it's difficult to pin down one cause," the *Post* added. "Bad teaching, chaotic home lives, low expectations for some students, cultural bias, the fact that older students simply don't read enough—all have been faulted." "Kids who are struggling readers have developed strategies to avoid reading," Sylvia Edwards, a reading specialist with the Maryland State Department of Education, told the *Post*. "They are under the radar, scraping by" (Aratani 2006, B1).

Also under the radar—where it had been too long—was the entire issue of adolescent literacy. As early as 1999, Carol Santa, then president of the International Reading Association, had said, "Adolescents are being shortchanged. Nobody is giving their literacy needs much press; there is little funding for adolescent literacy, and the topic is not a priority among educational policy makers or in the schools" (*Reading Today* 1999, 1).

To redress this oversight, the IRA issued its first position statement on adolescent literacy that same year, flatly asserting, "The reading, writing, and language development of adolescents is just as important and requires just as much attention as that of beginning readers" (*Reading Today* 1999, 22).

In a field that had always focused on elementary school reading instruction, the idea that literacy might be a developmental process and the acquiring of its skills a continuum was a new one that began exciting considerable professional attention. In 2004, for example, the National Council of Teachers of English issued a position-action statement of its own, "A Call to Action," which stated, "Reading is not a technical skill acquired once and for all in the primary grades, but rather a developmental process. A reader's competence continues to grow through engagement with various types of texts and wide reading for various purposes over a lifetime."[3]

The new focus on adolescent literacy seems to have arrived in the nick of time, for testing by the National Assessment of Educational Progress (the so-called Nation's Report Card) soon revealed the critical nature of this problem. The NAEP scores, released in 2007, showed that an alarming 65 percent of the nation's high school seniors and 71 percent of eighth graders were reading below grade level, and only 2 percent read at an advanced level.

As literacy skills have continued to stagnate or decline, both the IRA and the NCTE have begun searching for ways to engage students with books and other means of reading. Marsha Sprague, author of the IRA-published book *Their Voices: Engaging Adolescent Girls with Young Adult Literature*, suggests that teachers "give adolescents books that help teens make sense of their lives, with the idea that if they see reading as meaningful, they will want to read more" (*Reading Today* 2007, 12).

What better books to serve this indispensable purpose than those published for and about young adults?

Jonathan Eakle, director of the Reading Program at Johns Hopkins University agrees, saying, "One of the key pieces that must be present in the instruction of adolescent readers is authenticity. Reluctance is often related to relevance. Students don't see how what they're being asked to do is related to their lives, in the present or the future. Making the connection between literacy education and real life means teaching students how to gather, organize and design multimedia texts . . . to navigate the architectures of digital and real space" (Flanagan 2008, 7–8).

The Rise of Multiple Literacies

Multimedia texts, the architectures of digital and real space—what do such esoteric terms have to do with reading? Well, quite a lot, apparently.

"Now, at the start of the 21st century," writes Howard Gardner, a professor of cognitive psychology at Harvard's Graduate School of Education, "there's a dizzying set of literacies available—written languages, graphic displays, and notations. And there's an even broader array of media—analog, digital, electronic, hand-held, tangible, and virtual—from which to pick and choose" (2008, B01).

Annette Lamb, professor of library and information science at Indiana University, agrees: "I think we're already moving through a redefinition of 'literacy.' Computer literacy is only a small part of what young people need to be learning. I think information fluency is much broader than computer literacy. People who consider words on a paper page as the only form of 'real reading' are missing a large part of what people need to be information fluent in today's society" (Hill 2009, 112).

Some experts argue that young people need to be masters of visual literacy, media literacy, information literacy, technological literacy, and more— "all of which require the ability to read and write in multiple contexts across diverse media" (Carter 2009, 114–15).

No wonder YALSA chose "How We Read Now" as the theme of its first-ever YA Literature Symposium, held in Nashville in 2008. Or that Gardner predicts that "literacy—or an ensemble of literacies—will continue to thrive but in forms and formats we can't yet envision" (2008, B01).

In the meantime, according to the Pew Internet and American Life Project, 93 percent of twelve- to seventeen-year-olds presently go online, 63 percent of those on a daily basis. And according to the Kaiser Family Foundation (Foehr 2006), the amount of media content that eight- to eighteen-year-olds are exposed to each day has increased to eight and a half hours, but because young people multitask, they pack that content into an average of six and a half hours per day, including three hours of watching television, two hours listening to music, more than an hour spent on the computer (outside of home-work), and just under an hour playing video games. Surprisingly, nearly three of four also read for pleasure, averaging forty-three minutes per day, though how much of this reading is done while multitasking, the report does not say, nor does it say whether any of this pleasure reading is done online—which raises yet another question.

Is Reading Online Actually Reading?

Reading online is actually reading, but apparently it differs significantly from traditional reading on a printed page. The renowned web researcher Jakob Nielsen, who tested 232 people to determine how they read pages on screens, found they followed a pattern that looks like a capital letter *F*. Mark Bauerlein, author of *The Dumbest Generation,* explains: "At the top [of the screen] users read all the way across, but as they proceed, their descent quickens and hori-zontal sight contracts, with a slowdown around the middle of the page. Near the bottom eyes move almost vertically, the lower-right corner of the page largely ignored" (Bauerlein 2008). Speed is the hallmark of such reading, and—no surprise—another Nielsen test has found that teenagers skip through the Web even faster than adults do, but with a lower success rate for complet-ing tasks online (55 percent compared to 65 percent).

A recent study from University College London (2008) reports similar findings: "It is clear that users are not reading online in the traditional sense; indeed, there are signs that new forms of 'reading' are emerging as users 'power browse' horizontally through titles, contents pages, and abstracts going for quick wins. It almost seems they go online to avoid reading in the traditional sense."

"The result," Nicholas Carr (2008) wrote in his influential *Atlantic Monthly* article "Is Google Making Us Stupid?" "is to scatter our attention and diffuse our concentration. In Google's world, the world we enter when we go online, there's little place for the fuzziness of contemplation. Ambiguity is not an opening for insight but a bug to be fixed."

If true, this finding will be particularly disturbing to fans of the newly literary young adult fiction that has finally, *finally*, made a place in its pages for just such ambiguity, a staple of artful fiction, but one that—apparently—commands no place in fiction or other literary forms that one might find online.

Indeed, it seems the Internet is no friend to any kind of complex or long-form reading. Naomi Wolf, author of *Proust and the Squid: The Story and*

Science of the Reading Brain, "worries that the style of reading promoted by the Net, a style that puts 'efficiency' and 'immediacy' above all else, may be weakening our capacity for the kind of deep reading that emerged when an earlier technology, the printing press, made long and complex works of prose commonplace" (Carr 2008).

What the Internet favors instead, it seems, is the presentation of information, and the most successful information is that which is immediately available and in bite-size form. The long-range consequence of this may actually be a change in cognition. "What the Net seems to be doing," Carr laments (almost confessionally), "is chipping away my capacity for concentration and contemplation. My mind now takes in information the way the Net distributes it: in a swiftly moving stream of particles. Once I was a scuba diver in the sea of words. Now I zip along the surface like a guy on a jet ski."

Not everyone agrees with this gloomy assessment, of course. Writing in the *New Yorker,* for example, Caleb Crain (2007) says, "The Internet, happily, does not so far seem to be antagonistic to literacy." In support of his claim he cites a recent study of Michigan children and teenagers that found "grades and reading scores rose with the amount of time spent online. Even visits to pornography Web sites improved academic performance.

"Of course," he allows, "such synergies may disappear if the Internet continues its YouTube-fuelled evolution away from print and toward television."

Even more optimistic than Crain is Steven Johnson, author of the recent book *Everything Bad Is Good for You: How Today's Popular Culture Is Actually Making Us Smarter,* a paean to video gaming, film, television, and the Internet. But even Johnson (2005, 185), while claiming that, "thanks to e-mail and the Web we're reading text as much as ever, and we're writing more," admits that "it is true that a specific, historically crucial kind of reading has grown less common in this society: sitting down with a 300-page book and following its argument or narrative without a great deal of distraction. We deal with text now in shorter bursts, following links across the Web, or sifting through a dozen e-mail messages."

E-Books and the Future of Print

As technology continues to evolve, another digital form of reading has recently emerged: the e-book. Thanks to Amazon.com's introduction of its electronic book reader Kindle in October 2007 and the corollary popularity of the Sony e-book reader, the electronic book may have finally—after nearly a decade of failed efforts—become a viable alternative to the paper book, a prospect made even more probable by the introduction, in 2009, of both the third-generation Kindle DX (which can hold 1,500 titles and wirelessly download books in sixty seconds) and Barnes & Noble's first electronic book reader.

Nevertheless, it is doubtful that many teens will be engaged by this particular "new" way of reading. According to a recent survey conducted by Teenreads.com, 46 percent of teens, when asked about "their affection for a digital reading device for fun reading (not schoolwork) if the price were affordable," replied they preferred print books! While nearly one-quarter (24 percent) have read an e-book and 27 percent would like to, almost half (49 percent) said "they have no interest in reading e-books" (Fitzgerald 2009).

However, even if the YA book, printed and published on paper, is in no immediate danger of obsolescence, the form and format in which its content is presented and its story told are already being reimagined, thanks to the influence of the Internet. One of the earlier examples of this was Paula Danziger and Ann Martin's collaborative novel *Snail Mail No More* (Scholastic, 2000), which is told in the form of e-mail exchanges between best friends forever Elizabeth and Tara. As this suggests, authors were beginning as early as a decade ago to write books in the same way that teens themselves were writing online. Another example of this was Lauren Myracle's *ttyl* (Abrams Amulet, 2004), the first novel to be told entirely in the form of instant messages. An instant success (John Green [2004]—who has gone on to fame and fortune as a YA novelist—said in his *Booklist* review, "Myracle cleverly manages to build rich characters and narrative tension without ever taking the story outside of an IM box"), the book has spawned two sequels: *ttfn* and *18r, g8r* (Amulet, 2006 and 2007, respectively). In her novel *Heart on My Sleeve* (Simon & Schuster, 2004), the popular author Ellen Wittlinger also experimented with telling a novel in the form of traditional letters, e-mails, and instant messages, while in her earlier, Printz honor–winning *Hard Love* (Simon & Schuster, 1999), she had, of course, experimented with telling a novel in the form of excerpts from zines, handwritten poems, and letters. Similarly, Hillary Frank, in her novel *I Can't Tell You* (Graphia, 2004), tells her story in notes and drawings exchanged among the various characters, a technique that I called "story as assemblage" in my *Booklist* review (Cart 2004, 232).

Such assemblage also informed the construction of Australian author Jaclyn Moriarty's *The Year of Secret Assignments* and its sequel *The Murder of Bindy Mackenzie* (Levine/Scholastic, 2004 and 2006, respectively). In these two novels, Moriarty employed multiple bits and pieces that ranged widely from letters, diary entries, lists, and quizzes to mock subpoenas, school assignments, and transcripts. Steve Kluger, in his more recent *My Most Excellent Year* (Penguin,

2008), employed a similar strategy (and received the first Amelia Elizabeth Walden Award for his efforts), while Michael Spooner in *Entr@pment: A High School Comedy in Chat* (McElderry, 2009) wrote a novel almost entirely in the form of chats (interrupted by the occasional IM and blog entry).

These hectic, occasionally frenetic, sometimes stream-of-consciousness techniques are not always successful in aesthetic terms, but they all manage to capture the interactive, often interrupted, discontinuous ways in which contemporary young adults experience daily life.

Other online/digital activities—notably gaming—that occupy increasing portions of teens' waking hours have also begun to impact not only the narrative styles but also the plots of YA novels. In fact, the librarian Kelly Czarnecki did an extended feature about this for *Booklist*. Published in concert with YALSA's first-ever Teen Tech Week and titled "Books for Teen Gamers," it appeared in the March 1, 2007, issue and suggested that librarians "may find that young adult readers and gamers have a lot to teach you about learning and literacy through play" (Czarnecki 2007, 78–79).

Other novels, like Sean Stewart's *Cathy's Book* (Running Press Kids, 2006) and Patrick Carman's *Skeleton Creek* (and its sequel *Ghost in the Machine,* both from Scholastic, 2009) have incorporated elements that lead readers to websites specially created to augment the experience of reading the book. This has led to the more ambitious multiplatform experiences that are presently in evolution. By far the two most ambitious of these are Scholastic's 39 Clues and HarperTeen/Fourth Story Media's the Amanda Project.

The former is planned to consist of a projected ten-volume series of interrelated mysteries by such leading YA authors as Rick Riordan (who has plotted the story arc for the entire series and has written the first volume), Gordon Korman, Peter Lerangis, Jude Watson, Patrick Carman, and others. The premise is that the recently deceased matriarch of a prominent extended family, the Cahills, has left her survivors with a choice: each may accept either a bequest of $1 million or a clue. The first Cahill to assemble all thirty-nine clues, which are hidden all over the world, will, as Scholastic's promotional materials promise, "discover what makes the family so powerful—a reward beyond measure."

The series' interactive format involves reading the books, collecting game cards, playing "a fully immersive online gaming experience where players join the hunt for the 39 clues," and competing for more than $100,000 in prizes.

The latter project (Amanda) is aimed at seventh-grade readers and up, an older audience than Clues' eight- to twelve-year-old target audience. Like Clues, though, it is also a multivolume, multiplatform experience. The first volume, *invisible i*, published in the fall of 2009 will be followed by seven additional titles. The premise of this series is that Amanda Valentino, an enigmatic new girl at Endeavor High, has gone missing, and three students she befriended must attempt to find her by following a trail of cryptic clues. A dedicated website invites readers to participate, too, by signing on as a member and then posting comments, creating new characters that might be added to future volumes, participating in the Debate Club, and submitting art and original writing for possible publication in a forthcoming zine; there will also, it is promised, be videos, music playlists, and games at the website.

Though seemingly published for the retail market, libraries are purchasing both series (Clues publishes a library edition with a reinforced binding and without the game cards that are packaged with the retail edition). And teens are apparently welcoming such multiplatform experiences. A total of 56 percent of those who responded to the Teenreads.com survey mentioned previously said they would "like to see interactive online components and extras for books (e.g., website, YouTube videos, downloads) if they made sense with the content."

In a keynote address to the 2008 Ypulse Mashup, an annual event focusing on youth media, marketing, and technology, David Levithan, executive editorial director of Scholastic, stressed that "YA publishing needs to adapt to changes brought on by teens' use of technology." Publishers need to think of themselves as content providers," he continued, "which means exploring new options, from developing multimedia publishing projects [like 39 Clues] to getting ready for digital books and mobile reading devices. The big question is 'Can we go where teens live?'" (Pavo 2008).

That's exactly where YALSA intends to go, it seems, when it creates a new YA literature-focused blog with the mission of providing an online resource to teens for finding reading recommendations. It will also provide, YALSA promises, "a definitive web connection to blog posts, images, booklists, videos and more, all related to teen reading" (e-mail from Beth Yoke, YALSA executive director, September 15, 2009).

Authors and publishers are also going where teens live. "The online world has become *the* place to build book buzz and have it reach fever pitch more quickly than ever," according to Shannon Maughan (2007, 58), of *Publishers Weekly*. Among the major publishers, HarperCollins, Simon & Schuster, and Penguin have been particularly active, all three now having teen networking sites that offer myriad opportunities for reader interaction, message boards, contests, book trailers, video interviews with favorite authors, author blogs, advance looks at forthcoming books (usually in exchange for a posted reaction or review), and more.

Audiobooks

The sixteenth-century Spanish writer Francisco de Quevedo once said of reading that "it enables us to listen to the dead with our eyes." *Plus c'est ca change*—today's movement away from print is not only toward the visual but also toward the oral, as more and more people read with their ears. Recorded books are hardly a new phenomenon, however. They date to the 1930s and the establishment of the Library of Congress's program of recording for the blind, whereas Caedmon Records—the first to offer literature in the form of the spoken word—was founded in 1952. Nevertheless, most major publishers did not establish audio divisions until the mid-1980s; the Audio Publishers Association (APA) was founded in 1986, but it wasn't until the early nineties that recorded books became a significant industry that has, since then, grown apace. By 2006, sales were estimated at $871 million, and audiobooks accounted for 10–15 percent of a book's overall sales (Newman 2007).

In 2004 when the National Endowment for the Arts released that controversial assessment showing a precipitous decline in American reading, it also showed a more than 30 percent increase in the number of people listening to books on tapes, CDs, and iPods (Harmon 2005, E1). This came as no great surprise to librarians, who already knew that, with an increase of 13.5 percent in the circulation of adult audiobooks and 10.7 percent in children's, audio format materials were handily outpacing the overall circulation of materials. By 2008, 32 percent of all audiobook sales were to libraries (36 percent were to retailers; 16 percent, to wholesalers; 7 percent, direct to consumers; and 9 percent, to others). Seventeen percent of total sales were of audiobooks geared to children and teens, and the remaining 83 percent to adults. No surprise there—according to the APA, the majority of listeners are older than thirty. "They see audiobooks as a way to 'read' more while pursuing other lifestyle activities. The primary usage is while traveling and commuting."[4] Other activities while listening include exercising, relaxing, cooking, cleaning, gardening, crafting, walking the dog, and so on. In this sense, adults—like their teenage children—are becoming dedicated multitaskers.

But, people inevitably ask, is listening to a text actually reading? The *New York Times* published an amusing article in 2007 about the hot debate over this issue then occurring in the growing ranks of America's book discussion groups. Though the jury is still out, the reporter Andrew Adam Newman (2007) quoted one expert witness, Daniel T. Willingham, a University of Virginia cognitive neuroscientist, thus: "If the goal is to appreciate the aesthetic of the writing and understand the story, then there won't be much difference between listening and reading. The basic architecture of how we understand language is much more similar between reading and listening than it is different."

Pam Spencer Holley, a former president of YALSA and reviewer of audiobooks for *Booklist*, agrees: "The more I listen, the more ready I am to accept that listening can be interchanged with reading" (e-mail interview with Holley, December 6, 2009). When I asked her why audiobooks have become so popular with teens, she pointed to "the increase in the number of titles, which affords teens a wide range of selections from teen issues to vampires, werewolves and now angels. For pleasure or school assignments, listening is a natural for this teen population."

Indeed, more and more librarians are becoming—along with teachers— staunch advocates of the viability of listening as a literary experience. As a result, in 2006 YALSA and the Association for Library Service to Children jointly created a new annual prize for excellence in audiobook production. Called the Odyssey Award and sponsored by *Booklist*, it was first presented in 2008. Holley, one of the creators of the award, explains that it "gives recognition to the entire audiobook from ensuring that there are no distortions of sound, mispronunciations, or variations in sound quality to acknowledging the seamless partnership created by the best readers with their texts."

With this demonstration of increasing library interest, the producers of audio for children and teens have dramatically increased their output and, aided by technology, have also increased the number and variety of formats in which audiobooks are available.

New ground in this connection was broken in 2008 by Brilliance Audio, one of the major producers of audio, when it released its audio version of John Green's novel *Paper Towns* simultaneously with the print edition and in a record number of formats, including CD, MP3-CD, Playaway, and Audible and Overdrive downloadable options.

"I have all these resources—a plethora of platforms—at my fingertips," Brilliance vice president Tim Ditlow told *Publishers Weekly*, "and I can get listeners a book where they live and breathe" (Maughan 2008).

With ever-better and more dramatic production values, audiobooks' entertainment value has become a given. But what about their educational value? The creators of the Odyssey Award have an answer for this. "It's important," they write, "that we, as a group of professionals committed to lifelong literacy, recognize the role of audiobooks in the development of literacy."

In support of this stance, spokespersons cite an influential article coauthored by Sharon Grover and Lizette D. Hannegan that appeared in *Book Links* in May 2005. Titled "Not Just for Listening," the article discussed the growing integration of audiobooks into school curricula. "Educators," Grover and Hannegan (2005, 16) write, "know that one of the most important reasons for the increasing interest in audiobooks for young people is the research demonstrating that listening to audiobooks fosters reading comprehension, fluency, language acquisition, vocabulary development, and improved achievement."

"Listening," the Odyssey Award founders conclude, "is an important skill to be both taught and learned." Their conclusion seems to prove that all old is new again! As long ago as 1985, the poet Donald Hall (who went on to serve as America's poet laureate in 2006) wrote the essay "Bring Back the Out-Loud Culture" in *Newsweek*. In it, he noted that "before the late 1920s and 1930s American culture was *out loud*. We continually turned print into sound. Mother read or recited to infant (memorization allowed entertainment even while both hands made bread). Grandfather read from Prophet and Gospel; his grandson performed chapters from Scott and Dickens. . . . When we stopped memorizing and reciting literature, our ability to read started its famous decline" (Hall 1985, 12). As children speak poems and stories aloud," he continued, "by the pitch and muscle of their voices they will discover drama, humor, passion and intelligence in print. In order to become a nation of readers, we need again to become a nation of reciters."

And the French educator and author Daniel Pennac wrote compellingly in his book *Better Than Life* about his success, through reading aloud to them, in instilling a love of reading in his formerly book-hating students.

The nationally known reading expert Kylene Beers (1998, 31) saw further evidence of this in practice, as she reported on her field research in the article "Listen While You Read": "Soon I began to understand how certain students were able to connect to reading through listening." She offers this telling excerpt from one of her conversations with a teacher:

> *Teacher:* Listening to the English language is one of the best ways to improve their [students'] vocabulary, their usage, and their comprehension. Just reading books doesn't help these kids very much. They need to hear the language. So I put them with books on tape.
>
> *Beers:* Are you seeing that listening to the books improves their reading interest?
>
> *Teacher:* Sure. More important, because these kids have to pass tests, listening to books helps their comprehension.

Grover and Hannegan (2005, 16) concur, writing, "Many instructional standards, especially in English and language arts, refer to listening skills students need in order to be successful readers." They then offer an extensive annotated bibliography of books on tape that "have strong connections to classroom and instructional use."

Let ALA's Odyssey Award founders have the penultimate word here: "Children of this century live in a world where media is a dominant form of communication, and imagination's greatest champion in this technological realm is the spoken word. Through the years our cultures have been nurtured and our customs passed on by storytellers—audiobooks carry on that tradition."[5] To which Holley adds: "All of us who read form images in our minds of what we've read; the same thing occurs while listening. So I think that for most purposes listening to a book is using one's ears and imagination while reading is using one's eyes and imagination."

To which one can only add a hearty, "Hear, hear!"

If You Are Here, Where Is There?

Surely, it's obvious by now that story, in whatever form or format it may be presented, will survive. But so, I predict, will paper. Ease of access offered by technology is one thing; the aesthetic pleasure of the book as a physical object, as an artifact, is quite another, however. Nothing in my experience can beat the tactile and visual pleasure of holding, examining, and reading a beautifully designed, bound, and printed book. By comparison, the act of reading a book on a screen is a cold, sterile, and eyestrain-inducing exercise. And I suspect that enough other people share my sympathies to ensure that the book, as a physical object, will be around for a while, quite a while. What is interesting, even exciting, in this context, though, is the perhaps unintended impact that the omnipresence of the digital in the lives of today's young netizens is having on the design of books. More and more publishers, it seems, are finding the future in the past, as books begin to replicate the visual appeal of illustrated books from the nineteenth century.[6]

The best case in point at the moment of the new-old aesthetic importance of books for young readers may be Scott Westerfeld's new novel *Leviathan* (Simon Pulse, 2009), a book that—though aimed at young adults—is lavishly illustrated and features beautifully intricate, full-color endpaper maps. It's also printed on seventy-pound paper, the whole point of the obviously expensive exercise being Westerfeld's desire to re-create the look of Victorian books, as his novel itself is a work of steampunk science fiction (though set during an alternate World War I instead of the more customary Victorian era). Happily, Westerfeld has the best-selling clout with his publisher to make such an expensive publishing event happen (even if he did, as one reads, have to pay for a large part of it himself). Another recent case in point is Chris Wooding's *Malice*, a shiver-inducing story that combines traditional text-driven narrative with comic book elements. At the same time, its three-dimensional cover—while giving librarians fits—reminds us that reading is not only an intellectual but also a tactile experience!

Text and image, which can be enjoyed both visually and tactilely, offer an agreeable combination. But the most agreeable combination imaginable is that of young adults and young adult literature. When I wrote the first edition of this book in the 1990s there was widespread doubt that half of this equation—young adult literature—would survive, but as I hope I have demonstrated in the preceding pages, not only has the genre survived; it has thrived! Despite some temporary problems with the economy—both here and abroad—the future of YA literature seems secure.[7] Publishers continue to add new YA imprints and new means of distribution continue to develop—Borders bookstore chain, for example, added a new teen section to its many stores in 2009 to capitalize on the strength of that category, and as "the walls between marketing channels are beginning to crumble," the new mass merchandise market is also proving especially beneficial to teen book sales (Rosen 2009a).

As a result, juvenile and young adult sales for 2009 are expected to increase 5.1 percent, whereas virtually every other category is stagnant or in decline. Although it's hard to break out YA-specific statistics, *Publishers Weekly* reports that fiction, fantasy, and science fiction for older readers remains the strongest category in children's books (Roback 2009). This category will remain exceptionally strong until at least 2013, when sales are expected to total $861 million, a 30.6 percent increase over 2008 (Fitzgerald 2009).

As for teen demographics, YALSA reported in a 2007 press release that there were more than 42 million teens in America. But perhaps most promising of all is that the National Center for Education Statistics (2009) forecasts record levels of total elementary and secondary enrollment through at least 2017; indeed, new records are anticipated every year until then. Overall, public school enrollment is expected to increase 9 percent between 2008 and 2017, and secondary enrollment will grow by 5 percent.

At this rate, the golden age of young adult literature promises to become a permanent fixture of publishing, libraries, bookstores, and teen lives. It will be fascinating to watch the field continue to grow; continue to invite creative and technological innovations; continue to welcome traditional and nontraditional means of sharing stories and information in ways that will delight our imaginations, expand our minds, teach us new means of cultivating empathy and understanding; and—perhaps above all else—secure a civilization of enlightenment, comity, and compassion for future generations yet to come of teens and young adults.

Notes

1. See Michiko Kakutani, "The Age of Irony Isn't Over After All," *New York Times*, October 9, 2001; Brian Unger, "The Age of Irony Is Alive and Well," *Unger Report*, NPR, September 11, 2006, www.npr.org/templates/archives.php?thingId=4465030 &date=05-10-2010&p=106.

2. Nancy Kaplan, executive director of the School of Information Arts and Technologies at the University of Baltimore, offered a particularly withering analysis, "Reading Responsibly." See www.futureofthebook.org/blog/archives/2007/11/reading_responsibly _nancy_kaplan.

3. "NCTE Guideline: A Call to Action," National Council of Teachers of English, www .ncte.org.

4. Audio Publishers Association, "APAFAQ," www.audiopub.org/faq.asp.

5. American Library Association, "YALSA Odyssey Award," www.ala.org/yalsa/odyssey.

6. One of the best books on this subject is Percy Muir's *Victorian Illustrated Books* (Praeger, 1971).

7. A September 16, 2009, article by Caroline Horn in Britain's *The Bookseller* was head-lined "Children's Publishers Cutting Acquisitions and Advances."

references

Abrahamson, Richard. 1998. Back to the Future with Adult Books for the Teenage Reader. *Journal of Youth Services in Libraries* 11 (Summer): 383.

Abramson, Jane. 1976. Playing It Safe: Restricted Realism in Teen Novels. *School Library Journal* 22 (May): 38.

Alderdice, Kit. 1996. How Random Created a YA Crossover. *Publishers Weekly,* April 1, 24.

———. 2004. Chick Lit for Teens and Tweens. *Publishers Weekly,* November 15, 26.

Allen, Rachel. 2006. From Comic Book to Graphic Novel: Why Are Graphic Novels So Popular? CBSNews.com, July 31, www.cbsnews.com/stories/2006/07/27/entertainment/main1843318.shtml?tag=mncol;1st;1.

Alm, Richard S. 1955. The Glitter and the Gold. *English Journal* 44 (September): 315.

American Bar Association. 2006. Teen Dating Violence Facts. www.abanet.org/unmet/teendating/facts.pdf.

American Library Association Washington Office Newsline. 1977. News release, August 21.

Anonymous. 1998. *Go Ask Alice*. New York: Aladdin.

Aratani, Lori. 2006. Upper Grades, Lower Reading Skills. *Washington Post,* July 13, B1.

Arnold, Andrew D. 2003. The Graphic Novel Silver Anniversary. *Time,* www.time .com/time/columnist/arnold/article/0,9565,542579,00.html.

Aronson, Marc. 1995. The YA Novel Is Dead, and Other Fairly Stupid Tales. *School Library Journal* 41 (January): 36.

Association of American Publishers. 2006. December Sees Steady Rise in Book Sales. Press Center, January 31, www.publishers.org/main/PressCenter/ Archicves/2005_Jan/Jan_01.htm.

Avery, Gillian. 1995. The Beginnings of Children's Reading to c. 1700. In *Children's Literature: An Illustrated History,* ed. Peter Hunt. New York: Oxford University Press.

Bacon, Perry. 2002. Libraries, Stores Face a Teenage Mystery. *Washington Post,* July 13.

Baldwin, Neal. 1984. Writing for Young Adults. *Publishers Weekly,* October 19, 15.

Bantam Doubleday Dell. 1994. *Fall Catalog.*

Barr, Donald. 1986. Should Holden Caulfield Read These Books? *New York Times Book Review,* May 4, 1, 50–51.

Barson, Michael, and Steven Heller. 1998. *Teenage Confidential: An Illustrated History of the American Teen.* San Francisco: Chronicle Books.

Bass, Dina. 1997. Poll Finds Sharp Rise in Drug Use among Youngsters. *Los Angeles Times,* August 14, A4.

Bauerlein, Mark. 2008. Online Literacy Is a Lesser Kind. *Chronicle of Higher Education,* September 19, http://chronicle.com/article/Online-Literacy-Is-a -Lesser/28307/.

Beers, Kylene. 1998. Listen While You Read. *School Library Journal* 44 (April): 30.

Bellafante, Gina. 2003. Poor Little Rich Girls Throbbing to Shop. *New York Times,* August 17.

Berger, Laura Standley, ed. 1994. *Twentieth Century Young Adult Writers.* Detroit: St. James.

Bernstein, Elizabeth. 1996. Don't Throw the Small Ones Back. *Publishers Weekly,* November 18, 25.

Bickers, James. 2007. The Young and the Graphic Novel. *Publishers Weekly,* www .publishersweekly.com/article/CA6417183.html.

Billman, Carol. 1986. *The Secret of the Stratemeyer Syndicate.* New York: Ungar.

Blume, Judy, ed. 1999. *Places I Never Meant to Be.* New York: Simon & Schuster.

Bolle, Sonja. 2008. Why 'Twilight' Isn't for Everybody. *Los Angeles Times,* December 14, www.latimes.com/entertainment/la-caw-wordplay14 -2008dec14,1,3382735.story.

Bott, C. J. 2008. Bullybooks. *VOYA* 31 (June): 118.

Boylston, Helen. 1936. *Sue Barton Student Nurse.* Boston: Little, Brown.

Brill, Ian. 2006. A New Era in Comics Publishing. *Publishers Weekly,* June 27, www.publishersweekly.com/article/CA6347385.html.

Brown, Jennifer M. 2006. The CBC Grows Up. *Publishers Weekly,* November 13, 24.

Burton, Dwight L. 1951. The Novel for the Adolescent. *English Journal* 40 (September): 362.

Calvino, Italo. 1988. *Six Memos for the Next Millennium.* Cambridge, MA: Harvard University Press.

Campbell, Patty. 1993. The Sand in the Oyster. *Horn Book* 69 (September/October): 568.

———. 1997. Rescuing Young Adult Literature. *Horn Book* 73 (May/June): 365.

Carlsen, G. Robert. 1980. *Books and the Teen-age Reader.* 2nd ed. New York: Harper.

———. 1984. Teaching Literature for the Adolescent: A Historical Perspective. *English Journal* 73 (November): 29.

Carpenter, Dave. 2000. When Teens Spend, Business Listens. *Sacramento Bee,* November 20.

Carr, Nicholas. 2008. Is Google Making Us Stupid? *Atlantic Monthly,* July/August, www.theatlantic.com/doc/200807/google.

Cart, Michael. 1995a. Of Risk and Revelation: The Current State of Young Adult Literature. *Journal of Youth Services in Libraries* 9 (Winter): 151.

———. 1995b. The Stinky Cheese Man Goes to College. *Booklist,* December 15, 695.

———. 1996. *From Romance to Realism: 50 Years of Growth and Change in Young Adult Literature.* New York: HarperCollins.

———. 1997a. Let's Do a Month. *Booklist,* May 15, 1570.

———. 1997b. Not Just for Children Anymore. *Booklist* 93 (November 15): 553.

———. 1999. TO COME

———. 2000a. The Dream Becomes a Reality. *Booklist,* March 15.

———. 2000b. Robert Cormier Remembered. Eulogy delivered at St. Peter's Church, New York City, December 6.

———. 2001. Poetry Changes the World. *Booklist,* March 15, 1390.

———. 2002a. Eyewitness Books. *Booklist,* October 15, 399.

———. 2002b. Got Graphic? *Booklist,* www.booklistonline.com/default .aspx?page=show_product&pid=1536187.

———. 2004. Review of *I Can't Tell You,* by Hillary Frank. *Booklist,* September 15.

———. 2005. New Things under the Sun. *Booklist,* January 1–15, 838.

———. 2007. Teens and the Future of Reading. *American Libraries* 38 (October): 42.

———. 2009. Core Collection: Crossovers. *Booklist*, February 15, 74.

———, and Christine A. Jenkins. 2006. *The Heart Has Its Reasons*. Lanham, MD: Scarecrow Press.

Carter, Betty. 1988. Let's Take Taitte to Task. *School Library Journal* 35 (November): 60.

———. 1994. *Best Books for Young Adults: The Selections, the History, the Romance*. Chicago: American Library Association.

———. 2000. *Best Books for Young Adults*, 2nd ed. Chicago: American Library Association.

———. 2008. The Alex Award. In *The Official YALSA Awards Guidebook*, ed. Tina Frolund. New York: Neal-Schuman.

Carter, Kim. 2009. It's a Web 2.0 World. *VOYA* 32 (June): 114.

Carvajal, Doreen. 1997. Book Chains' New Role: Soothsayers for Publishers. *New York Times*, August 12.

Cavanna, Betty. 1946. *Going on Sixteen*. Philadelphia: Westminster.

Centers for Disease Control and Prevention. 2009. Youth Violence: Facts at a Glance. www.cdc.gov/violenceprevention.

———. 2010. Trends in the Prevalence of Sexual Behaviors. National Youth Risk Behavior Survey: 1991–2010. www.cdc.gov/HealthyYouth/yrbs/pdf/us_sexual_trend_yrbs.pdf.

Children's Software Revue. 1997. A Conversation with Dorling Kindersley's Peter Kindersley. November/December, www.childrenssoftware.com/kindersley.html.

Comerford, Lynda Brill. 2009. Q and A with Virginia Euwer Wolff. *Booklist*, February 5, www.publishersweekly.com/pw/by-topic/new-titles/adult-announcements/article/3348-q-amp-a-with-virginia-euwer-wolff-.html.

Cooke, Rachel. 2003. It Ain't Half Hot, Mum. *Manchester Guardian*, February 23, http://books .guardian.co.uk/departments/childrenandteens/story/0,6000,900845,00.html.

Corliss, Richard. 1995a. Elegies for Degeneration X. *Time*, November 6, 77, www.time.com/time/magazine/article/0,9171,983677,00.html.

———. 1995b. To Live and Buy in L.A. *Time*, www.time.com/time/magazine/article/0,9171,983251,00.html.

Cormier, Robert. 1974. *The Chocolate War*. New York: Pantheon.

———. 1998. Probing the Cellars of a Young Adult Writer's Heart. Frances Clarke Sayers Lecture, University of California, Los Angeles, May 17.

Cornish, Sarah, and Patrick Jones. 2002. Retro Mock Printz. *VOYA* 25 (December): 353.

Craig, Amanda. 2008. Crossover Books—Time Out. www.amandacraig.com.

Crain, Caleb. 2007. Twilight of the Books. *New Yorker,* December 24, www
.newyorker.com/arts/critics/atlarge/2007/12/24/071224crat_atlarge_crain?.

Czarnecki, Kelly. 2007. Books for Teen Gamers. *Booklist,* March 1, 78.

Daly, Maureen. 1942. *Seventeenth Summer.* New York: Dodd, Mead.

———, ed. 1951. *Profile of Youth.* Philadelphia: J. B. Lippincott.

Daum, Meghan. 2006. Middle School Confidential. *Los Angeles Times,* www
.latimes.com/news/opinion/commentary/la-oe-daum11mar11,0,3150641
.column?coll=la-home-commentary.

Davis, Terry. 1997. Chris Crutcher. In *Writers for Young Adults,* vol. 1, ed. Ted
Hipple. New York: Scribner's.

Deahl, Rachel. 2007. DC Goes Where the Girls Are. *Publishers Weekly,* April 20,
www.publishersweekly.com/pw/by-topic/1-legacy/24-comic-book-reviews/
article/12082-where-the-girls-are-.html.

Denizet-Lewis, Benoit. 2004. Whatever Happened to Teen Romance? *New York
Times Magazine,* May 30, 30–35, 54, 56–58.

DiMassa, Cara Mia. 2001. New Chapter for Young Adult Books. *Los Angeles
Times,* January 29.

Du Jardin, Rosamund. 1949. *Practically Seventeen.* Philadelphia: Lippincott.

Dunleavy, M. P. 1993. The Crest of the Wave. *Publishers Weekly,* July 19, 31.

Eaglen, Audrey. 1990. Don't Argue with Success. *School Library Journal* 36
(May): 54.

Edwards, Margaret A. 1954. The Rise of Teen-Age Reading. *Saturday Review,*
November 13, 88.

———. 1969. *The Fair Garden and the Swarm of Beasts.* New York: Hawthorn.

Egley, Arlen, Jr., and Christina E. O'Donnell. 2009. Highlights of the 2007 National
Youth Gang Survey. *OJJDP Fact Sheet.* Washington, D.C.: U.S. Department
of Justice.

Egoff, Sheila. 1980. Beyond the Garden Wall. In *The Arbuthnot Lectures
1970-1979,* comp. Zena Sutherland, 190–96. Chicago: American Library
Association.

Elleman, Barbara. 1998. To Market, to Market. *School Library Journal* 44 (April):
44.

Engberg, Gillian. 2004. Choosing Adult Romances for Teens. *Booklist* 101
(September 15): 237.

Epstein, Connie. 1990. A Publisher's Perspective. *Horn Book* 66 (March/April):
237.

Erikson, Erik. 1950. *Childhood and Society.* New York: W. W. Norton.

Estrada, Jackie. 2006. The Rise of the Graphic Novel. *ForeWord,* January/February,
C4.

Fitzgerald, Carol. 2009. What Do Teens Want? *The Book Report Network*, October 26, http://news.tbrnetwork.com/2010/03/what-do-teens-wantby-carol-fitzgerald.asp.

Flanagan, Anna. 2008. The Role of Research in Improving Adolescent Literacy. *Council Chronicle* 17 (March): 6.

Flanagan, Caitlin. 2006. Are You There God? It's Me, Monica. *Atlantic*, www.theatlantic.com/doc/200601/oral-sex.

Foehr, Ulla G. 2006. Media Multitasking among American Youth: Prevalence, Predictors, and Pairings. Kaiser Family Foundation Report, December, www.kff.org/entmedia/upload/7592.pdf.

Forman, Jack. 1994. Paul Zindel. In *Twentieth-Century Young Adult Writers*, ed. Laura Standley Berger, 931–933. Detroit: St. James.

Freedman, Russell. 1994. Bring 'Em Back Alive. *School Library Journal* 40 (March): 138.

Frolund, Tina, ed. 2008. *The Official YALSA Awards Guidebook.* New York: Neal–Schuman Publishers.

Frost, Helen. 2006. *The Braid*. New York: Farrar, Strauss & Giroux.

Fry, Richard. 2009. Latino Children: A Majority Are U.S.-Born Offspring of Immigrants. Pew Hispanic Center, http://pewhispanic.org/reports/report.php?ReportID=110.

Gallo, Don, ed. 1990. *Speaking for Ourselves.* Urbana, IL: National Council of Teachers of English.

Gardner, Howard. 2008. The End of Literacy? Don't Stop Reading. *Washington Post*, February 15, B01, www.washingtonpost.com/wp-dyn/content/article/2008/02/15/AR2008021502898.html.

Getlin, Josh. 1997. Future of Books Isn't Written in Stone. *Los Angeles Times*, October 1.

Giblin, James Cross. 1988. The Rise and Fall and Rise of Juvenile Nonfiction, 1961–1988. *School Library Journal* 35 (October): 27.

Gray, Paul. 1993. Carnage: An Open Book. *Time*, August 2, 54.

———. 1999. Wild about Harry. *Time*, September 20, 67.

Green, John. 2004. Review of *ttyl* by Lauren Myracle. *Booklist* 100 (May 15): 1615.

Grover, Sharon, and Lizette D. Hannegan. 2005. Not Just for Listening: Integrating Audiobooks into the Curriculum. *Book Links*, May, 16.

Hall, Donald E. 1985. Bring Back the Out-Loud Culture. *Newsweek*, April 15, 12.

Hall, G. Stanley. 1904. *Adolescence: Its Psychology and Its Relations to Psychology, Anthropology, Sociology, Sex, Crime, Religion and Education.* 2 vols. New York: D. Appleton.

Harmon, Amy. 2004. Internet Gives Teenage Bullies Weapons to Wound from Afar. *New York Times*, August 26.

———. 2005. Loud, Proud, Unabridged: It Is *Too* Reading. *New York Times,* May 26.

Havighurst, Robert J. 1950. *Developmental Tasks and Education.* New York: McKay.

———. 1988. Developmental Tasks and Education. Quoted in David A. Russell, The Common Experience of Adolescence. *Journal of Youth Services in Libraries* 2 (Fall): 61.

Hendricks, Tyche. 2008. Obama Raises Profile of Mixed-Race Americans. *San Francisco Chronicle,* July 21.

Hentoff, Nat. 1967. Tell It As It Is. *New York Times Book Review,* May 7, 3.

Hertz, Sarah H., and Donald R. Gallo. 1996. *From Hinton to Hamlet: Building Bridges between Young Adult Literature and the Classics.* Westport, CT: Greenwood Press.

Hesse, Monica. 2009. When Romance Writers Gather. *Washington Post,* July 18.

Hill, Rebecca S. 2009. The New Literacy Equation. *VOYA* 32 (June): 112.

Hine, Thomas. 1999. *The Rise and Fall of the American Teenager.* New York: Avon Books.

Hinton, S. E. 1967a. *The Outsiders.* New York: Viking.

———. 1967b. Teen-Agers Are for Real. *New York Times Book Review,* August 27, 26.

Hochschild, Adam. 1994. War and Peace, Part II. *Los Angeles Times Book Review,* August 7, 1, 11.

Hu, Winnie. 2009. Gossip Girls and Boys Stop to Empathize. *New York Times,* April 5.

Huntwork, Mary M. 1990. Why Girls Flock to Sweet Valley High. *School Library Journal* 36 (March): 137

Hutchinson, Margaret. 1973. Fifty Years of Young Adult Reading 1921–1971. *Top of the News* 30 (November): 27.

Italie, Hillel. 2008. Teen Sensation Writes Adult Novel. *San Francisco Chronicle,* April 30, www.chron.com/disp/story.mpl/fn/5742787.html.

Ivins, Molly. 1997. America Turns on Its Kids. *San Francisco Chronicle,* July 2.

Jackson, Richard. 1998. The Beast Within. *Booklist* 94 (August): 1985.

Jacobs, Thomas A. 1997 What Are My Rights? 95 Questions and Answers about Teens and the Law. Minneapolis, MN: Free Spirit.

Jefferson, Margo. 1982. Sweet Dreams for Prom Queens. *Nation,* 234 (May 22): 613.

Jenkins, Christine. 1999. Two Hundred Years of Young Adult Library Services History. www.voya.com/2010/03/30/chronology.

Jennings, Frank G. 1956. Literature for Adolescents—Pap or Protein? *English Journal* 45 (December): 226.

Johnson, Steven. 2005. *Everything Bad Is Good for You: How Today's Popular Culture Is Actually Making Us Smarter.* New York: Riverhead.

Kantrowitz, Barbara, and Karen Springen. 2005. A Teen Health Gap. *Newsweek,* December 12, 65.

Kantrowitz, Barbara, and Pat Wingert. 1999. How Well Do You Know Your Kid? *Newsweek,* May 10, 39.

Kellogg, Mary Alice. 1983. The Romance Book Boom. *Seventeen* 42 (May): 158.

Kett, Joseph F. 1977. *Rites of Passage: Adolescence in America 1790 to the Present.* New York: Basic Books.

Kimmel, Michael. 2008. *Guyland: The Perilous World Where Boys Become Men.* New York: HarperCollins.

Klein, Norma. 1991. Thoughts on the Adolescent Novel. In *Writers on Writing for Young Adults,* ed. Patricia E. Feehan and Pamela Petrick Barron, 20–29. Detroit: Omnigraphics.

Koelling, Holly, ed. 2007. *Best Books for Young Adults.* 3rd ed. Chicago: American Library Association.

Kohlberg, Lawrence, and Carol Gilligan. 1971. *The Adolescent as Philosopher.* New York: Daedalus.

Kraus, W. Keith. 1975. Cinderella in Trouble Still Dreaming and Losing. *School Library Journal* 21 (January): 18.

Kushman, Rick. 1999. Youth Market. *Sacramento Bee,* May 28.

LaFeria, Ruth. 2004. Generation Mixed. *San Diego Union-Tribune,* January 4.

Lane, Rose Wilder. 1933. *Let the Hurricane Roar.* New York: Longmans, Green.

Larrick, Nancy. 1965. The All White World of Children's Books. *Saturday Review,* September 11, 63–65.

Latrobe, Kathy Howard. 1994. Report on the Young Adult Library Services Association's Membership Survey. *Journal of Youth Services in Libraries* 7 (Spring): 238.

Lawrence-Pietroni, Anna. 1996. The Tricksters, the Changeover, and the Fluidity of Adolescent Literature. *Children's Literature Association Quarterly* 21 (Spring): 34.

Levithan, David. 2009. *Love Is the Higher Law.* New York: Knopf.

Lewin, Tamar. 2005a. Are These Parties for Real? *New York Times,* June 30.

———. 2005b. Nationwide Survey Includes Data on Teenage Sex Habits. *New York Times,* September 16.

Lipsyte, Robert. 1967. *The Contender.* New York: Harper.

Lodge, Sally. 1992. The Making of a Crossover. *Publishers Weekly,* November 23, 38.

———. 1998. Breaking Out of Format Formulas. *Publishers Weekly,* November 9, 31.

————. 2008. Gossip Girl Dishes On. *Publishers Weekly*, www.publishersweekly .com/article/CA6547202.html?

Los Angeles Times. 1994. Youth Crime, Workplace Violence Rising, Studies Say. February 1, A15.

Lynch, Chris. 1994. Today's YA Writers: Pulling No Punches. *School Library Journal* 40 (January): 37.

Macaulay, David. 1991. Caldecott Medal Acceptance Speech. *Horn Book*, 67 (July/ August): 419.

MacDonald, Heidi. 2008. Big NYCC Crowds Enjoy Good Mood, Weather, Comics. *Publishers Weekly*, www.publishersweekly.com/article/CA6553777.html.

————. 2008. ICv2 Confab Reports 2007 Graphic Novel Sales Rise 12%, *Publishers Weekly*, April 18, www.publishersweekly.com/pw/by -topic/1-legacy/24-comic-book-reviews/article/8185-icv2-confab-reports -2007-graphic-novel-sales-rise-12-.html.

————, Calvin Reid, Douglas Wolk, Laura Hudson, Wil Moss, and Erin Finnegan. 2008. Big NYCC Crowds Enjoy Good Mood, Weather, Comics. *Publishers Weekly*, April 22, www.publishersweekly.com/pw/by-topic/book-news/comics/ article/757-big-nycc-crowds-enjoy-good-mood-weather-comics-.html.

MacDonald, Scott. 2005. YA for Everybody. *Quill & Quire*, February.

Maguire, Gregory. 2009. *Making Mischief.* New York: Morrow.

Marano, Hara Estoff. 2007. Trashing Teens. *Psychology Today*, March 1, www .psychologytoday.com/node/23774.

Marcus, Leonard. 2008. *Minders of Make-Believe*. Boston: Houghton Mifflin.

Marschall, Richard. 1989. *America's Great Comic Strip Artists*. New York: Abbeville Press.

Mathews, Virginia, et al. 1990. Kids Need Libraries. *Journal of Youth Services in Libraries* 3 (Spring): 197–207.

Mattson, Dirk. 1997. Should We Beware of Donors Bearing Book Prizes? Questioning the Walden Award. *School Library Journal* 43, no. 9 (September), 115–17.

Maughan, Shannon. 1999. The Harry Potter Halo. *Publishers Weekly*, July 19, 92.

————. 2000. Teenage Growing Pains. *Publishers Weekly*, October 23, 28.

————. 2007. Way Cool: Marketing and the Internet. *Publishers Weekly*, www .publishersweekly.com/article/CA6417182.

————. 2008. All Ears on 'Paper Towns.' *Publishers Weekly*, www.publishers weekly.com/article/CA6605848.html.

————, and Jim Milliot. 2001. Time-Life Trade, Teen People Book Club to Close. *Publishers Weekly*, April 2, 12.

McElderry, Margaret E. 1994. Across the Years, Across the Seas. *Journal of Youth Services in Libraries* 7 (Summer): 369–80.

McGrath, Charles. 2004a. Not Funnies. *New York Times Magazine,* July 11.

———. 2004b. The Short Story Shakes Itself out of Academe. *New York Times,* August 25.

———. 2004c. What Johnny Won't Read. *New York Times,* July 11.

Miller, Laura. 2004. Lad Lit. *New York Times,* May 23.

———. 2005/2006. Far from Narnia. *New Yorker,* December 2005–January 2006, 52.

Mondale, Sarah, and Sarah B. Patton, eds. 2001. *School: The Story of American Public Education.* Boston: Beacon Press.

Moore, John Noell. 1997. *Interpreting Young Adult Literature: Literary Theory in the Secondary Classroom.* Portsmouth, NH: Boynton/Cook Heinemann.

Morales, Robert. 1997. That's Entertainment. *Publishers Weekly,* June 30, 49.

Mydans, Seth. 1993. A New Tide of Immigration Brings Hostility to the Surface, Poll Finds. *New York Times,* June 27.

Myers, Walter Dean. 2008. Margaret A. Edwards Award Acceptance Speech. In *Official YALSA Awards Guidebook,* ed. Tina Frolund, 98–101. New York: Neal-Schuman.

Nation. 1997. The Crushing Power of Big Publishing. March 17, 3–4, 11–29.

National Center for Education Statistics. 2009. Digest of Education Statistics: 2008. March, http://nces.ed.gov/programs/digest/d08/.

National Endowment for the Arts. 2004. *Reading at Risk.* Washington, DC: National Endowment for the Arts.

———. 2009. *Reading on the Rise.* Washington, DC: National Endowment for the Arts.

Navarro, Mireya. 2003. Census Reflects Hispanic Identity That Is Hardly Black and White. *New York Times,* November 9.

New York Times. 1993. The Children of the Shadows: Shaping Young Lives. April 4–25, www.nytimes.com/1993/04/04/us/the-children-of-the-shadows -shaping-young-lives.html?scp=5&sq=%22children%20of%20the%20 shadows%22&st=cse.

Newman, Andrew Adam. 2007. Your Cheatin' Listenin' Ways. *New York Times,* August 2, http://www.nytimes.com/2007/08/02/fashion/02cheat.html?_r=1.

Nilsen, Alleen Pace. 1994. That Was Then, This Is Now. *School Library Journal* 40 (April): 30.

———, and Kenneth L. Donelson. 1988. The New Realism Comes of Age. *Journal of Youth Services in Libraries* 1 (Spring): 275.

———. 1993. *Literature for Today's Young Adults.* 4th ed. New York: HarperCollins.

———. 2009. *Literature for Today's Young Adults.* 8th ed. Boston: Pearson.

O'Connor, John J. 1994. Is the BBC Too Adult for American Viewers? *New York Times,* December 29.

Ohanian, Susan. 1991. Learning "Whole Language." *Publishers Weekly,* February 22, 127.

Olsen, Ray. 2002. The *Booklist* Interview: Neil Gaiman. *Booklist* 98 (August): 1949.

Palladino, Grace. 1996. *Teenagers: An American History.* New York: Basic Books.

Pareles, Jon. 1995. They're Rebels without a Cause and Couldn't Care Less. *New York Times,* July 16.

Paterson, Katherine. 1999. Historical Fiction: Some Whys and Hows. *Booklist,* April 1, 1430.

Pavo, Kate. 2008. Embracing Technology in a YA World. *Publishers Weekly,* www.publishersweekly.com/article/CA6579337.html.

Peck, Richard. 1993. The Silver Anniversary of Young Adult Books. *Journal of Youth Services in Libraries* 6 (Fall): 19–23.

———. 1994. *Love and Death at the Mall.* New York: Delacorte.

Pierce, Tamora. 1993. Why Kids Read It, Why Kids Need It. *School Library Journal* 39 (October): 50.

Pogrebin, Robin. 1996. Magazines Learning to Take Not-So-Cluless (and Monied) Teen-Agers More Seriously. *New York Times,* November 4.

Pollack, Pamela D. 1981. The Business of Popularity: The Surge of Teenage Paperbacks. *School Library Journal* 28 (November): 25.

Poniewozik, James. 1999. Their Major Is Alienation. *Time,* September 20, 77–78.

Ponton, Lynn. 1999. Their Dark Romance with Risk. *Newsweek,* May 10, 55.

Publishers Weekly. 1991. Future Tense. February 22, 12.

———. 2008. NYCC; ICv2 Briefs. www.publishersweekly.com/article/CA6553798.html.

Rabb, Margo. 2008. I'm Y.A. and I'm O.K. *New York Times Book Review,* July 20, 23.

Raeburn, Paul W. 2004. Too Immature for the Death Penalty? *New York Times Magazine,* October 17, 26, 28–29.

Rafferty, Terrence. 1994. Superhero. *New Yorker,* May 23, 93.

Ramsdell, Kristen. 1983. Young Adult Publishing: A Blossoming Market. *Top of the News* 39 (Winter): 177.

———. 1987. *Happily Ever After.* Littleton, CO: Libraries Unlimited.

Rapp, Adam. 2002. *Little Chicago.* Honesdale, PA: Front Street.

———. 2003. *33 Snowfish.* Somerville, MA: Candlewick.

———. 2004. *Under the Wolf, Under the Dog.* Somerville, MA: Candlewick.

———. 2007. Adolescent Literacy: The Hottest Topic. 25 (February/March): 12.

———. 2009. *Punkzilla.* Somerville, MA: Candlewick.

Reading Today. 1999. Adolescent Literacy Comes of Age. 17 (August/September): 1.

Reed, J. D. 1982. Packaging the Facts of Life. *Time,* August 23, 65.

Reid, Calvin and Heidi MacDonald. 2000. The Literature of Comics. *Publishers Weekly* 247 (October 16): 44–45.

———. 2009. BookExpo America 2009: Despite No-Shows, Many Comics, Graphic Novels at BEA, *Publishers Weekly,* May 26, www.publishersweekly.com/pw/by-topic/new-titles/adult-announcements/article/9365-bookexpo-america-2009-despite-no-shows-many-comics-graphic-novels-at-bea-.html.

Resnick, Michael D., Peter S. Bearman, Robert Wm. Blum, Karl E. Bauman, Kathleen M. Harris, Jo Jones, Yoyce Tabor, Trish Beuhring, Renee E. Sieving, Marcia Shew, Marjorie Ireland, Linda H. Bearinger, and J. Richard Udry. 1997. Protecting Adolescents from Harm. *Journal of the American Medical Association* 278 (September): 823.

Rich, Motoko. 2007. Study Links Drop. *New York Times,* November 19.

———. 2008. An Author Looks beyond Age Limits. *New York Times,* February 20.

Rinaldi, Ann. 2009. In Defense of Historical Fiction. *Publishers Weekly,* www.publishersweekly.com/Article/CA66486223.html?.

Roan, Shari. 1994. Next! When Abnormal Becomes Normal. *Los Angeles Times,* September 6.

Roback, Diane. 2009. Children's Sales to Stay Soft. *Publishers Weekly,* www.publishersweekly.com/article/CA6655846.

Rochman, Hazel. 1993. *Against Borders: Promoting Books for a Multicultural World.* Chicago: American Library Association.

———. 1998. The Art of the Anthology. *Booklist,* March 15, 1234.

Rodriguez, Roberto, and Patrisia Gonzales. 1994. Censorship by Omission. *Los Angeles Times,* December 30.

Roiphe, Katie. 2009. A Lovely Way to Burn. *New York Times Book Review,* April 12, 14.

Rollin, Lucy. 1999. *Twentieth-Century Teen Culture by the Decades: A Reference Guide.* Westport, CT: Greenwood Press.

Rosen, Judith. 1997. Breaking the Age Barrier. *Publishers Weekly,* September 8, 28.

———. 2003. Selling Graphic Novels to Retailers. *Publishers Weekly,* October 20, S2.

———. 2005. Growing Up. *Publishers Weekly,* February 21, 79.

———. 2008. Going YA2. *Publishers Weekly,* www.publishersweekly.com/Article/CA6534266.html.

———. 2009a. Children's Books: Channel Surfing. *Publishers Weekly,* July 20, http://www.publishersweekly.com/pw/by-topic/1-legacy/23-children-s-book-reviews/article/2314-children-s-books-channel-surfing-.html.

————. 2009b. McNally Jackson Books: Turn, Turn, Turn. *Publishers Weekly*, May 12, www.publishersweekly.com/pw/by-topic/new-titles/adult-announcements/article/10914-mcnally-jackson-books-turn-turn-turn-.html.

Rosen, Julia. 1998. Mature Young Adult Books Are Given a Bad Reputation. *VOYA* 21 (December): 347.

Rudman, Masha Kabakow. 2006. Multiculturalism. In *The Oxford Encyclopedia of Children's Literature*, vol. 3, ed. Jack Zipes. New York: Oxford University Press.

Salinger, J. D. 1951. *The Catcher in the Rye*. Boston: Little, Brown.

Saricks, Joyce. 2008. Revisiting Historical Fiction. *Booklist*, April 15, 33.

Schiffrin, Andre. 1995. Between Us. *American Bookseller*, April, 17.

Schuker, Lauren A. E. 2009. Harry Potter and the Rival Teen Franchise. *Wall Street Journal*, July 9, http://online.wsj.com/article/SB10001424052970204261704574276261288253316.html.

Seldes, Gilbert. 1924. *The Seven Lively Arts*. New York: Harper & Brothers

Sellers, John A. 2008. Scholastic Report. *Publishers Weekly*, www.publishersweekly.com/article/CA6569106.html.

Shaffer, Kenneth R. 1963. What Makes Sammy Read? *Top of the News* 19 (March): 9.

Silvey, Anita. 2006. The Unreal Deal. *School Library Journal* 52 (October): 45.

Smith, Henrietta. 1995. African American Children's Literature. In *Children's Books and Their Creators*, ed. Anita Silvey, 4–7. Boston: Houghton Mifflin.

Smith, Karen Patricia. 1993. The Multicultural Ethic and Connection to Literature for Children and Young Adults. *Library Trends* 41 (Winter): 341.

Smith, Lynn. 1997. What Americans Say about Their Children. *Los Angeles Times*, E3.

Spitz, David. 1999. Reads Like Teen Spirit. *Time*, July 19.

Springen, Karen. 2009. A New Look for 'Liar.' *Publishers Weekly*, www.publishersweekly.com/pw/by-topic/childrens/childrens-book-news/article/2366-a-new-look-for-e2-80-98liar-e2-80-99-.html.

Stavn, Diane Gersoni. 1969. Watching Fiction for Today's Teens: Notes of a Critical Voyeur. *School Library Journal* 16 (November): 139.

Stepp, Laura Sessions. 2000. Teen Problems Not Linked to Race, Income, Study Finds. *Sacramento Bee*, November 30.

Stevenson, Nanette. 1997. Hipper, Brighter, and Bolder. *Publishers Weekly*, February 17, 139.

Sutton, Roger. 1982. The Critical Myth: Realistic YA Novels. *School Library Journal* 29 (November): 33.

Tarkington, Booth. 1916. *Seventeen*. New York: Harper.

Thompson, Bob. 2007. A Troubling Case of Reader's Block. *Washington Post*, November 19.

Thompson, Bob. 2009. Unexpected Twist: Fiction Reading Is Up. *Washington Post*, January 12, www.washingtonpost.com/wp-dyn/content/article/2009/01/11/AR2009011102337.html.

Thompson, Jason. 2007. *Manga: A Complete Guide.* New York: Del Rey.

Time. 1993. The Numbers Game. Fall Special Issue, 14.

Toffler, Alvin. 1970. *Future Shock.* New York: Random House.

Townsend, John Rowe. 1980. Standards of Criticism for Children's Literature. In *The Arbuthnot Lectures, 1970–1979,* compiled by Zena Sutherland, 26–33. Chicago: American Library Association.

Trites, Roberta Seelinger, ed. 1996. Critical Theory and Adolescent Literature. Special issue, *Children's Literature Association Quarterly* 21 (Spring).

Tucker, Ken. 1993. Nameless Fear Stalks the Middle-Class Teen-Ager. *New York Times Book Review,* November 14, 27.

Tunis, John R. 1977. What Is a Juvenile Book? In *Crosscurrents of Criticism,* ed. Paul Heins, 22–26. Boston: Horn Book.

Unger, Brian. 2006. The Age of Irony Is Alive and Well. *Unger Report,* September 11, http://www.npr.org/templates/archives.php?thingId=4465030&date=05-10-2010&p=106.

University College London. 2008. Information Behavior of the Researcher of the Future. January 11, www.bl.uk/news/pdf/googlegen.pdf.

Valby, Karen. 2008. Stephanie Meyer: Inside the 'Twilight' Saga. Entertainment Weekly, July 31, www.ew.com/ew/article/0,,20211938,00.html.

Van Gelder, Robert. 1942. An Interview with Miss Maureen Daly. *New York Times,* July 12.

Waddle, Linda. 1991. Just Say Know. *Journal of Youth Services in Libraries* 4 (Summer): 361.

Waters, Harry F. 1994. Teenage Suicide: One Act Not to Follow. *Newsweek* 123 (April): 49.

Weisman, Kay. 2006. An Inside Look at Series Nonfiction. *Booklist,* October 15, 58.

Wertham, Frederick. 1954. *The Seduction of the Innocent.* New York: Rinehart

Westphal, David. 2001. Giant Leap in U.S. Diversity. *Sacramento Bee*, March 13.

Winerip, Michael. 2008. In Novels for Girls, Fashion Trumps Romance. *New York Times,* July 13.

Wojciechowska, Maia. 1968. An End to Nostalgia. *School Library Journal* 15 (December): 13.

Wolf, Naomi. 2006. Young Adult Fiction: Wild Things. *New York Times,* March 12.

Woods, George. 1966. Screening Books for Review. *Wilson Library Bulletin* 41 (October): 169.

Wren, Christopher. 1997. Drugs Common in Schools, Survey Shows. *New York Times*, September 19, A12.

Yao, Lauren. 2008. Bitten and Smitten: Readers Crave Stephenie Meyer's 'Twilight' Tales of Vampire Love. *Washington Post*, August 1, www .washingtonpost.com/wp-dyn/content/article/2008/08/01/AR2008080100064 .html.

Yardley, Jonathan. 1994. The Moral of the Story. *Washington Post Book World*, April 17, 3.

Yep, Laurence, ed. 1993. *American Dragons*. New York: Harper.

Yolen, Jane. 1994. An Empress of Thieves. *Horn Book* 70 (December): 705.

Zindel, Paul. 1968. *The Pigman*. New York: Harper.

index

You may also be interested in

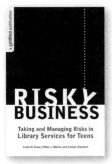

Risky Business: Real-world examples of risky change in action from librarians and authors of YA lit enrich this exploration of a topic rarely discussed in depth, but central to YA services in school and public libraries today.

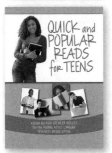

Multicultural Programs for Tweens and Teens: A one-stop resource that encourages children and young adults to explore different cultures, this book includes dozens of flexible programming ideas which allow you to choose a program specific to your scheduling needs; create an event that reflects a specific culture; and recommend further resources to tweens and teens interested in learning more about diverse cultures.

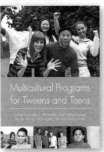

Quick and Popular Reads for Teens: This resource compiles bibliographic information about the books honored by YALSA's *Popular Paperbacks for Young Adults* and *Quick Picks for Reluctant Readers.* Make choosing titles for teens fun, quick, and easy with this one-of-a-kind resource!

A Year of Programs for Teens 2: This volume offers several new themed book lists and read-alikes as well as appendices with reproducible handouts for the various programs. Also included is a section of introductory material that includes general programming advice, information on teen clubs, and marketing ideas, and more than 30 programs cleverly organized around a calendar year, including several that focus on technology, with many other ideas that can adapted year-round as needed.

Order today at www.alastore.ala.org or 866-746-7252!

ALA Store purchases fund advocacy, awareness, and accreditation programs for library professionals worldwide.